# ADAPTATION AN

# ADAPTATION AND INNOVATION

## Theory, Design and Role-Taking in Group Relations Conferences and their Applications

## Volume II

*Eliat Aram, Robert Baxter and Avi Nutkevitch*

Routledge
Taylor & Francis Group
LONDON AND NEW YORK

First published 2009 by Karnac Books Ltd.

Published 2018 by Routledge
2 Park Square, Milton Park, Abingdon, Oxon OX14 4RN
711 Third Avenue, New York, NY 10017, USA

*Routledge is an imprint of the Taylor & Francis Group, an informa business*



British Library Cataloguing in Publication Data

A C.I.P. for this book is available from the British Library

ISBN-13: 9781855756779 (pbk)

Typeset by Vikatan Publishing Solutions (P) Ltd., Chennai, India

# *CONTENTS*

# PREFACE AND ACKNOWLEDGEMENTS

This book, the second in an emerging series based on the Belgirate conferences, could not have been written without the devotion to task of numerous people.

We are deeply grateful to all participants who made the journey to the conference and contributed with their feet, experience, thinking and writing to keeping alive the movement of Group Relations theory and practice.

Our special thanks go to the contributors, without whom there wouldn't have been this book, a testimony to the ongoing unravelling creative potential in the Group Relations network;

To Louisa Brunner, our enthusiastic Italian colleague who bridged the language boundary and supported our administrative effort when organising the conference;

To Anne-Marie Kirkpatrick, who contained us by holding the administrative boundary before, during and post the conference, and provided the best of 'good-enough mothering';

To Miri Tzadok, who joined the administrative team during the conference for the invaluable task of containing and managing us, as well as the conference boundaries;

To Mannie Sher, who was a great partner in the decision to mount a second Belgirate conference and in the initial planning of it; and when stepping away from organising and managing the conference and offering it to Eliat, created for us this unique opportunity;

To our institutions—The A. K. Rice Institute, OFEK and The Tavistock Institute of Human Relations—which authorised and supported us in this effort;

To our families, who had to constantly compromise on our attention.

This book includes all papers that were presented at the Belgirate II conference in November 2006. They are divided into three sections according to their focus on adaptations and innovations in theory, design or application, and role taking.

The fourth and final section consists of four post-conference reflections written by participants of the conference.

Avi, Bob and Eliat
November 2008

# FOREWORD

Almost two decades ago, on a trip to London from my hometown in Perth, Western Australia, I was fortunate to meet the late Eric Miller. Perth is known to be the most isolated capital city in the world, and I expressed to Eric my envy of colleagues in London, who are so close to the nucleus of group relations—the Tavistock Institute. Eric replied wryly that he envied those of us in the Antipodes, far away from institutionalised pressures and with the apparent frontier freedom to explore.

I think he would have been stirred by the exciting developments and explorations that have emanated from the institutional heart of group relations, and which are so robustly evident in the Belgirate conferences and the gathering of group relations representatives from around the globe.

I feel very privileged to have been invited by the editors of the book to write this foreword. The breadth and depth of original and creative thought about, and application of, group relations theory, design, role-taking and application that I see in this book is a clear embodiment of its core theme, 'innovation and adaptation'.

In a Festschrift on the 65th birthday of Gouranga Chattopadhyay, I published a somewhat impassioned plea for the application of this inspired framework to the exploration of authority, leadership and organisation to the social and political world. I have, in the past, wondered what factors have constrained group relations work from deeply penetrating new arenas such as the corporate world and also the socio-political sphere. What boundary conditions might have restrained its proponents?

Although the authors in this volume may be seen to represent group relations in England, Israel, Australia, the USA, Italy, South Africa, India, the Netherlands, and Greece, it is clear from these fascinating chapters that representation is never simple. On the contrary, what is revealed is the complexity of 'boundaries' of identity, geography, sexuality, race, religion, and ethnicity, among other elements that weave into the fabric of Belgirate II and group relations internationally. Perhaps one of the key motifs to emerge from this book is the critical examination of what constitutes a 'boundary', and, by implication, whether—and how—adaptation and innovation involve boundary violation, penetration, expansion, destruction, or creation.

The exploration of the theme of 'adaptation and innovation' also draws vital attention to the exacting, complex and paradoxical nature of the evolution of group relations: continually adapting to what is 'known' inside and outside assumed boundaries. At the same time, challenging them, venturing into the unknown and, indeed, into the realm of the unknowable. This is the primary challenge exemplified in this volume.

Dr Allan Shafer
Clinical Psychologist and Socio-analyst
January 2009

# *ABOUT THE EDITORS AND CONTRIBUTORS*

## *Editors*

**Eliat Aram**, PhD, is the Director of the Tavistock Institute of Human Relations, which she leads through a new phase of change and growth. A practising chartered psychologist (BPS)—British Psychological Society and a UKCP (United Kingdom Council for Psychotherapy) registered psychotherapist and supervisor, with interests in team/organisational development and transformation, diversity and multiculturalism, she consults and coaches drawing on group relations theory and practice, systems psychodynamics, Gestalt therapy theory, and Complexity theory. She also works as a staff member on group relations conferences regularly nationally and internationally, and has directed the Tavistock Institute's group relations conference 'Authority, Role and Organisation' (the 'Leicester' conference) since 2007. She was born and raised in Israel and lives in London with her husband and two children.

**Robert Baxter**, MD, is a retired Professor of Psychiatry at the University of Louisville where he was Director of the Division of Child and Adolescent Psychiatry and Executive Director of the Bingham Child Guidance Center. He is a Fellow of the American Psychiatric

Association and the A.K. Rice Institute for the Study of Social Systems. He formerly served on AKRI's Board of Directors and was its President for eight years. He also directed AKRI's National Conference for four years, and he currently chairs AKRI's Training and Certification Committee. He now divides his time between Bonita Springs, Florida and Santa Fe, New Mexico.

**Avi Nutkevitch,** PhD, is a clinical psychologist, psychoanalyst and organizational consultant. He is a full member of the Israel Psychoanalytic Society and teaches at the Israel Psychoanalytic Institute and other postgraduate programs for psychotherapy. He is a founding member and former Chair of OFEK, the Israel Association for the Study of Group and Organisational Processes. He is currently Co-Director and Faculty of the Program in Organisational Consultation and Development: a Psychoanalytic-Systemic Approach. He holds a senior teaching position on the MBA programme of the College of Management in Rishon Le'Tzion.

## *Contributors*

**David Armstrong,** BA, is an organizational psychologist and Principal Consultant at the Tavistock Consultancy Service, the Tavistock Centre, London. He is a member of the International Society for the Psychoanalytic Study of Organizations (ISPSO). A collection of his occasional papers from the past 15 years, edited by Robert French, was published in Armstrong, D. (2005) *Organization in the Mind: Psychoanalysis, Group Relations and Organizational Consultancy.* London: Karnac.

**John Bazalgette,** MA, Dip Ed, is an organisational analyst. He is a senior member of staff of the Grubb Institute, London, UK and works as a consultant and researcher in a wide range of professional settings, both in the UK and other countries. He directs the Institute's innovative and practical Professional Development and Formation Programme, which leads to a Master's degree in Organisational Analysis from the University of East London. This multidisciplinary programme pays special attention to the practical application of beliefs and values in organisational life. He has particular responsibility for leading the Institute's work with institutions which initiate young people into the adult world. He has published several books and articles in this field. He has designed, directed and administered group relations conferences and applied variations in several different countries.

**Louisa Diana Brunner**, MSc, is a management and organizational consultant. She carries out selection and career counseling for the MBA Courses at the Bocconi School of Management, Milan. Her main areas of intervention and interest are leadership, family business, generational transitions, organizational culture, group relations, team-building and executive coaching. She is Treasurer of Partners in Confronting Collective Atrocities and a member of OFEK, Associazione il NODO Group, OPUS and CSGSS—The Boston Affiliate of AKRI.

**Willem de Jager**, PhD, is a consulting psychologist in organisational development, research and design. At the time of the project described in his paper, he was a specialist organisation development consultant in leadership and culture change for the ABSA Bank in South Africa where he oversaw large scale culture change and transformation projects affecting up to 55,000 employees. In this role, he developed interventions to build high performance cultures to deal with the demands of globalisation and democratisation of the workplace, talent and performance management and reward. He currently works for The Resolve Group in South Africa as an associate consultant in leadership and culture change.

**Doris L. Gottlieb**, MSc, is an organizational consultant based in Amsterdam, the Netherlands and is the founder of Contorno Consulting, a company working to stimulate organizational and professional development in (culturally) complex settings. She has a Master of Science in Mass Communication and is a graduate of the advanced program "Working on the Boundary" created by IAS International in Haarlem, The Netherlands. She is a member of the International Society for the Psychoanalytic Study of Organizations (ISPSO) and an associate of the Organisation for Promoting Understanding of Society (OPUS). She is also a Board member of Group Relations Nederland.

**Zachary Gabriel Green**, PhD, is a Fellow of the A.K. Rice Institute and an associate of the Washington-Baltimore Center. As a senior scholar at the Academy of Leadership, University of Maryland and an executive coach for the World Bank, he offers applied learning experiences and interventions that support and impact international leadership and development initiatives. He is also a member of the graduate faculty of the Leadership Institute, School of Leadership and Educational Sciences, at the University of San Diego. Zachary and his husband, Rene Molenkamp, are co-founders of Group Relations International and co-authors of numerous articles in the fields of identity analysis, leadership and group relations. They and their two sons reside in the Netherlands.

**Charla Hayden**, MA, has extensive experience in applying the "Tavistock" approach to teaching about leadership and authority and in consulting to issues in leadership, intergroup conflict, and organizational culture. She has been a member of the A.K. Rice Institute for the Study of Social Systems (AKRI) since it was established. She chaired the Institute's Committee on Training and Certification and served as Director of the AKRI National Conference from 1998–2000. Currently she is directing a series of residential conferences for the Boston Affiliate of AKRI.

**Yoram Lahav**, PhD, is a clinical psychologist, organizational consultant, and Lecturer, Graduate Program for School Counseling, Constantiner School of Education, Tel-Aviv University. He is a former board member of OFEK and was the Director of the first International Conference on Jewish Identity, Belonging and Leadership: Israel and the Diaspora.

**Susan Long**, PhD, is Professor of Creative and Sustainable Organisation with the Creative Organisational Systems Group (COS) at RMIT University in Melbourne, Australia. She has many years of experience with group relations methodologies working on conferences in Australia, New Zealand, the UK, Israel, the Netherlands and Germany. She was the inaugural President of Group Relations Australia, is currently on its Committee of Management and is a Board member of the International Society for the Psychoanalytic Study of Organisations (ISPSO). She has published five books and many articles in the field, the latest being *The Perverse Organisation and its Deadly Sins* published by Karnac, London, 2008.

**Mary B. McRae**, EdD, is an Associate Professor in Counseling Psychology, Department of Applied Psychology in the Steinhardt School of Culture, Education and Human Development at New York University. She is a licensed psychologist and practitioner who does individual/group psychotherapy, coaching and leadership development. She has served on the board of the A.K. Rice Institute for the Study of Social Systems and is presently a member of the New York Center for the Study of Groups, Organizations and Social Systems.

**Nick Papadopoulos**, MA, works as an executive coach, an organisation development and change consultant specialising in organisational culture, leadership and the people side of management, and a facilitator on leadership and people development programs. His professional interests lie in organisational culture, group and inter-group dynamics, learning conversations and the organisational design structures, systems and conversations that facilitate trust, collaboration and initiative between people. He has an MA in Advanced Organisational Consulting from the Tavistock Institute and an MA in Executive Coaching. In his prior career, he trained and worked as a psychotherapist in psychoanalytic psychotherapy, systemic family therapy, psychodrama and Gestalt therapy. He is a managing partner of People Savvy Consulting. He lives in Athens, Greece and works across Europe.

**Mario Perini**, MD, is a psychiatrist, psychoanalyst and organizational consultant. He is Chair of IL NODO Group, a member of the Italian Psychoanalytic Association (IPA), and the scientific advisor for the Italian Group Relations Conferences Programme ("Seminari di Arona"). He has been working for many years as a consultant in the public, private and voluntary sector and also as a trainer, a group supervisor, and a Balint group leader. He works in private practice as a psychotherapist and a personal coach, and he teaches group dynamics and team work at the Post-Graduate School of Health Psychology, Turin University.

**Mannie Sher**, BA, TQAP, FBAP, is a Principal Social Scientist and Director of the Group Relations Programme at the Tavistock Institute, London. He manages organisational development and change projects and consults to top management of organisations on the role of leadership in effecting strategic change. He is a Fellow of the British Association of Psychotherapists and a practicing psychoanalytical psychotherapist. He has published on subjects of consultancy, leadership, organisational development, ethics and corruption. He is a Board Member of ISPSO and a member of OFEK and OPUS.

**Ellen L. Short**, PhD, is currently an Assistant Professor at Long Island University, Brooklyn Campus, in the Department of Human Development and Leadership, Counseling Programs. She received her MA in Counseling Psychology from Northwestern University and her PhD in Counseling Psychology from New York University. Her areas of specialization in teaching, scholarly research and publishing are: group dynamics, focusing on race, ethnicity, gender, and culture; HIV, substance abuse and high-risk behavior among heterosexual populations; and multicultural assessment of intelligence tests.

**Gordon Strauss**, MD, is Professor of Psychiatry and Director of Student Psychiatric Services for the Campus Health Service at the University of Louisville. After joining the psychiatry faculty of the University of Louisville School of Medicine in 1992 he has been the training director and the director of emergency psychiatry. A graduate of New York University School of Medicine and of Stanford University, he was formerly on the faculty at UCLA where he was the founding director of the Center for the Study of Organizational and Group Dynamics. He is President of the Midwest Center for Group Relations, one of seven affiliated centers of the A.K. Rice Institute for the Study of Social Systems. He was a Board member of AKRI from 2005–08 and was the Director of the Leadership Institute, AKRI's annual group relations conference, from 2007–09.

**Josef Triest**, PhD, is a clinical psychologist, a Training Analyst of the Israel Psychoanalytic Institute (IPA), and an organizational consultant. He is the owner of the Triest-Sarig private clinic and a lecturer at Tel-Aviv University where he teaches at the psychology department, the general BA programme and the Group Facilitators Programme. He supervises and teaches also at the Israel Psychoanalytical Institute and at the psychotherapy school of Tel-Aviv University. He is a Member of OFEK, the Israel Association for the Study of Group and Organisational Processes, and is a Co-director and Faculty member in the Program in Organisational Consultation and Development: a Psychoanalytic-Systemic Approach (P.O.C.D.). He has taken up a variety of roles in group relations conferences, including the director's role in three of them. He is the author of several papers in the field of group relations.

**Gerard van Reekum**, CMC, is an organisation scientist and consultant and co-founder of InterSysteem Consulting Partners in Amsterdam. His professional practice ranges from organizational observation through group intervention to role transformation. He is certified with the OOA, a professional association of consultants in the Netherlands. He is a member of the International Society for the Psychoanalytic Study of Organizations (ISPSO), an associate of the Organisation for Promoting Understanding of Society (OPUS), and a Board member of Group Relations Nederland.

**Elio Vera** spent most of his working life working in marketing and communication in multinational companies like Henkel, Unilever, Young & Rubicam, and Chesebrough Pond's before becoming Executive and Intercultural Education Director of CESMA, the *Centre for Experiences and Studies in Management*, in Milan. He is one of the Founders of GRC in Italy, the "Seminari di Arona", and has contributed very actively to their development. He specializes in executive education and generational transition for medium and small entrepreneurs. He is a member of OPUS, EATGA (European Association for Transcultural Group Analysis) and EFMD (European Foundation for Management Development) and a past president of ETDF-FEFD (European Training and Development Federation).

**Rosemary Viswanath**, BSc, PGDBM, is an accredited professional member of the Indian Society of Applied Behavioural Sciences and a Member of the Orientation Committee of IFSI, France. She founded Learning Network, an organisation focussing on organisation change and strategic management with non-profits involved in social justice issues in India and internationally. She also heads EQUATIONS, a national non-profit organisation working for the rights of local communities impacted by mass tourism. She has been involved in group relations work in India and internationally for many years.

**Jeanne Woon**, PhD, is a psychologist at the University of Central Missouri. In addition to her counseling work with students there, she also provides training and consultation on group and organizational processes to other organizations. She has been involved in group relations since 1994, while a graduate student at Teachers College, Columbia University. She is an associate of the A.K. Rice Institute and of its Midwest and New York affiliates. She currently serves on AKRI's Training and Certification Committee.

*INTRODUCTION*

# Adaptation and innovation: Theory, design and role-taking in group relations conferences and their applications

*Eliat Aram, Robert Baxter and Avi Nutkevitch*

## *From two to three sponsoring institutions: From the personal duo to the organisational trio*

When Avi Nutkevitch and Mannie Sher got together after the first conference at Belgirate ended, in November 2003, they felt that the conference was successful in providing a space full of potential for emerging ideas and advancing the theory of Group Relations Conferences and their applications. It was then that they began the conversation around offering a second conference of this nature, perhaps three years later, to provide a space for the emerging international Group Relations network to continue working on relevant tasks.

Whereas Avi and Mannie's collaboration was institutional (OFEK and the Tavistock Institute), its origin was personal to a great degree, based on familiar inter- organisational and individual connections. A key question that emerged for them had to do with the temptation of institutional possessiveness versus the value of institutional generosity. Would they hold on to the 'patent' initiated through their personal authority, fed by the institutional authority of the Tavistock Institute and OFEK? Or would they open the boundaries of institutional authority (which we know is inherently unstable) and share the success they experienced as organisers of the first Belgirate conference by including a larger segment of the global network of GR organizations in the process of maintaining and taking forward this enterprise?

In parallel another question that emerged from the conference dynamics for the pragmatic Avi and Mannie was regarding the place of the large American GR contingency. In reflecting on these questions they thought it useful to consider the A.K. Rice Institute, the largest GR organisation in the world, as the third sponsor for the development of the second conference in Belgirate and as a likely candidate for increasing the participation of the American GR practitioners in this conference.

The move from two partner organisations to three symbolised the transition from the personal, yet not private, connection that gave birth to the first conference for GR practitioners to an international cross-institutional collaboration of persons-in-role.

A formal invitation was then issued to the president of AKRI, Bob Baxter, and its Board of Directors authorised him to hold an exploratory meeting with Avi and Mannie.

The three men met in February 2005, following which they then formally agreed to collaborate in working towards the task of providing a space for furthering GR international work for the second time in Belgirate in November 2006. They were all authorised by their respective institutions, and this collaboration was supported by a formal Memorandum of Agreement between AKRI, OFEK and the Tavistock Institute (TI).

Another change awaited the trio however. After that February, Mannie Sher, struggling under an increasing workload, wrote an email to the other two one day in June to say that he proposed a change to the management. He couldn't invest the time required to participate in this production but a newcomer to the TI, his colleague Eliat Aram, was willing and able to take this on.

So now, with Eliat Aram coming on board the Belgirate II management became gender mixed, cross generational and more formally a representation of this unique cross institutional collaboration among organisations that, to our knowledge, have never collaborated in this way before.

The three of us established regular telephone-conference calls which provided the space for all of the pre-conference work.

One of the first decisions we took was for AKRI to take up the leading administrative function, which included handling the budget for the conference the registration and payments. The only area where we found that the personal still prevailed was in liaison with the Hotel Villa Carlotta in Italy, where the owner paid little attention to anyone but Avi and, to a lesser degree, to Anne-Marie Kirkpatrick, one of the administrators.

While we joked and still joke about this, there might be some insight here to do with cultural and inter-cultural dialogue and connection. In addition, the Italian hotel owner's connection was with Avi, as if he knew—unconsciously—that OFEK symbolises the partner organisation that holds the authority for the history and the genesis of these conferences.

So, OFEK through Avi held the history of the Belgirate conferences; AKRI through Bob and Anne-Marie held the financial aspects of this enterprise; and Eliat- well, with her arrival we began to deal with the complexities of the history and tradition as represented through the Tavistock Institute at the same time as she, being a younger female newcomer to the TI, brought a sense of freedom to experiment with tradition and expand the boundaries of the GR network.

As we write about our experience of working together, we find it quite interesting. Two of us had never met before (Eliat and Bob); two of us had worked together once before (Avi and Eliat); and two met before in one or two conferences in NYC that they can't recall in the same way (Bob and Avi). Nevertheless, we have established a very satisfying working relationship, task-focused and clear on purpose, which was sustained throughout the conference and its dynamics. We had no director although we worked with Avi as convenor of the management based on his authority of history, but our decision making was joint and collaborative. Our experience of each other was one of trust and generosity; it was open and often filled with humour.

### *How come it worked?*

We believe that before and during the conference we represented movement: across age, ideas, traditions, succession. We came together fully authorised by our organisations to carry out the task of putting together this conference, and we were committed to working on this task with full and authentic collaboration.

We still hold as true our sense that the GR international network will only survive through collaboration, generosity of sharing and joint innovation and application. Despite the conference competitive and envious dynamics that are always part of this kind of work, the system-as-a-whole had the desire for this conference to succeed in providing the space for the GR network to grow and deepen.

This brings us to a key question in this chapter, namely to do with understanding the emerging **identity** of this enterprise, which we refer to as the Belgirate conferences.

## *Identity in relation to the Belgirate conferences: The notion of "organizational identity"*

The notion of organizational identity is a complex one that has been an emerging and interesting area of exploration and articulation in the last 25 years (Hatch & Schultz, 2004). We will not get into an extensive review of this notion, but highlight a few points that will provide a conceptual framework for our delineation of what we consider to be some important elements of the Belgirate conferences' identity.

The notion of identity of an organization or an enterprise (like the Belgirate conferences) answers the questions "who are we?" or "what do we want to be?" Concurrently the external world carries notions, images, phantasies, wishes, projections and projective identifications that are related to the questions "who are they?" or "what do they want to be?" Thus from a Socio-Psychological-Organizational perspective, the concept of identity is understood in relational terms. We assume that these two sets of images and definitions—the internal ones and the external ones—are reciprocally influencing each other, both consciously and unconsciously, and are thus related to the formation and development of the organizational identity, An organizational identity is a dynamic process that evolves and devolves over time and can be a source of some stability and coherence for those who depend on it. Hatch and Schultz (2004) offer a model where a formulation of an organizational identity is based on three sets of criteria: those related to the organization's **central character**; those related to the organization's **distinctiveness**; and those related to the organization's **temporal continuity**. However, there is no one objective way of defining what a "central character" is or what elements of "distinctiveness" or "temporal continuity" entail. There are endless aspects of an organization that can be related to its identity. In the literature on this subject, we find references to the organization's goals, culture, tasks, values, vision, membership, geographical location, ideology, and products or output, to mention a few. In group relations language we might talk about various **boundaries**: of primary task, of time, of territory, of membership, of structure and design, of ways of taking up roles, etc. Yet different people within or outside of the organization might define or interpret these things differently. The various elements related to the above are therefore not objective. They are related to the context and purpose of defining it, hence to conscious and unconscious dynamics of power and political agendas.

The way an organization's identity is defined and perceived by its management and members influences continuously its decisions both in the short and in the long run.

Organizational identity is therefore a heuristic concept—like a primary task—that serves as a compass for structuring, designing, managing and planning for the future.

Now, after a second Belgirate conference we feel we are in a place where describing some aspects of what transpired in the Belgirate II conference can be understood in relation to or in the context of the **emerging identity** of the Belgirate conferences as an organization or enterprise in-the-mind[1] (Armstrong, 2005).

## *Elements in the Belgirate conferences identity: Issues of place, time, participants, primary task, design, role taking and their meanings*

### *Place and time*

Clearly, the Belgirate conferences' identity is integrally related to space and time. The practical, rational reasoning of the location and the three years gap have an underlying meaning related to human beings attachment to the place where things have happened before and influence the developing psyche of the conferences through the rhythm of every three years return. This attachment may be understood differently from different perspectives, but we believe that naming the conference Belgirate II and hence making a strong connection to the place where the event takes place, and having it return to this place periodically, has meanings which are linked to experiencing an evolving tradition, history and roots, emerging identity and also spiritual associations (e.g. 'coming back' to a 'promised land', 'holy', place of worship' etc.)

Holding the Belgirate conferences in Italy regularly adds to the symbolism of a place in time which is a 'neutral' territory, or at least, not as contested as would be the homeland of any of the three sponsoring institutions.

### *The participants*

As was true for the first Belgirate conference, Belgirate II was designed for people who had held staff roles—directorial, consultative and/or administrative—in Group Relations conferences. This was an important aspect of the conference's identity, and it created a boundary that had to be managed. In the end, two applications to participate were rejected because the individuals indicated that they had had no staff role experience. However, given the fact that we had decided to take people's statements on their applications at face value, we did have at least one participant who had not taken up a staff role, despite stating otherwise on the application.

Delineating and managing this boundary around participation created a boundary around a subgroup of individuals associated with, and interested in, Group Relations. In drawing and holding this boundary, dynamics of inclusion and exclusion, of being chosen or rejected, emerged and carried a world of associations and fantasies in the life of the conference. Some of these are addressed by writers in the Post-conference Reflections section of the book.

In the pre-conference phase, the registration process was remarkably different from that experienced in many experiential Group Relations conferences around the globe today. Rather than being anxious about the sufficiency of participants, the Management Team ultimately had to struggle with the problem of space limitations. By the end of the early registration period, 95% of the total participants had registered for the conference, and in the weeks just prior to the conference, there was a waiting list of 14 individuals, three of whom were finally able to attend.

In total, 86 individuals, inclusive of the Management (3) and Administrative (2) Teams, participated in the conference. They represented 11 countries (Australia, Denmark, Finland, Germany, Israel, Italy, the Netherlands, South Africa, Sweden, the United Kingdom and the United States). One other person (from India) had to withdraw at the last minute. Of the participants, 46 had previously directed Group Relations conferences, 79 had served in consultant roles and 37 had administered one or more Group Relations conferences. Five individuals had taken up administrative roles exclusively.

The age distribution among the participants was of interest. Two did not indicate their age, but of the others, only 16 were younger than 50. Three were 70 or older; 32 were aged 60–69; 33 were aged 50–59; 15 were aged 40–49; and one person was aged 30–39. This distribution poses questions about where the younger generation of Group Relations practitioners is and how to include these individuals in future events such as this.

Many of the participants took up specific roles during the conference. Fourteen individuals presented papers while 10 others chaired their presentations. Two of the participants served as convenors for the morning reflections and associations events. The Management Team included the three of us, and the Administrative Team included Anne Marie Kirkpatrick and Miri Tzadok; collectively, we referred to ourselves as the MATS. In total, 31 participants held specifically authorized roles during the conference. This reflected an element of the culture and identity of the conference: the fact that this was a meeting of colleagues, created by a small group but implemented and sustained through collective participation. Perhaps the best analogy is that of an extended family dinner party; the Management Team planned and hosted, but did not direct, the event as would be expected in a group relations conference.

### *The primary task*

We stated in the brochure that the primary task of this conference was:

> *To provide opportunities to learn about and explore innovations and adaptations in theory, design and role taking in GR conferences and their applications.*

Whereas the first Belgirate conference was about exploring and reviewing 'what is' a GRC, the second one looking at innovations and adaptations was a natural and logical extension to that. The Group Relations Conference concept, including its theoretical underpinnings, structure, design and applications are at the heart of the conceptualisation and delivery of the Belgirate conference. It is a statement, co-created by the participants of the conference as members of the global GR community, regarding the GRC as the main meeting ground of theory, design, values, ways of taking up roles, GR principles and practices. In other words, the practice of a GRC is the core aspect of identity of the Belgirate conference.

The question of how to work on the primary task of these conferences, which deal with GRCs and their applications, is directly related to the question of how the Belgirate conferences' identity develops and expresses itself over time. Some of the answer is in the design.

### *Design of the conference*

The conference combined both the traditional scientific mode of formal paper presentations with discussion and a here-and-now exploratory event. This design attempted to meet the primary task of this conference as well as hold and contain the tension embedded between the two modes of engaging with the conference task. Weaving together these two modes of exploring, learning and engaging is another major aspect of the identity of Belgirate, which doesn't go without challenge.

The **exploratory event**, with the task of exploring conscious and unconscious forces and meanings underlying the conference and its themes, included both an opening and a closing plenary with five 90-minute sessions in between. While others were free to constitute (or not) their own groups for exploration, the MATs announced that they would fully participate but would remain together in order to carry out their specialized functions as management of the event and the conference. The MATs intention was to participate in the exploration with transparency but to not explore the familiar authority relations in the here-and-now, as would be expected in an experiential Group Relations conference.

This, however, proved confusing. It was in this event that the tension between the primary task of the conference and the habitual primary task of an experiential Group Relations conference became most apparent. As management, we felt a continual pull and expectation for us to take up roles as consultants and management to an institutional event and to provide hypotheses to the membership about the state of the conference institution.

The MATS' dilemma was complex, indeed. We were committed to providing a space for exploration but were equally committed to not intruding actively on the participants' experiences. Therefore, we often did not know what those experiences were. We did not own the event; we did not see that our role was to work toward an over-all sense of the system. We did not see that our task was to collect data, integrate it and offer hypotheses to the system as a whole.

Our management of the boundary of the event included a high degree of participation, or the desire at least, to be part of the experience with little attempt to control the learning.

We anticipated that collective learning would come out in the collaborative and iterative process of the event and in its subsequent plenary. However, in failing to provide interventions from an assumed knowing position that would interpret the unconscious processes that were taking place, we were perceived as not managing well and even criticized for not leading well.

### *Management and leadership at Belgirate II*

#### *The way we took up our role*

As MATs working together in this way for the first time we were exploring the nature of the conference and its management as part of our work in this event. The discussions we had during the event included debating the nature of MAT in a conference such as this, how it was done before and how we would like to do it now. We were keen to operate as collaborative management and participants, trying to constantly deal with tension between participation, and its meaning, and management, and its meaning, during the event.

In exploring the hidden dynamics that informed our work, we think that the challenge and possible anxiety in containing such an international gathering of GR practitioners also led us to work in this way. An example of this could be our decision to stay together as MATs in the EE instead of participating fully in the groupings of this event and delegating the MAT, should this be management?? function to the administrative team.

In addition, the fear of an envious attack, the experience of being humbled by 86 people coming to work together in a communal spirit for Group Relations for four days, our sense of purpose as hosts in service of the task of the conference, and the transition from the pre-conference leadership work into the conference management work mixed together to lead us to downplay our leadership in the exploratory event. We focused instead on managing and containing the boundaries to allow the 'extended family dinner party' to fulfil itself.

Since our clarity of role in this event emerged as the event progressed, we understand that the experience of the participants was ambivalent. It seemed that there was a lack of clarity about us as management and hence the criticism (is this the management we want and/or need?) at the same time as we were experienced as enabling an authentic exploration of the nature of this conference.

### *The question of leadership in the GR network in this conference*

This was a prominent issue at this conference: the wish for the old leadership style, where one strong leader is loved and hated, whilst recognising the transition in the world towards leadership through networking and collaboration, where survival is determined through interdependent relationships and not through linear hierarchies.

It was brought up in one morning reflections and associations session through a dream in which two conference participants were standing on a balcony and one showed the other the night sky, which was clear without stars.

This dream could be seen as touching the question of leadership as it was perceived or wished for in the conference as well as the question of leadership in GR network, which was alive in Belgirate I as well as in this second Belgirate conference. The dream can be interpreted as either a wish for stardom in GR work and a rejection of the collaborative networking leadership, or vice versa, a wish for collaborative leadership with no stars in it.

### *From temporary to permanent: Expressing the Belgirate identity through the written word*

As it happened, the book based on the Belgirate I conference that Karnac was happy to publish was ready just in time for this second Belgirate II conference. The shipment of books arrived for the last evening of the conference, enabling us to hold a lovely book launch ceremony. This book continued to sell after this conference and led to Karnac being pleased to offer a contract for the second book.

The connection between Belgirate conferences and book publications, which through this second book is now being established, is meaningful. The Belgirate conferences seem to be providing a scholarly greenhouse for the articulation and continued originality of group relations practice, theory and methodology, and offers a permanent space in the life of the otherwise 'temporary' nature of GR conferences.

### *A final word*

The first Belgirate conference was an innovation. Belgirate II adapted the structure of that conference in order to explore different themes, and it returned to the same venue for that exploration, thereby establishing a sense of continuity and, perhaps, the beginning of a tradition. The notions of continuity and tradition are intimately related to the notion of this enterprise's identity.

We believe that our exploration and attempt to articulate various elements of the Belgirate conferences' identity not only is an interesting and important way of describing an enterprise and a modest contribution to the research regarding this powerful notion of 'organizational identity', but is also a statement for the future—for those future group relations organizations and persons-in-role that will be involved in planning, managing and developing creatively this enterprise named the Belgirate conferences.

### *Note*

1. The organisation-in-the-mind is the person's initial emotional and mental reading of the organisational system as emerging from the evidence the person has collected.

## *References*


Armstrong, D. (2005). *The organisation in the mind: Psychoanalysis, group Relations and organisational consultancy*. London: Karnac.

Hatch, M.J. & Schultz, M. (2004). The dynamics of organizational identity, In *Organizational Identity: A Reader*, Hatch & Schultz, Oxford University Press.

Hatch, M.J. & Schultz, M. (2004). *Organizational Identity: A Reader*. Oxford University Press.

# SECTION I

## ADAPTATION AND INNOVATION IN THEORY

Each of the three chapters in this section has taken a key aspect of Group Relations Conferences and offered a rigorous discussion of it.

In the first of these David Armstrong takes a fresh and creative look at the Large Study Group (LSG) event, which has always been pivotal to a Group Relations Conference. Drawing on James Joyce's concept of 'plurability of experience', Armstrong explores the LSG as a paradoxical experience in place and time where, he says, what may be most feared is also what may be most generative.

The second of these chapters, by John Bazalgette, draws on the Grubb Institute's 'Transforming Experience Framework' to substantiate the understanding of Leadership, a key concept for exploration and experimentation in a Group Relations Conference. Bazalgette suggests that a Leader is someone who is a full human being in role, from which s/he is able to take action into the world with a physical, intellectual and spiritual sense of purpose, drawing on the rich resource within oneself, one's environment and society and one's world of faith.

The third and final chapter in this section, by Avi Nutkevitch and Joseph Triest, is an examination of a core theory underlying and informing the Group Relations Conference practice, namely Psychoanalysis. Starting with a provocative question—'Doth my father yet live?'—Nutkevitch and Triest examine the place of our "theoretical fathers" in light of developments in psychoanalysis. They explore critically the perception of authority and its representation in the unconscious, the question regarding the validity of the consultants interpretations, as well as the unconscious place of narcissistic needs and their unacknowledged appearance in conference life.

Put together, the chapters in this section excite the brain and stimulate our collective thinking. They all reflect the rich and in-depth thinking that exists within the Group Relations community around the world.

CHAPTER ONE

# The 'plurability of experience': Looking afresh at the large group

*David Armstrong*

The neologism in this title was first coined I believe by James Joyce. I came across it last summer, together with the phrase in which it appears, when, during an enforced absence from work, I happened to pick up the Penguin edition of Ulysses and started reading. It is cited in the Introduction to this edition by the Irish academic, Declan Kiberd (Kiberd, 2000).

One might take this phrase as referring to the capacity of the novelist (or dramatist) to enter into the multiple worlds of his or her characters; something akin to Keats's description of Shakespeare as a 'Man of Achievement' and his famous characterisation of 'negative capability' as the means of entry to such, imaginative, achievement (Forman, 1931, pp. 69–72). However, Kiberd makes clear that for Joyce this capacity refers equally to the ability and readiness of the author to enter into the multiple worlds, the multiple 'characters', one might say, of himself.

This is how Kiberd puts it, drawing on a distinction initially made by the American literary critic, Lionel Trilling, between sincerity and authenticity:

> "Sincerity, a congruence between avowal and feeling, is based on the Romantic idea of truth to the self and it presupposes a

> definite identity which it becomes the task of a lifetime to be true to. Authenticity … a more exclusively modern demand … makes the congruence between avowal and feeling difficult: it recognises that the issue is not truth to the self but the finding of the many selves that one might wish to be true to. It makes the liberating concession that a person, or a nation, has a plurality of identities, constantly remaking themselves as a result of perpetual renewals".
>
> "The romantic writer says: there is an essential Ireland to be served and a definite Irish mind to be described. The modernist rejoins: there is no single Ireland, but a field of force subject to constant renegotiations; and no Irish mind, but Irish minds shaped by a predicament which produces some common characteristics in those caught up in it" (Kiberd, 2000, pp. xxvii–iii).

One might perhaps compare this, at the level of the individual, to the distinction between the psychoanalytic romanticism of, say, Winnicott's formulation of the 'true self' and Wilfred Bion's more layered picture, most strikingly on display in his psychoanalytic dialogue, *"A Memoir of the Future"*, (Bion, 1991), of the many voices out of whose imagined conversation a personality evolves, develops, regresses, is conflicted, continually renegotiating its own boundaries: the group in the mind.

I want to suggest that this literary formulation, captured in Joyce's neologism, the 'plurability' of experience, has a particular aptness in relation to the phenomena of the Large Group, as we encounter this in conference settings, illuminating both its constructive potential and the more destructive shadow that potential elicits and evokes. I want, then, to use this perspective to raise a number of questions and reservations, both about how we may work as consultants in and to the Large Group and about certain limitations that a Group Relations perspective may set, implicitly if not explicitly, on the boundaries of exploration. I hope this may in turn open up broader questions of areas of possible innovation in design and technique.

## *Images of configuration*

While Joyce's neologism and its augmentation in Kiberd's comment helped to stake out the territory I am seeking to explore, the immediate origin of this paper I owe to the impact of two images offered by members during successive conferences at Leicester, in which I was working as a consultant in the Large Study Group. Both of these images referred to the physical configuration of the LSG and each was presented in a session shortly after the mid conference break. Together they seemed to give birth to the "germ of an idea" which I am trying to articulate here and now. Whether it will turn out to add something new or fresh or simply be another way of saying what we already know, I remain unsure.

Both images shared something, in being brief, unexpected and apparently disregarded. Each however differed in their emotional tone: the first suffused with hope, the second with despair.

The first image was offered by a member, excitedly, at the start of I think the second LSG following the break. The group had been, both for members and for consultants, a pretty turbulent ride so far. In the middle of the first week one member had had to withdraw from the conference. The shock waves were still around. Staff, consultants and sponsoring institution were all under intense scrutiny; issues of safety and dependability at a premium. There was also, as normally in recent years, a sharp and noticeable differentiation between second and first timers, the 'knowing' and the 'innocents abroad'.

The image was presented by a first timer, whose background and profession owed little or nothing to potential conference know how. He had been pretty active in the Large Group, sometimes welcomed for speaking his mind, sometimes consciously or unconsciously somewhat patronised. The physical configuration of the Large Group was the familiar (at least in Leicester Conferences) spiral. During the Large Group there had been a good deal of the sharing of dreams, often quite lengthy, offered mainly if not exclusively by second or third timers. What the new member now offered was not a dream he said, but an image that had come to him that morning and had excited him. It was simply this: that he had seen the lay out of the group as an **image of the brain.** Although I cannot exactly recall what he went on briefly to say, the import seem to be of a many faceted and differentiated vehicle for registering experience, which if it could be accessed would offer ...? It wasn't exactly clear what, but something additive: an enlargement.

In the session the conversation moved swiftly on, the image and its offerer, apparently discounted or ignored. But the image stayed with me, unusually vivid, intense and apparently suggestive, throughout the day and subsequently. Sometime, during a gap in the programme, I jotted down the following train of thought. I am leaving it more or less as it came out at the time.

> "One image that will stay with me (from this conference) is the image of the Large Group as a brain—with all its separate layers, cortices, left and right sides, cerebral and basal.
>
> It was offered as an image of enlargement, of collaboration and connection (but I wonder) if this image is at the same time terrifying (maybe this is why it is not picked up and built on). Does it arouse a fear that in trying to connect with all these parts, one's own sense of separateness and identity will dissolve?
>
> At the same time, it seems to me an image, (a potentially fearful image), of each one of us also, of the insides of our own heads. As if were we to conduct a conversation between all the parts of our own brains we too would dissolve into fragments and identity seem but a mirage.
>
> So better a contracting universe than an expanding one.
>
> Would this help to make sense of the boundaries we seem, as staff and members, to set up: me/not me;/us/not us; but also staff/member; male/female; my/our/your nationality/ethnicity etc, even on task/off task.
>
> They seem so reasonable, but are they also defensive: strategies of contraction, or boundaries of exclusion".

I will return to these somewhat unprocessed reflections in a moment, trying to locate them against what others have written and thought about Large Group dynamics. But first I need to share the second image that stuck in my mind, one year on. I referred to this earlier as an image of despair. It was offered, this time by a woman, who herself worked professionally with groups outside, towards the end of a session after the break, in which she had till then been silent.

To appreciate the image she offered I need to say something about the physical lay out of the Large Group on this occasion. One of the members attending the conference was disabled, as a result of an accident some while ago, and confined to a wheel chair. The LSG consultants wondered beforehand how best to arrange the Large Group configuration in a way that would enable her to locate a place, if not completely of her own choosing, at least within a range of options nearer or further from the centre. We eventually decided to preserve something of the familiar spiral, but to open up a gap from the door and through to the start of the spiral in a way that would allow her to move between the different layers or rings. One of us was to describe the arrangement as a bit like a keyhole. Correspondingly we took out one chair. In the event this arrangement was never made use of, the member in question, with the assistance of one or other participant, finding her own place somewhere, usually in the outer ring, with consequent reshuffling of chairs. Nor was the arrangement of the spiral ever referred to in the group except towards the end of the second week. Disability and staff's management attempt to accommodate for it went unacknowledged, in the Large Group at least, session after session. It was eventually to emerge in dramatic form during the Institutional Event, after which it did become possible to name in the LSG, but subsequent to the session I am referring to.

During this session the member offering the image in question arrived a little late and took a seat just to the left of the opening into the spiral near the door, with just two occupied chairs at the end of the spiral next to her. I cannot now remember the drift of the discussion preceding her comment, though I do recall noting her silence and a certain air of distress. What she said was that arriving late, she had taken this seat and had gradually begun to feel that it was as if she was at the tail end of a snake that had been bitten off. She conveyed a sense of disconnection and an attendant anxiety, as if she had been in some sense depleted or rendered silent.

After she had spoken I was aware of an association I was making to her offered image. This was to what I thought of as a kind of revisionist account of the story of the Garden of Eden, in which Eve instead of biting the proffered apple of knowledge, bites off the serpent's tail.

In his magisterial and to some degree still unsuperceded or outgrown account of Large Group dynamics, originally written in the early 70s, Pierre Turquet at one point comments on how, faced with the sense of bewilderment and bombardment attendant on membership of the Large Group (its 'disarroy' as he puts it), there may be the emergence of a:

> "paradise myth, the I M (individual member) seeing himself as being expelled from the Garden of Eden, with a loss of innocence and with knowledge as a feared, even unnecessary eruption into what should be a quiet and peaceful existence. At the same time there are present wishes to return to such a state of blissful ignorance, as if ignorance could be recreated" (Turquet, 1975/1994, p. 103).

Well, maybe. But on this occasion, it seemed and still seems to me, that this member's implicit reversal of the paradise story, with its accompanying aura of despair, expressed and drew attention rather to some sense of deadness in the rejection of knowing, whatever the burden of knowing might turn out to be. Something perhaps represented, though not named, in the silence around disability. Not so much then a regressive pull as a, partly vain, unconscious, developmental push.

The two images I have described I am taking to be work interventions, each of which potentially both posed and offered a developmental challenge, though neither at the time gained much of a purchase. I want to argue that between them they may serve not just to illustrate but to illuminate a paradox at the heart of the Large Group experience: that what may be most feared is simultaneously what may be most generative: to return to my starting point, the 'plurability of experience', in the individual as in the group, each of which may serve as a mirror to the other.

## *The problematising of identity*

There is nothing particularly new in the thought that the Large Group, with its multiple and not readily encompassable voices (or faces of experience, voiced or silent), challenges the individual's sense of identity. Pierre Turquet's pioneering account of the Large Group, which I cited a moment ago is after all itself, entitled 'Threats to Identity in the Large Group'.

In this paper Turquet refers to the "dislocation every conference member experiences as he takes himself into a world which transcends the usual parameters of his own individuality" and the ways in which this may threaten him or her with "annihilation", of "becoming other than himself (or herself), of being in some way altered, pressurised, even diminished" (Turquet, op cit, p. 94).

Later on he comments how:

> "the apparent vastness of the Large Group seems to give substance to a fantasy of the singleton/IM's internal world as also vast, unencompassable or boundless. The singleton requires of external life in groups a bounded experience to take in as an introject on which to build up his own psychic life-notions of internal boundaries or limitations. But the immediate external picture conjured up by the large group is one of vastness, if only because the boundaries do not seem to be directly or immediately visible" (Turquet, op cit, p. 117).

What I want to suggest, though, is that the 'fantasy' of unencompassability or boundlessness may be serving rather as a cover for what is, here and now, experienced as unencompassable, in the self as in the group: the unacknowledged or unconscious states of mind that go against the grain of our entertained sense of identity; states of mind, like all unconscious experience," not directly or immediately visible". To put this another way I suggest that it is precisely our "psychic life-notions of internal boundaries or limitations" that the experience of the Large Group challenges. It threatens our experience of identity one might say precisely because it problematises it. On this view the threat of annihilation Turquet refers to, is not so much of becoming other than one's self, as of the risk of discovering the unwanted selves lurking around in the shadows.

I believe that it is the anticipatory fear, or at the extreme the terror, of this unknown territory of the self that drives the drama of projection and projective identification in the Large Group that Turquet maps out, alongside the panoply of defensive strategies, e.g. sub group formation, the obliteration or alternatively the over accentuation of differences, the attempts to establish implicit or explicit rules of conduct etc. I would also think that what Turquet refers to as "errancy", the potential for violence that may erupt in the Large Group, is both an externalisation and a defence against the felt violence or potential for violence within each individual's inner world.

In one of the series of seminars Wilfred Bion conducted towards the end of his life, referring to his experience as an analyst, he comments:

> "the situation in analysis is misleading, because there is apparently only one person there with the analyst. I have found my experiences in groups useful—a group is almost like one person, character or personality spread out over a space" (Bion, 2005, p. 18).

The implicit quid pro quo is that the person is 'almost like' a group. One way of expressing what I am trying to draw attention to is just this: that what may seem to be spread out over the space of the Large Group is simultaneously experienced as evoking and gathering together the group within. The fear of and for the Large Group is then an echo of the fear of and for what might perhaps be termed the 'group of and in ourselves'.

I suggest that, whether it is a conscious intent or more likely an unconscious apprehension, it is our readiness to entertain the plurality of voices within the self that enables us as it were to negotiate and give value to the plurality of voices within the Large Group. It is this apprehension or readiness that I think is captured in Joyce's 'plurability'.

Earlier I referred to the situation in the Large Group as mirroring the situation in the individual and vice versa. But I am not suggesting that the plurality of voices in the Large Group and the plurality of voices in the individual member are one and the same. If that were so the Large Group would simply appear as a kind of vehicle for individual therapy. There are real differences in the Large Group, as many one might suggest as there are individual members. In a sense, the issue in the Large Group and its generative potential lies precisely in bringing these differences into view, to borrow a phrase from an Italian analyst as "the focal points of a multidimensional conversation" (Bion, 2005, p. 56). The point I am making is simply that the readiness to entertain these differences and explore their meaning-what they are saying about this gathering of people and the context in which they meet—turns on our capacity to tolerate, to entertain the differences, conscious and unconscious, in ourselves. And this is risky, precisely to the extent that it is unknown.

It is this fear of what is unknown, in one's self no less than in the group that in my view drives the regressive pull of the Large Group experience, the descent into Turquet's 'disarroy'.

And there is a sense in which, whatever its consequences, this fear may be said to be completely realistic, since we cannot foresee the spectres in ourselves, the unconscious, unacknowledged spectral selves that we may meet on the way, like the ghosts that haunt Dante's hell.

But it is equally important, though not I think equally acknowledged, that alongside this regressive pull there may also be a countervailing developmental push. And this is what I took to be represented, however obliquely, in the second image, offered by a woman, from which I started, where the rejection of knowing was felt as a deadness, a contraction: a movement or dynamic that foreclosed the possibility of an expansion, in one's acquaintance with and understanding of oneself, the group within one's being and one's being within the group.

I think there are occasions in the Large Group when this developmental push takes hold and indeed were this not the case it is quite hard to understand why people should stay the course, other than perhaps to feel at the end, 'well at least we have come through'. But in my experience for much if not most of the time it seems present more as a sensed, feared and never fully realised potential: one might say as an absent object!

Why? I am not convinced that this developmental difficulty is necessarily intrinsic to any large group experience. And during the last few years I have had experiences of consulting to large groups in other settings, where in spite of an undercurrent of anxiety, (as a participant in one such event put it, "our tendency to behave as if a large group is like facing the medusa"), the mutative potential of the large group as a vehicle for unlocking and communicating differences of experience within a bounded and shared setting (the membership of a professional society for example), for facing shared challenges or unravelling felt conflicts, has seemed to have more space in which to play.

There is a sense I think in which our conceptualisation of and approach to the Large Group is over-determined, in a way which both feeds into and in turn mobilises the regressive pull. In conference brochures for example the Large Study Group or the Large Study Event is regularly introduced as follows:

> "By contrast (to the Small Study Group) the LSG has more of the qualities of a crowd in which sub-groups and anti-groups, alliances and anti-alliances, fantasies and myths emerge"
>
> (The Leicester Conference brochure, 2003)

Or

> "The Large Study Event (LSE) is of a size where individual relations are difficult to form and sustain, being swamped by group myths, both conscious and unconscious, reflecting various assumptions and their impact on behaviour"
>
> (The Grubb Institute Conference brochure, 2006)

The language (crowd, swamped, anti-groups, difficult to sustain) seems well designed to arouse an anticipatory anxiety, a sense of getting into something exciting, unfamiliar, and maybe dangerous. Why do we feel the need to say any of this beforehand?

Well one answer could be that the conference organisers are simply alerting members to what will indeed be the case. And in one sense this is true. But it is true I think, not because a large group is exclusively characterised in these terms, but because it is precisely this feature or dimension of the Large Group that the conference explicitly sets out to frame and explore.

Here we come up against a dilemma which I have argued before may indeed be intrinsic, not so much to the theory or indeed the reality of Group Relations but rather to their institutionalisation in Group Relations conferences and events. The argument goes as follows:

> "Group Relations conferences, whatever the titles they trade under, are temporary training institutions set up to explore or study the tensions inherent in group life, using a method of experiential learning. This is their manifest intention or 'primary task'. In order to study these tensions a frame must be created which mobilises such tensions from the outset. In part this frame is created by the very definition of the task, since

> as Bob Gosling once put it with characteristic bluntness "setting up a group that studies its own tensions is a rather peculiar social experience". This peculiarity is in turn considerably compounded by the combination of under and over determination that, appropriately enough, characterizes the organisation and structure of the Conference and correspondingly the behaviour of staff in their work roles.
>
> By 'underdetermination' I am referring to the stance taken by consultant staff within the here and now events: the refusal to answer questions, to structure the conversation, to address members as individuals etc, all of which are aspects of the rejection of basic assumption leadership. By 'overdetermination' I am referring to the firmness, often felt to be rigidity, with which boundaries are observed by staff, in particular boundaries of time, which may be taken as the accentuation almost to the point of characiature, of a work group culture.
>
> Undue obtrusion of the basic group (or I might say here of the defensive strategies of the Large Group) are precisely what the design of such conferences seeks to sustain and hence make available for exploration. Inevitably then, attention tends to focus on this level of mental functioning. Correspondingly, the part played by work group mentality (the experiences, thoughts, associations, feelings of the group as an 'aggregate of individuals, or persons',) can slip out of view. It operates often I think as a silent factor, expressed in members' readiness to stay in the field of what can be an extraordinarily unsettling experience" (Armstrong, 2005, pp. 146–7).

Returning to this argument again, now in a different context, I would want to put it differently. I find myself wondering whether it is not so much that work group functioning slips out of view as that, paradoxically, it takes place below the surface, operating unconsciously as members get more in touch with the multiple voices in themselves and hence more able to acknowledge, to listen and give value to the multiple voices in the group. If so one might pick this up in the changing ways in which differences were being heard, built on, linked, associated to.

I am not always sure that as consultants in the Large Group we attend or find ourselves attending to this unconscious movement within what is happening. The focus on the relation to the consultant group gives what might be termed a certain steer to the distribution and flow of transference and counter transference phenomena. This steer and the accompanying emphasis on whole group interpretation may I think sometimes give rise to what a younger colleague, Simon Western, has referred to as a tendency towards 'totalisation', in which something of the variety or multi-dimensionality of the Large Group experience, as this is being refracted through the prism of its different members, is lost. If I am right about an unconscious movement in work group activity one might imagine that as this begins to take hold the working relation between consultants and the Large Group could shift. Towards something more collaborative and associative, less transferential or interpretative. Why, for example, was I not prepared to share my own associations to the two images I started from, at the time? What held me back?

The difficulty is perhaps not so much to do with our focus or preoccupation with group dynamics as such, but rather with our tendency to read group dynamics or group mentality too exclusively in defensive terms, rather than in terms of the tension between the developmental challenges of the work group, the resistances set up against these challenges and what it is that drives those resistances, Pierre Turquet's 'because clause'. In my view the 'because clause' will always have to do with the unconscious undertow of the work group, its sensed internal meaning. Just as in Isabel Menzies Lyth's path breaking study of nursing, the defensive mechanisms she identified in the structuring and dynamics of the hospital were seen to have arisen and be functioning as a resistance or defence against unconscious anxieties inherent in the task of nursing (Menzies Lyth, 1960/1988, pp. 43–85).

I do not think we have ever fully or adequately conceptualised the specific nature of the work group in conference settings and in the particular events which frame those settings. Hence perhaps the tendency as it were to leave the dynamics of the work group to one side (Armstrong, D. 2005, pp. 139–150).

In this regard one might read or hear this paper as one provisional attempt to locate the unconscious meaning or import of the work group within the Large Group event. To return to my starting point, that it challenges the singularity of our identity. To enter the large group as a member, that is to take up the role of member, necessarily and unconsciously involves encountering and engaging with that challenge. This is its unique particularity.

It is, in my view, this unconsciously sensed particularity that both limits but simultaneously evokes the transformational potential of the Large Group: to return to the quotation from which I began, the acknowledgement that a person or collectivity of persons, (family, tribe, organisation, nation) *"has a plurality of identities, constantly remaking themselves as a result of perpetual renewals"*, ... *"shaped"*, as the writer goes on to say *"by a predicament which produces some common characteristics in those caught up in it"* (Kiberd, op cit, p1xvii).

One might, then, think of the Large Group as a vehicle for the exploration of this predicament. And this leads to the last thing I want to say, concerning application. I am not quite sure how to put this. The idea of the Large Group as a vehicle for the exploration of plurability opens up new ways both of thinking about and probing the nature of our wider organisational and societal attachments. It expands or broadens the idea of the 'organisation (or society) in the mind', suggesting to paraphrase Kiberd's gloss on Joyce's enterprise in his novel, that we think rather in terms of a *"field of force, subject to constant renegotiations"*.

The Large Study Group **in** itself does not provide a vehicle for such an exploration, since the focus is simply **on** itself. There is, as it were, no third shared object in the wings. The conference as an organisation is not such an object. (The LSG is not about exploring the 'organisation in the mind' and the attempt to make it so, which may often surface at the beginning of a group, only serves as a defence against the anxiety membership of the Large Group elicits).

Moreover the focus on the 'here and now' and the interpretative stance taken by the consultants, however valuable in probing the nature of the anxiety membership of the Large Group elicits, tends, as I have already suggested, to get in the way of a more free floating, associative mode of working.

I am not suggesting that the experience of the Large Group is irrelevant to the kind of exploration I have in mind. On the contrary, to the extent that the Large Group opens up the territory of plurability and the resistances to which it may give rise, it may rather prepare the ground for such an exploration. But it does not itself constitute it.

Suppose, though, that one revisits the ways in which at present we think of plenary sessions, in particular those plenaries that take place towards the end of a conference, after the 'here and now' sessions have run their course. At the moment the focus of such sessions tends to be on sharing experiences of individual learning, or non-learning and working at endings.

Another way of construing and perhaps extending such sessions would be to frame them as an exploration of the conference itself as an organisation, as this has been and is being refracted through the minds of its participants, members and staff, meeting now, collaboratively, as co-workers or peers. Within such a meeting, the interpretative stance would be suspended, or carried as it were implicitly in the to and from of associative work, similar perhaps to what may happen in a Social Dreaming Matrix. (Lawrence, 2005).

Such an exploration could serve not only to continue but to test the learning, put it to work, introduce us afresh to the organisation or organisations in the mind we have been and are part off, the multiplicity of their identity, the developmental and counter developmental forces at work, the predicament at their heart. The analytic stance.

## *References*

Armstrong, D. (2005). The work group revisited: Reflections on the practice and reference of group relations. In: D. Armstrong, Organisation in the Mind: Psychoanalysis, Group Relations and Organisational Consultancy, (edited by Robert French) (pp. 139–150). London: Karnac.

Bion, W.R. (1991). A Memoir of the Future. London: Karnac.

Bion, W.R. (2006). The Italian Seminars. London: Karnac.

Forman, M.B. (ed.). (1931). The Letters of John Keats. London: Oxford University Press.

Kiberd, D. (2000). Introduction, in James Joyce, Ulysses. London: Penguin Books.

Lawrence, W.G. (2005). An Introduction to Social Dreaming: transforming thinking. London: Karnac.

Menzies Lyth, 1. (1960). A case study in the functioning of social systems as a defence against anxiety. Human Relations, *13*: 95–121. (Reprinted in: 1. Menzies Lyth, Containing Anxiety in Institutions. Selected Essays, *Vol 1* (pp. 26–44). London: Free Association Books, 1988.)

CHAPTER TWO

# Leadership: The impact of the full human being in role

*John Bazalgette*

*This paper describes work in progress at The Grubb Institute. Though I made the original presentation in November 2006, at Belgirate II, I spoke then and write now on behalf of my colleagues: Bruce Irvine, Rosy Fairhurst, Colin Quine, Jean Reed and Vega Roberts. At the heart of the Framework described here is the original thinking of the late Bruce Reed, the founder of The Grubb Institute, the fourth anniversary of whose death fell at the time of writing this paper.*

John Bazalgette

## *"He was their leader: He followed them"*

There is a mysterious symbiosis between *'leader'* and *'follower'* which is nicely summed up above by Christopher Hill (1972) in his description of the relationship between Oliver Cromwell and the Parliamentarians during the English Civil War in the middle of the seventeenth century.

But how does that symbiosis work out in 21st century practice?

When we allow ourselves beyond common thinking about leadership which embeds it primarily in working organisations, we find ourselves realising that this aphorism most accurately applies to experiences elsewhere—between parents and children, clinicians and patients, priests and congregations, and teachers and students. These relationships all contain an emotional exposure of oneness with the other, where oneness includes the linked electrical poles—positive and negative. This oneness has a greater depth than is common in relations between persons in organisations such as business, finance, government, the administration of justice or the military.

All human structures wrestle with the reality of life in organisations, where power frequently gets used to exercise control rather than to liberate.

In essence, what face to face encounters in families and human service agencies can have, is the experience of the impact of one *full human being* encountering another *full human being*. Each of us can surely remember being the object of a parent's or a teacher's rage, followed by the satisfying experience of reparation followed by the restoration of calm and respect, ideally of love in its fullest sense. What we have here is experience of the richness of the whole human being in consort with another human being, or in group situations whole human beings in consort with other whole human beings.

In such situations, where is the leader and where the follower? Those of us privileged to be parents know the richness of the melding of person with person, leader with follower, from another perspective. We know that we often follow the child's lead in the restoration of love, justice and peace.

Given the 'scale' of the family, the tension between the potential destructiveness and potential creativity of the dynamic is more manageable there than in our larger organisations. In those settings, knowing the scale of the power that can be generated, we yearn for a sense of wholeness and completion for ourselves and for others. But it is usually easier to adopt defensive rather than creative positions and strategies, to seek blandness or other recourses away from exposure.

## *Treasuring experience*

The 'Tavistock' tradition of group relations conferences is rooted firmly in the study of *experience* in the *here-and-now,* with all its riskiness. Key assumptions behind this position include:

- It is possible to study what one experiences as it is experienced;
- This approach to engaging with 'reality' in lived experience, despite the apprehension induced, reveals previously hidden treasures that are always present in the experience;
- This apparently 'strange' behaviour is worth engaging with, both for itself and with the conviction that what is learned from it can be used beyond the conference framework.

The tradition recognises that one's experience is not something tangible and open to simple observation. It is volatile; changeable when considered from different perspectives; it has greater or lesser impact on emotions, depending on a range of factors such as time, setting, others who are involved, responsibilities; it relates to one's current mental state. The novelist Henry James described experience as "... *never limited and never complete; ... a kind of spider's web of the finest silken threads suspended in the chamber of consciousness, catching every airborne particle in its tissue".* *(James, 1884)* For experience to be a resource enabling authentic action, certain perspectives and conditions need to be taken into account.

The *first condition* is that of valuing lived experience. This reflects a Sanskrit verse which says:

> *The Absolute is here in the present. See, enjoy and communicate with Him, and do not bother your head with the past or the future.*
>
> *(Saraswati, 1992)*

The implication of this idea is that the *here-and-now* is the best and the truest place to be in; being anxious about past and future achieves nothing, since these are beyond the control of the individual: given enough trust, everything that we need is with us in the present. This includes taking into full account our own emotions, views, remembered histories and imagined futures that we carry within us, recognising how they influence what we see and how we see it, making us who we are. This is not a relativist position because it takes full account of those factors for others—no one person has all the truth.

The Sanskrit Absolute is the same spirit to which Bion (1970) refers when, in following Plato, he writes of taking account of

> *"ultimate reality, absolute truth, the thing-in-itself, the infinite and 'O' ... which becomes manifest through the emergence of actual events." (p. 26–28).*

What is here in the present moment is 'perfect' in the sense of being 'fit for purpose'.[1] So, if we attend to our lived experience of the here-and-now with full care and attention, whatever is truly needed for our next step will present itself.

The *second condition* is that the *institutional* structure[2] of the conference creates a framework of sufficiently predictable circumstances under which staff and members, as persons, can create together patterns of mutual expectations of what they are there to do through their conference roles. This enables the purpose of the conference—its primary task—to be worked at together, exploring the experiences of love and hate, despair and hope, exhilaration and boredom, that constitute the realities of working life together.

This creates and focuses the *third condition,* which is *working in role.* Institutions, including group relations conferences, are made up of human beings, who bring themselves—hearts, minds and bodies—into those institutions. Working to understand and put into practice the purpose of the institution is a dynamic continuous process which catches up everyone consciously and unconsciously. This process of engagement can be described as that of *finding, making and taking one's roles in the here-and-now* of the conference. It creates opportunities for all the participants—staff and members—to work with each other as full human beings to the best of their ability. In writing about the conference that he had invented, Ken Rice underlined the central significance to group relations conferences of working professionally in role. (Rice, 1973) He pointed out that at the heart of the conference primary task, which the conference is designed to work to, is the spirit of enquiry. Consultant staff work at formulating and testing working hypotheses (interpretations) about the experience of being the active participants in the group or systems of the conference, inviting the members to learn to do the same. By working as a person-in-role, experience can be subjected to a disciplined search for meaning, designed to lead to action. In a group relations conference this includes speaking or remaining silent, making choices or leaving that to others, initiating a range of actions or leaving that to others.

The challenging question is:

> *What framework is there to enable us to be as trusting of the here-and-now when the conference's dependable structures are no longer available?*

## *The framework for transforming experience into authentic action through role*

Over the last thirty years a framework has slowly evolved at the Grubb Institute and with those associated with it, which now constitutes a robust *mental* structure for exploring one's lived experience in any setting. This framework can be internalised and can provide in everyday life that dependability which is provided by the *institutional* structure in a group relations conference.

The significance of this is that with this framework it becomes possible to treasure one's working experience as a rich resource to one's everyday work and life, and to delight in what it can offer us in terms of new creative opportunities for effective action through thinking of oneself in terms of being a *person-in-role.*

What we call the Grubb Institute's *Transforming Experience Framework* (using our abbreviation of the longer section title used above), has four domains from which experience can be viewed. Each domain engages with and is influenced by all three others and provides the underpinning ideas which one puts into action through one's behaviour in role.

A person with leadership responsibility can divine the meaning of their experience from the four domains. As a result they can

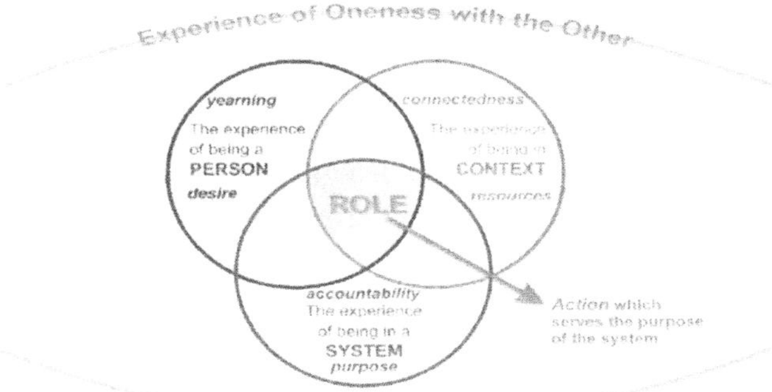

explore why they behave as they do when they take action through role. We will return to this later in this paper, but suffice it to say here that we think of role in dynamic terms: as a sailor constantly adjusts the course, the trim of the sails and boat's balance to reach the mark, so one's role-idea is expressed through continuously active behaviour.

We represent the Framework diagrammatically in the form of a Venn diagram with additions. While on paper each sector appears 'balanced' in relation to the others, in experience they engage dynamically, with shifting overlaps and differing balances between them.

### *Experience of oneness with the other*

Exploring our experience of Oneness with the Other[3] immediately opens up spiritual questions as our attention expands wider and wider. Here the boundedness of mechanistic thinking increasingly dissolves and integration becomes central to the leader's thinking, without denying differentiation. Boundaries are thought of as semi-permeable membranes rather than barriers; as points of transition between inside and outside; as parts whose essence is related to wholes. The concept of *'holon'* is important here: the part reflects the essence of the whole—for example, the holographic plate, from every fragment of which the whole image can be recovered (Koestler 1969).

Thinking inclusively can involve intense experiences, with a powerful impact on how one views oneself in relation to the world. Under these conditions differences can be thought of as resources rather than threats. This is the experience of Oneness with the Other, which includes other persons while going wider and wider as we permit ourselves to meditate in it (Bion, 1970).

There is a growing body of thinking about ways of leading which is referred to as 'action logics'. Broadly, levels of leadership are categorised into 'pre-conventional' (reductionist thinking), 'conventional' (rational/linear thinking) and 'post conventional' (systemic thinking). The highest level of leadership in action logics (in systemic thinking) is variously named 'alchemist', 'magician' and 'shaman', bringing metaphysics into the territory of thinking about leadership. (Cook-Greuter, 1985, Rooke and Torbert, 2005, Sharmer, 2000) It is also the area that Gordon Lawrence has in mind when he refers to the significance of the Cosmos (Lawrence, 2000).

In our twenty-first century experience, we can see how leaders of world stature such as the Dalai Lama, Nelson Mandela and Archbishop Tutu affect us by drawing on metaphysical points of reference as they speak about the relevance of their philosophies to present day circumstances.

Parallel thinking is emerging in the physical sciences at the same time. Quantum physics is opening up understanding of the necessary links between the very small and the very large. Physicists explore how the universe consists of two central elements: energy and consciousness. These elements are being researched in ways that suggest that every particle has an effect upon every other particle, thus influencing the universe as a whole. That influence may seem small but is not to be ignored if we are to understand reality. (Blake, 1991)[4] Quantum thinking means that the well known story of the butterfly on China bringing about hurricanes in the Caribbean gains credibility (Al-Kalili, 2003).

Further, there is a growing search to bring the physical sciences and theology into closer conjunction with each other. These include writers in both Vedic (Bhaumik, 2005) and Christian traditions. John Polkinghorne (2007) makes the point that both science and theology are searching for truth on the basis of "motivated belief"; John Bowker (2007) explores the relatedness between theology and the neural sciences.

Seeking to integrate these different disciplines we need not restrict ourselves to thinking at high levels of abstraction alone or to the realms of the quantum physics. When the transcendent and the immanent coincide we are brought into touch with the experience of integration, integration which is not the product of our own will, but which presents itself to us, often taking us by surprise. We experience these conjunctions in significant moments of everyday life: being present at the birth of a child, grieving together at the loss of a loved one, hearing the news of the success of one's offspring, seeing a beautiful sunset, or hearing a telling phrase of poetry or music.

This first domain of *Experience—the experience of Oneness with the Other*—is both transcendent in that it lies outside the control of the person, yet is also immanent within them, raising resonances. We become alert to this as we pose ourselves with the question 'why' and thus become aware of our spiritual capacity: the function of theology and religion is to offer the words, concepts and structural forms that make these felt experiences meaningful and capable of being worked with.

## *The experience of being a Person: The locus of desire*

In the second domain of experience being a *Person*, a key distinction needs to be made. This differentiates between what might be called experiencing oneself and others as an ***'individual'*** and experiencing oneself and others as a ***'person'***.

To experience oneself in terms of ***individual*** is to consider oneself a separate being. Considering numbers of individuals in statistical terms is to see human beings as separated integers, like marbles in a box rattling around with no sensitivity to one another. Most governments tend to think of and treat their citizens as individuals. For some purposes the 'individual perspective' can be valuable—for example in asking what is our level of unemployment? What is the incidence of infection in our hospitals? What are the levels of racial abuse? However, this is not adequate for leaders and managers who seek to intervene in and to transform dynamic processes, conscious and unconscious. To engage actively means asking the question 'why' and to go on asking it: numbers provide data but may not advance understanding.

For this latter purpose it helps if we use the term ***'person'***, referring to a nexus of relationships. Here, within our inner world, we carry our personal images of parents, siblings, children, colleagues, memories, aspirations and fears. One phrase which well describes a person is as a *'being-in-a-relationship-of-communion'*. (Marist Brothers, 1993) As persons we experience loving and being loved, giving and receiving, losing and being lost. A 'person' is vibrant, a constant source of desire, energy and drive, as well as being constantly open to stimuli from our rich and varied context.

Experiencing oneself as a person is continuous: we cannot exist without other human beings who serve our needs in a myriad of ways, providing us with food, water, warmth, shelter or even clean air. Thus we are in a continual state of *'lack'* (Gutmann (2005) or as Reed calls it *'in-neediness'* (Reed, 1996). So ***desire*** is a normal feature of human life: we experience gaps in ourselves in the forms of hunger and thirst; seeing others with gifts we wish we had; needing others to work and live with us; and some gaps which cannot be filled. This need is not simply libidinal: it is biological; it is social; it is spiritual. As we mature we can learn to live creatively with our state of in-neediness.

In the previous section, we noted those experiences, which are seldom easy to put into words; those universal experiences of longing, which are beyond 'desire'. Moments when we sense ourselves wishing for something, *'we know not what'*. In English the word that effectively expresses this is ***yearning***, a word whose sound expresses the feeling. It is this deep sense that goes beyond the rational and takes us into that visceral sense of humans being bound together for good and for ill.

In one sense, being aware of this yearning is to be the fullest human being that we can be. It drives the work of human beings to repair, heal and transform both ourselves and the world we live in.[5] That would be vain if we sought to do that as individuals—such wholeness can only be realised as we together and singly seek to understand ourselves as *person,* finding our own 'personal' meaning. An essential human characteristic is to ask the question 'why' and this second domain is also concerned with that question.

### *The experience of being in context—the reservoir of abundant resources*

So we come to the third domain of *Context* from which to explore our lived experience. From our context we receive the diverse ***resources*** that we need for us to survive and prosper. These include physical and social resources. Our relatedness to the context and the resources it has to offer is not bland but a living, dynamic relatedness.

None of us exists without contexts and we are essentially engaged with our context. This unity is beautifully explored by Bateson in several different writings. (Bateson 1972, 1985) James Lovelock (2006) has explored the idea of the globe as a living entity whose survival is under threat because of our rapacious attitude towards natural resources and which is now in a process of retaliation against us.

Not many of us will have read Bateson or Lovelock and other such writers and thinkers. But the majority of us have been influenced by the accounts of the creation of the world—our whole context—in a range of philosophies and religions. Few take these as literal, 'scientific' accounts, but they do influence our frames of mind at subconscious levels.

Religious metaphors provide rich allegories with which to explore the third domain of meaning from the external world's perspective, which are also significant to human well-being. This perspective concerns the responsiveness of sentient human beings to their overall context. We use a wide range of categories to make the context comprehensible, each category with its own principles, values, priorities and beliefs. We use words such as 'family', 'tribe', 'market', 'nation', 'profession', 'friend' and 'foe', 'competitor' or 'partner' to bound particular parts of the context. We use different ways to inform ourselves: press, radio, conferences, reading and writing. We have techniques of analysis and ways of making decisions in the light of the analysis

Words and phrases frame and differentiate our feelings about the nature of our ***connectedness*** with those other occupants of the context and how we expect to relate to them. (Cook-Greuter, 1995) And that connectedness is not solely with us: the occupants of the context connect with each other, affecting survival and prosperity.

The prevailing mode of connectedness with context is not adequately summed up as the 'survival of the fittest'—though some would like it to be so. As Bowker points out, 'survival of the fittest' equips us to answer the 'how' questions but does not equip us to explore the 'why' questions. To do that we must also take into account the *transcendent*[6]—that for which we yearn but for which we have not adequate words, that which we experience as bringing us together in our human-ness in the world rather than sundering us apart.

We have explored at greater length elsewhere how the spiritual perspective begins from the assumption that the context is of its essence benign, which is the message of the book of Genesis in the Judaeo-Christian Bible and the way the allegory tells the tale of the consequence of using the fruit of the tree of 'knowledge of good and evil' as the principal criterion of choice, rather drawing on the fruit of the tree of life, what we might call the 'reality tree'

(Bazalgette, Irvine and Quine, 2006). The lesson the Adam and Eve allegory offers us, alerts us to the danger of seeking to simplify how we understand our context by sorting it into 'good' and 'evil'. This is the trap of thinking in a bi-polar fashion, setting up oppositions as our default position. By so doing we create destructive conditions which we then fail to manage.

This allegory encourages three valuable understandings about context:

- Context is of its nature *good* and is a store of all the real resources necessary for survival and prosperity;
- Context has become *contaminated* and therefore also contains dangers;
- Were we to *have faith in the inherent goodness* of our context and the essential *connectedness* of all its parts and learn to manage our feelings of panic, guilt and shame about our destructiveness, we would find ourselves able to pierce through the context's threatening aspects and access the real *resources* present there.

We will then find the value of our mutual connectedness with all parts of the context. From that connectedness we can discover and receive the resources we need in the here-and-now, not simply to survive, but to prosper.

In 1975 Emery and Trist, taking a biologist's approach to environments, wrote a trail-blazing book about the dynamics by which an organism, in its search for sustenance, relates to its environment. The ease or otherwise with which sustenance can be won depends upon the state of the environment. They describe four environmental states: ranging from the placid random environment, to the turbulent environment. They describe different ways in which organisms respond to the state of environment they experience.

What Emery and Trist tell us is that, though it is tempting to see one's environment as a series of unrelated entities, this is to ignore systemic reality. Environments may contain other organisms that are more than simply potential 'friend' or 'foe'. Life in context is not a matter of simple, linear cause and effect, or a gentle search for goodies; it is a living and lively engagement, multivalently taking place at all levels, consciously and unconsciously. The values, beliefs, assumptions, myths and stories of the culture(s) in which we live pervade each one of us and shape our particular senses of identity and/or alienation, affecting how we approach our contexts.

## *System—the structure for achieving shared purpose*

'Context' is an enormous idea, too extensive to be comprehended as a totality: so we need a way of focusing our attention so that we can handle the question of meaning and taking action more discretely. Thus we come to our fourth domain, the domain of *system*.

It is important to recognize that 'systems' only exist in the mind: they are not in themselves tangible 'things'. A 'system' is a construct which assembles entities in a person's mind, including persons, equipment, finance, buildings, and resources. A system is a powerful mental construct, held in common by a group.[7]

We need a simple definition of a system. The following serves well.

> *Human activities within a boundary, which differentiates them from other systems in their context.*

This definition offers a frame for thinking about the kind of engagements a 'person' makes within and between the system's parts by postulating that every activity within the system boundary is reflected in the system as a whole. To study a system's part can lead to an understanding of the whole. A metaphor for this is the broken holographic plate, from every fragment of which the hologram can be reproduced. Of course, the 'whole' of a micro-system is itself also 'part' in a macro-system.

In practice the way we use the idea of a system to engage with context is to draw boundaries around parts of our specific context in order that we can focus our attention with greater precision, drawing on specific desires as sources of energy for action.[8] Thus we bring our desire into conjunction with the desires of others. Examples of the systems through which we engage with context include family, school, company, hospital, church, club, political party and so on.

Now we need to answer the question 'What holds these people, resources and activities together?—What difference does it make?

How does it continue in existence and prosper?' This is the ***purpose*** of the organization. Its purpose makes the system coherent in itself, providing a focal point towards which personal desires can be directed. Personal, financial, physical and social resources can be mobilized to realise those desires.

In essence focusing on purpose is not a new idea. 'Management by Objectives' and 'Mission Statements' are amongst various historic ways of approaching the question. The latest thinking is taking us to thinking about more than just the survival and flourishing of the organisation itself, but taking account of the impact it has on the needs of the context. Thus, businesses contribute to the wealth of a community, hospitals to its health, and education to its overall capacity to be creative, together they all contribute to the experience community well-being.

The reality is that there are always diverse desires in any system, relating to purpose. This diversity is one contributing factor to the potential chaos referred to at the opening of this paper. In order that a synergy can be derived from the energies brought together in a system by all those engaged in a venture we need the idea of ***accountability***—accountability for how what each person does contributes to the purpose of the system. There is a range of ways that are used to bring the accountability of persons into view in relation to the system's purpose, including performance appraisal, performance management, reviews, annual general meetings, inspections and so on.

These are externally exercised accountability procedures. But persons also hold themselves accountable: here the concept of 'duty' is valuable—duty to ones sense of self, others and—for those with that faith—in God.

## *Role: Action which serves the system (Reed and Bazalgette, 2006)*

Seeking to take action, a person uses their multifaceted experience as a resource in deciding what to do. They also draw from it the energy they need to take action. The consequence is a dynamic interaction in their mind between the four domains of the Framework, resulting in a behavioural process which can be summed up as *finding, making and taking one's role*. These steps may take place in a few seconds, or they may be slowly deliberated upon, but those three steps bridge the space between the idea in the mind and the physical action in the context.

*Role* is inextricably related to behaviour and action: it can be continuously examined in a dynamic and iterative process of finding, making and taking a role. As was said earlier in this paper, taking a role is comparable to a sailor sailing a boat, responding to currents and wind change, whilst continuously holding in mind the place for which one is aiming.

What is critical here is that any one who finds, makes and takes their role on the basis of their perception of contributing to the purpose of the system and is willing to be held accountable for what they do is offering leadership. Leadership is not restricted to 'senior' positions: a child who grasps what the school is for and responds from the role of student as an accountable learner offers leadership to everyone else, teachers, administrators and other students (Kirk undated).

We are not suggesting that this mental process is a wholly conscious or even a sub-conscious one: intuitive may be a better word to use. (Atkinson, and Claxton, 2000) At its heart this concept of role concerns working actively with experience.

Given that human beings are always in relatedness with other human beings one's experience is affected by what is happening in those relations, affecting the way one behaves in two ways. In one, one's behaviour expresses the internal image of the purpose of one's system. We call this perception the person's *psychological role*. Secondly, one's behaviour is a response to expectations that others have of how one should behave, reflecting their desires and their perception of the purpose. We call this the person's *sociological role.*

The following further points can be made about role from each of the domains:

From the domain of *Person*:

- One's behaviour in organisations is not haphazard or disconnected but reflects a coherent pattern in the mind which can be traced out in a disciplined way;
- Feelings are important evidence in relation to taking a role, providing a potent resource for both offering leadership and responding to it;
- The impact of one's desires and yearning on behaviour in role can be explored and related to other domains with objectivity;

thus motivations may be surfaced which have hitherto been unrecognised and hence not fully mobilised or taken into account;
- The person's understanding about the first domain can be used to explore actions, including both internal and external judgements on oneself, including the influence of one's thinking about duty.

From the domain of *Context*:

- Seeing the context as the primary fount of resources encourages a constructive rather than destructive position to be taken towards it; the function is that of 'creator' not 'defender';
- Giving thought to context effectively mobilises one's capacity to differentiate and categorise it, bringing different judgements to bear on the resources it offers; the function is that of 'judge' or 'liberator', not 'prison guard' or 'executioner';
- The impact of actions upon the context can be taken into account, seeking to make a difference to it in more ways than simply seeing it a forum for competition; one's function becomes one of 'collaborator' not 'competitor';
- By recognising the state of the context or parts of it, appropriate courses of action can be planned; one's function is as 'realist' rather than 'determinist'.

From the domain of System:

- Role is an idea in the person's mind, which is expressed in action which serves the purpose of the system—which is also an idea in the mind; one's function is that of active 'leader' rather than passive 'follower';
- Role is a function of *'organisation-in-the-mind'* , the mental picture of how all the system's parts work together, continuously evolving; one's function is as 'clarifier' or 'integrator', rather than 'confuser' or 'separator';
- Since behaviour is related to the purpose of the system, *all* behaviour can be seen as being in role and can be explored in relation to how purpose is understood;[9] the function here is as 'analyser';
- By analysing and exploring one's experience of working in role from these perspectives, issues which are normally hidden come into view and are thus available for further and deeper work; the function here is as 'enricher'.

From the domain of *Oneness with the Other:*

Here deep-seated values and beliefs about life's meaning influence how one finds, makes and takes the role. For those drawing on a faith perspective, this is the domain which includes spirituality.

- Taking a role is affected by how a person's desires and yearning are framed. For example, the 'Golden Rule', which is embedded in one form or another in virtually all religions, can pervade a person's characteristic approach to any action; (Covey and Merrill, 2006) here one's function might be 'disciple', 'priest' or 'prophet'.
- The current thinkers about leadership, developing 'action-logics', call this the 'post conventional' position, from which human activities are perceived in terms of a universalist or cosmic perspective; using their terminology, the function might be 'strategist' or 'alchemist'.

## *Working with the Framework: The full human being in role*

The Framework provides an instrument with which to explore and investigate one's experience. In particular it enables a disciplined approach. It enables one to adopt a spirit of enquiry into both one's own actions and the actions of others. The discipline of formulating and testing hypotheses makes it possible to reframe current challenges and tensions, opening up new possibilities for strategic thinking, action and innovation.

- A person can access their role Idea through examining their thoughts, actions and feelings about the inter-relations between the four domains of the Framework;
- Working hypotheses can be used to explore the realities that affect why the person-in-role finds themselves in current situations and behaving as they do;
- Working hypotheses can explore the functioning (behaviour) of the system as a totality in its context, with interdependent parts, which mutually affect the functioning of every part in relation to purpose.

But this disciplined curiosity is not a matter of being tentative, presenting oneself as not being able to make up one's mind till everything has been 'properly investigated'. The Framework creates conditions in which working in role need not be thought about as being artificial, contrived or inhuman. In particular a leader working in role, from wherever they may be in the system, *'senior'* or *'junior,'* will be experienced as a passionate human being, expressing a full range of emotions which give depth, substance and meaning to the purpose of a system in its context. This frees others in their in turn to be passionate, discovering themselves as full human beings through their roles.

I began with a quotation about the leadership of Oliver Cromwell. My own study of this remarkable man—who was and still is both loved and hated—has expanded my own thinking about the Transforming Experience Framework and of the incredible power that flows from a deep understanding of how to find, make and take one's leadership role. With Cromwell, as others have found, figures from history can illuminate our present day concerns sometimes with greater clarity than a study of our contemporaries. Readers may wish to explore the same territory as I have done in order to discover across 250 years, how coming to know Oliver Cromwell as a leader, is to discover new aspects of our own humanity. (Bazalgette, 2004, Gould, 1999, French and Vince, 1999, Hill, 1972).

## Notes

1. In classical Greek the word 'perfect' can be translated as 'fit for purpose'.
2. The *institutional* structure is provided by factors such as the statement of the conference primary task in the brochure, the tasks of events, the professional and administrative skills and values of the staff, and the timetable, combined with the administrative/physical provision.
3. It does make a difference to use an upper case or lower case 'O', and that will emerge later.
4. This is the same understanding as William Blake had when, in *Auguries of Innocence,* he wrote *"To see a World in a Grain of Sand, and heaven in a wild flower, Hold Eternity in the palm of your hand, and Eternity on an hour."*
5. *Tikkun olam* is a Hebrew religious duty to heal and repair the world. Visit the website www.tikkunolam.com and many similar websites.

6. See Archbishop Tutu who said in a speech at the launching of the Tutu Foundation in London "*We are transcendent beings … . God's dream is that you and I and all of us will realise that we are family; that we are made for togetherness, for goodness, and for compassion. In God's family there are no outsiders, no enemies. Black and white, rich and poor, gay and straight, Jew and Arab … all belong. When we start to live as brothers and sisters and to recognize our interdependence, we become fully human.*" Author's personal note 18 July 2007.
7. An airline—say BA—consists of aircraft, staff to fly them and to service passengers on the ground and in the air, timetables, equipment and so on. What makes BA an entity is an idea shared by thousands of people that informs their behaviour and brings about co-ordination in how they behave.
8. It is important to recognise that it is natural to draw boundaries and we learn to do this from early childhood. The danger—sometimes almost irresistible—is that we then reify and concretise those boundaries. The late Bruce Reed used to say often that boundaries are drawn like lines in the sand below the high water mark; they need to be redrawn as the context changes, seen as temporary human creations, constantly open to revision in the light of changing purpose and context.
9. Because the substrata of personal histories from family systems are so powerful these can overlay other overt systems in which persons participate, diverting from the purpose of one system to the purpose of another. Hence the significance of working with the *here-and-now.*

## *Bibliography*


Al-Kalili, J. (2003). *Quantum, a Guide form the Perplexed,* Weidenfeld and Nicholson, London UK.

Atkinson, T. & Claxton, G. (eds.). (2000). *The Intuitive Practitioner: On the value of not always knowing what one is doing,* Open University Press, Maidenhead, UK.

Bateson, G. (1972). *Steps to an Ecology of Mind,* Ballantine Books, Random House, New York USA.

Bateson, G. (1985). *Mind and Nature: A necessary unity,* Flamingo Books, London UK.

Bazalgette, J.L. (2004). *King David and Oliver Cromwell: Authority and Power in Scripture and History, A tribute to David Armstrong on his 70th birthday,* The Grubb Institute, London UK.

Bazalgette, J.L., Irvine, G.B. & Quine, C. (2006). The Absolute in the Present: Role, the hopeful road to transformation. In: Mathur A.N. (ed.), *Dare to think the unthought Known*, Aivoairut Oy, Tampere, Finland.

Bion, W.R. (1970). *Attention and Interpretation*, Jason Aranson, New York pp. 26–28.

Bhaumik, M. (2005). *Code Name God the spiritual odyssey of a Man of Science*, Penguin Books, India.

Blake, W. (1991). *Auguries of Innocence*, King's College, Cambridge.

Bowker, J. (2007). *The Sacred Neuron: Discovering the Extraordinary Links between Science and Religion*, IB Taurus, London and New York.

Cook-Greuter, S. (1985). *Ego Development: Nine Levels of Increasing Embrace*, scookgreuter@ii.org.

Cook-Greuter, S. (1995). *Comprehensive Language Awareness*—scookgreuter@integralinstitute.org.

Cook-Greuter, S. (2004). *Making the Case for a Developmental Perspective*—Industrial and Commercial Training, Vol 36 No. 7 pp. 275–281.

Covey, S.M.R. & Merrill, R. (2006). *The Speed of Trust: the one thing that changes everything*, Simon and Schuster, London UK, p. 145.

Emery, F. & Trist, E. (1975). *Towards a Social Ecology*, Plenum Press, London UK.

Fraser, A. (1973). *Cromwell: Our Chief of Men*, Phoenix Books, London UK.

French, R.B. & Vince, R. *Group Relations, Management and organization*, Oxford University Press, UK.

Gould, L.J. (1999). 'A political visionary in Mid-Life: Notes on Leadership and the life cycle' in French, R.B. & Vince, R. *Group Relations, Management and organization*, Oxford University Press, UK.

Gutmann, D. (2005). *Disillusion: Dialogue of Lacks*, Karnac Books, London UK.

Hill, C. (1972). *God's Englishman: Oliver Cromwell and the English Revolution*, Penguin Books, London UK, p. 86.

James, H. (91884). *The Art of Fiction*, Longmans Magazine 4.

Philip Kirk (undated), *Voice and leadership: achieving distributed leadership through organisational role leadership and organisational conversation*—unpublished paper, Bristol Business School, University of the West of England.

Koestler, A. (1969). *Some General Properties of Self-Regulating Open Hierarchical Order (SOHO), at* www.panarchy.org.koestler/holon.1969.html.

Lawrence, W.G. (2000). *Tongued with Fire: groups in experience,* Karnac Books London UK.

Lovelock, J. (2006). *The Revenge of Gaia,* Allen Lane, London UK.

Marist Brothers. (1993). *Formation Guide,* available on line at http. champgnat.org/en/doc/GuiaFormazioneEN.pdf.

Mathur, A.N. (2006). (ed.), *Dare to think the unthought Known,* Aivoairut Oy, Tampere, Finland.

Moltmann, J. (1985). *God in Creation: The Gifford Lectures,* SCM Press London UK.

Newton, J. et al (2006). *Coaching in Depth: The Organisational Role Analysis approach,* Karnac, London UK.

Polkinghorne, J. (2007). *Quantum Physics and Theology: an unexpected kinship,* Yale University Press, USA.

Reed, B.D. (1996). *The Psychodynamics of Life and Workshop,* The Grubb Institute, London UK.

Reed, B.D., and Bazalgette, J.L. (2006). *Organizational Analysis at The Grubb Institute of Behavioural Studies: origins and development,* in (pp. 43–62).

Rice, A.K. (1973). *Learning for Leadership: interpersonal and intergroup relations,* Tavistock Publications, London.

Rooke, D., and Torbert, W. (2005). *Seven Transformations of Leadership,* Harvard Business Review, April.

Shantanand Saraswati, (1992). *Good Company. Sayings, Stories, Answers—* Element Books, Shaftesbury, Dorset, UK (p. 69).

Sharmer, O. (2000). *Presencing: Learning from the future as it emerges, Lecture to MIT Sloan School of Management,* scharmer@MIT.EDU.

CHAPTER THREE

# "Doth my father yet live" Psychoanalysis and group relations conferences: Revisited

*Avi Nutkevitch and Joseph Triest*

Long before we knew what the exact content of this lecture, now a book chapter, that we had agreed to prepare and present jointly was going to be, we chose the title of the lecture, "Doth my father yet live?" We did that because of time constraints. In other words, the urgent need to respond to the demand of the organizers of the Belgirate II conference and to provide a title, which would allow them to complete the brochure. What was it about this title that suggested itself as an organizing framework for a discussion of a subject as wide as "how have the major developmental changes that have occurred in psychoanalytic theory over the past 50 years influenced meta-psychology and the practice of group relations conferences"?

We will therefore open with a word about the title, since it is impossible not to recognize that unconsciously we seem to have found it a pointer that could lead us to the entire discussion. All that remains is to decipher what it was that we had discovered without knowing.

So, the first association to the question, "Doth my father (or more accurately, our father) yet live?" was of course the "fathers" of our theory. Insofar as this refers to psychoanalysis and "Group

Relations", we're talking about Freud, Bion and Klein (from the perspective of "the name of the father"—Klein may be thought of as a "father" too), Eric Miller and A.K. Rice. We know that a theory is not just a body of knowledge and a collection of information, but a whole world of object relations. A group of professionals that organizes itself under a single theoretical model, by definition accepts the "father's name" of the theorist who is identified with the model, and generates a relationship of love-hate, admiration and competition. In short, a group regards itself for better or for worse as a kind of family. A professional community, like ours, that analyzes the relevance of the theory that represents its guiding light, cannot avoid the Oedipal dynamic of sons who challenge their fathers, and daughters who wish to differentiate themselves from their mothers (and vice versa). In this respect, we found the question "Doth my father yet live?" sufficiently relevant and challenging. But that's not all.

From another perspective, this chapter's title touches on one of the central issues that have engaged group relations conferences from the start, and have almost become their most obvious hallmark—the exploration of authority: how is it represented in the Unconscious, and how does it appears in the different cultures where our conferences are held. It asks: have any genuine changes occurred in our perception of authority since we began exploring the depths of the unconscious? Have any changes occurred in the perception of the consultant as an epistemological and professional authority?

However, when we began examining the scriptural sources of this quote, we discovered an additional, incredibly rich layer of meaning. The highly touching Bible story tells of how Joseph, the arrogant and best-loved son of Jacob, meets his brothers who sold him as a slave, and who discover him years later as the unchallenged ruler of the Pharaoh's court, exactly as his troubled dreams had prophesied. We may look at the story not only as telling a piece of "real" history but also as a kind of "power-relations" phantasy; a description of the internal drama of a person who assumes a position of authority, in that case. A grandiose and ambitious lad is cast into the pit of slavery, emerges with a regal crown on his head, and finds himself face-to-face with the same brothers who had previously betrayed him. Now they have to overcome their resentment and jealousy and accept him as their leader. At this point the family saga reaches its climax that is so surprising mainly because it is so expected.

In different variations, this story will be familiar to anyone who has ever taken upon themselves a leadership role in an organization or a group.

But above all, Joseph's story is a story of dreams that are fulfilled in reality after they have been deciphered, received meaning, and translated from the language of fantasy into the language of action. It is the story of the relationship between the inner world—the world of fantasy—and the world of reality. What really gave him his influence and power as the king of Egypt's highly influential consultant, a consultant that no group relations organization would be ashamed of, was his impressive ability to listen most attentively to Pharaoh's dreams as an expression of the organization in the mind, as articulated by the unconscious matrix. Not only does he not totally dismiss and de-legitimize the dream about the seven lean cows that devour the seven fat cows, and the seven dried sheaves that devour the seven fresh sheaves; he is skilled enough to translate them into a highly workable action plan that stands the test of rapidly changing circumstances. We're talking about a visionary and daring all-encompassing economic-social-political strategy that starts with fantasy and ends with a practical plan of action, a strategy that allows Egypt not just to survive the seven lean years of drought and famine, but also to emerge with considerable political and economic gain.

The question "Doth my father yet live?"—which is the question Joseph finally dares to ask his brothers, will be adopted as our leitmotif for examining the influences of our past legacy on our present traditions. More specifically, we will explore the contribution of developments in psychoanalytic theory that represent one of the two central foundations of the group relations model, in relation to the conceptualization and practice that we adopt today. When we ask "Doth our father yet live?", we will refer not only to Freud, Melanie Klein, Bion, whose ideas and thoughts most of us know by reading but also to Eric Miller and A.K. Rice, whose memory we retain in our hearts, and whose written and oral teachings we have incorporated both in our learning and in our joint work. We will dare to ask whether their spirit, that gave birth to the model of group relations as is implemented in the Leicester model that has been used around the world for the past several decades, is still with us, or whether new winds are blowing in the Tavistock empire. And maybe we will discover that we have remained frozen in time. Maybe we were afraid to depart for foreign lands, or maybe in the process we have held back from preparing for the seven lean years, and we have failed to create new models that are relevant to the modern era and to the changes that have occurred in the half a century that has elapsed.

## *Developments in psychoanalysis*

In the years that Bion (1961) developed his group relations theory, there were two major approaches in the psychoanalytic world that seemed to evolve from the Freudian drives theory. The Ego Psychology, whose American variation mainly emphasized man's desire for ***autonomy, separation and mastery***; (Hartmann, 1932a; Mahler, 1974) and the Kleinian (1935, 1946, 1950) approach that produced the object relations theories, and regarded man as basically ***"Object Related"***, and not the release of drives and/or tensions. Bion grew up in this greenhouse, which eventually produced later the Middle Group, whose main spokesman was Winnicott (1971). Winnicott presented a developmental theory that, more than its predecessors, emphasized the critical importance of the mother and of the environment in the development of the infant. Concepts such as "holding environment" or "a good enough mother" gradually became the stock in trade of clinical psychoanalytic work (Winnicott, 1956, 1961, 1967, 1969, 1975).

It was at the end of the sixties and the early seventies that Kohut's theory of the self appeared as the fourth actor on the psychoanalytic stage (Kohut, 1971, 1977). This emphasized concepts such as narcissism (which was not perceived as an insult anymore), a sense of self-worth and self-image, empathy and empathic failure (Kohut, 1982) and regarded man as being perpetually in need of a self-object to serve as a mirror so as to enable him to build a ***coherent, cohesive and integrative self*** (Kohut, 1977).

The 80s and 90s saw the start of the development of the intersubjective/relational approach, a new and influential school that first developed in the USA, especially in New York, and which gained a firm foothold in the theory and practice of psychoanalysis (Greenberg & Mitchell, 1983; Mitchell & Aron, 1990). This approach challenged the classic analyst's role and derived technique as being based on the principles of "neutrality, anonymity and abstinence" (Freud, 1912; 1915; Greenberg, 1986). The intersubjective school taught that the analyst can never be a "tabula rasa", an objective researcher of the patient's unconscious. The object of analytic exploration is therefore, not only the patient's unconscious, but the therapeutic dyad—the intersubjective field—that is **created while it is being discovered**. This is a field that contains the analyst's unconscious just as much as the patient's unconscious. In order to explore it, and further the treatment, the analyst takes responsibility and ownership for his own unconscious parts and projections, and in appropriate circumstances allows these to be transparent to the patient by proactively revealing them.

Obviously, we can only survey the very tip of the changes that have happened in psychoanalysis, and we can only explore a few of the implications on our work. Our main intention is to point out areas where we believe there are solid grounds for a re-examination of our traditional positions and conceptualizations—and even here, we admit to some doubt whether the "traditional positions" exist at all, or whether they are the fruit of our imagination and projections.

In any case, the way theory conceptualizes man is not only a matter of philosophy. It has a direct impact on the way we understand and interpret the phenomena we are exploring. [For example—the Kleinian model tends to emphasise the destructive power of envy as a derivative of the death instinct. The Kohutian theory, in contrast, questions the primacy of envy as a central nuclear motivation. Is man bound to be born envious or is he made envious when he feels himself not recognized and acknowledged?]

To answer questions of that kind, we choose to focus on three major areas:

a. The perception of authority and its representation in the unconscious.
b. The role of the consultant; what does the consultant know? In this part we will deal with the issue of projective identification and its implications for the perception of reality.
c. The self and the experience of learning from experience.

## *The perception of authority and its representation in the unconscious*

Although it is common to identify Bion, with his Kleinian roots, as the analyst who more than any others contributed to the theorization of the group relations model—in all that regards the perception of authority, it seems that the Freudian perception has no less discernible influence.

The representation of authority in the unconscious, according to Freud (1921), is undoubtedly the figure of the Archaic Father. For both men and women, this figure represents the Omnipotent authority. The mythological saga that is quoted in Group Psychology and the Analysis of the Ego (1921) presents women as the purchase of the early man, and man as his castrated subjects. The Oedipal drama—in which Freud sees the cornerstone of man's soul and the basic mould from which identity is formed, is described as a copy of the hierarchical ancient tribal structure. The father figure is incorporated as the superstructure of the ego—the Über Ich, and represents the law (1921, 1923). It is also responsible, according to the Lacanian commentary, for the caesura—a symbolic act that is analogous to the cutting of the umbilical cord between the mother and infant. This is the act that will give birth to the infant as a human subject and will demarcate the boundary to the symbiotic yearning to be incorporated inside the mother, in an oceanic space-time, that does not recognize the laws of the external reality.

When we look at the Oedipal Myth (as told by Freud) as a reflection of the way in which the internal authority is represented and "registered" in the unconscious, there is no way of avoiding seeing this as a phallic authority figure, that is characterized by an ability **to point and to cut**. In other words, this authority is phallic, even in the way it sets out specific targets and has the ability to indicate direction and to take decisions, to choose and to decide between options. Its symbol is the arrow.

Klein's work revealed a world of pre-Oedipal and preverbal relations, and created a revolution in psychoanalysis (Klein, 1975a; 1975b). After all, the first authority that the infant meets is the mother and not the father. But how is the mother characterized as an authority? Or in other words, how do mother-infant relations shape the perception of the representation of authority in the unconscious? It seems that these issues have remained quite impenetrable, partially because the impact of the mother on the mental structure is stamped during the preverbal period and therefore, cannot be conceptualized by the infant. It can be recognized only as body impressions, as an existential experience.

In our opinion, it was Bion more so than Klein who first presented the option of exploring the relations with the archaic female authority in group setting (Bion, 1961)—even though to the best of our understanding, he never specifically stated this (in a generalized form). Bion, the master of turning upside down the thought gestalt, focuses his mental microscope lens on an apparently marginal figure in the Freudian Oedipal story—the figure of the Sphinx. The Sphinx is a woman. She posed a puzzle for all mankind—the puzzle of birth and existence. Her power does not lie in castration but in her ability to "swallow" the space that she rules over, the power of annihilation.

Bion (1961) alludes to this authority in his writings on groups when he proposes the revolutionary idea that the group as a whole is not based only on the hierarchical tribal structure or the patriarchal family—where brothers struggle for the mother's attention, try to kill the father and are afraid of his castrating power. This layer certainly exists and is relatively easy to identify. Bion's revelation was that all the members of the group create and re-enact in an unconscious fashion the primal connection to the mother's body as a partial object—in their connection to the group. This is what represents for them—the (body of the) archaic mother, the Sphinx; and this is what offers the matrix from which all culture can develop—including, of course, the culture of leadership in its Freudian, phallic and patriarchal variation.

And now, just as apparently the Eskimos have thirty seven (?) words to describe snow, while Western man has just one word—so our discourse culture is rich with several words that describe the masculine-father authority, while it has far fewer words to describe feminine authority. The word "Director" is a prime example of this. It comes from the function of pointing a direction, the arrow, the phallus of the leader. What is the female equivalent for representing authority and leadership?[1]

If we try and derive the qualities of female leadership from the biological qualities in an analogy to the phallic-male, then we have to talk about the qualities that characterize the womb and ovaries. If male authority, which is defined in terms of **doing,** has been blessed with the ability **to cut, to choose, to indicate, the ability to take decisions** on the basis of preferring one option at the expense of rejecting the other options, and **pointing out a direction**—then female authority will probably be based on the potential of ***creating options***. These last are like ovules that are awaiting to be fertilized in the ovaries. This is nothing like the passivity that Freud mistakenly ascribes to the woman's role—but rather a receptive role. Even though receptiveness is a quality that can be described in terms of ***Being***, it is never passive. Containment and receptiveness could be the qualities of female leadership.

It is superfluous to mention that the distinction between the Psychological aspects of female and male authority does not necessarily point to a distinction between men and women. Thought is not possible without the simultaneous existence of both qualities.

Has the Tavistock establishment assimilated the innovations and contributions of feministic perspective in its depth?

We are doubtful about this. When it comes to conceptualization, it is true that **Containment** (Bion, 1959) has achieved a place of honour as representing female authority. But we suspect that Containment suggests an empty vessel that will be filled with something from outside. Containment is not the only quality that the woman's biological anatomy could contribute to the psychological representation of female authority and leadership. What, for example, represents female fertility (as an analogy to creativity), the ability of egging, in the jargon that serves us as descriptions of authority and leadership?

It is true that we have noticed just how many women have run conferences in recent years—but the question remains whether someone who directs a conference continues to be a woman. Or has the conference culture changed so much that it now allows women to be activists and "wear the pants" without the essence of female management, authority and leadership receiving proper representation in theory as well as in practice? In other words—have the changes occurred in "conference culture," as an analogy to Bion's "group culture", while the "mentality"—the unconscious registration in the fantasy world of the group—remains as it was, that is: authority = father. We assume that female-mother representation does exist in the Unconscious, but is not yet recognized enough by us—or by our culturally-influenced ego—as representing female authority.

It therefore seems that one of the areas that awaits re-examination and development is the linguistic range that serves us for the purpose of exploring the characteristics of female leadership and authority and its inter-connection to male leadership and authority. A wider choice of more accurate research tools could throw new light on the way unconscious representations of male and female authority and leadership influence the culture of groups and organizational management.

### *What does the consultant know? Projective identification and its implications for the perception of reality*

Mitchell, who is one of the foremost spokesmen for the relational or intersubjective approach of psychoanalysis, had a chapter entitled: "What does the analyst know?" in his book '*Hope and Dread in Psychoanalysis*' (Mitchell, 1993). The complex answer that emerges from this epistemological and clinical examination symbolizes one of the main developmental and changing paths of psychoanalysis in recent decades. The intersubjective approach claims that the meaning of the clinical phenomenon is not discovered but rather constructed. In Winnicott's dialectic language we could say that the infant discovers reality while creating it, and creates reality while discovering it, and he adds: "An essential part of my formulation of transitional phenomena is that we agree never to make the challenge to the baby: did you create this object, or did you find it conveniently lying around?" (Winnicott, 1971, p. 96).

### *And what about us?*

In the introduction of Bion's groundbreaking book, '*Experiences in groups*' he writes: "My contemporary work convinces me of the critical importance of Klein's theory of projective identification and the mutual relations between the paranoid-schizoid positions and the depressive position" (Bion, 1961, p. 8.) In practice, in his creative daring, Bion departed in his conceptualizations regarding projective identification from those of Klein. Whilst Klein defined projective identification as an intra-psychic mechanism in 1946, Bion (1961) had already related to projective identification as an interpersonal mechanism in the beginning of his work with groups in the Tavistock (during the late forties and early fifties). This mechanism has real emotional and cognitive impact on the object towards which the projection is directed.

This is not the place to survey the vast literature on the notion of projective identification. We will limit ourselves to stating the following: both Bion and the neo-Kleinians make much use of projective identification in order to understand the patient and what is happening in the countertransference process. However, the essence of the interaction that has projective identification in it, tends to be uni-directional, namely, the analyst is perceived as an "empty container" which absorbs the projective identifications of the patient.

The relational approach offers a different perspective on what is happening in the analytical interaction (Greenberg, 1986).

The assumption lying at the core of this approach is that in the consulting room, there are two subjects that influence each other. This mutual influence is never without unconscious mutual projection. There exists an encounter of the "unconscious" of both subjects, a meeting of the minds (Aron, 1996). And so, just as the denied and split-off parts of the patient are projected into the analyst, so the denied and unlinked parts of the analyst could lodge themselves in the patient.

The distinction between the internal reality and the external reality, and between self and the other, therefore, becomes a challenge, which is far from simple.

What could be the implications of this for the stand and position of the analyst or the consultant? An important aspect of the technique, as proposed by the relational approach to this question, touches on the issue of the analyst's initiated Self-revelation (Aron, 1991) . The classic approach tries to handle the problem of the influence of the subjectivity of the analyst by neutralizing and removing it as much as possible from the intersubjective field.

According to the relational approach, however, the way to increase the patient's ability to recognize one's unconscious split parts is for the analyst to reveal, or rather own, one's own part in the situation—even if only in essence—thus taking responsibility for the impact of one's unconscious projective identification on the patient. So, for example, if the patient believes that the analyst is angry, the analyst will not rush to explain this as an expression of the patient's projected anger, but will examine oneself—maybe there is real anger of which one is unaware. If that's the case one will reveal to the patient an aspect of one's subjectivity and work on it.

How is the role of the consultant characterized in the world of group relations?

A K Rice writes in his seminal book:

> "The mature ego is one that can differentiate between what is real in the outside world and what is projected onto it from the inside, what should be accepted and incorporated into experience and what should be rejected. In short, the mature ego is one that can define the boundary between what is inside and what is outside, and can control the transactions between one and the other" (Rice, 1965, p. 11).

Is this really the case? Can we indeed differentiate—even if we assume a mature ego—between our subjective dynamics and what is projected into us?

It seems that on this point, there is something of a split between the different aspects of the theory, as well as between our theoretical approach and the nature of the socialization that we give the consultants—in all that pertains to our perception of reality and the epistemic authority of the consultant.

In one central aspect, the conceptualization of the group relations model retains its humility in relation to the ownership of the truth and the reality testing. At a time when analysts are involved in giving interpretations—the consultant proposes 'working hypotheses'—these are hypotheses that encourage a continuation of the exploration, and do not claim a monopoly on the perception of reality, as is inferred by using the word 'working'.

But when we look at practice, when we examine our socialization, however hard it may be to generalize, it seems to us that the tone in which we articulate our interventions is usually not so tentative. Group consultants—especially when working in a large group that naturally does not tend towards tentativeness—often sound, at least to us, as being absolute regarding the exclusive ownership of the truth.

Eric Miller, for example, writes in his interesting and important manuscript about the Leicester workshop (Miller, 1989):

> "The capacity to be in touch with one's shifting experience in relation to the group—of being pushed and pulled, attacked

> and ignored—and to reflect that back to the group, preferably with some explanation of why it might be happening—that of course remained the central criterion" (Miller, 1989, pp. 15–16). He also adds that the interpretation or working hypothesis "should contain a because clause" (ibid.)—a possible explanation of why this dynamic is occurring.

But in our efforts to recall the stock of consultative interventions that the consultants gave or which we received as participants—we found that generally the consultants' interventions tend to draw the causal relationship between the group and the consultant in one direction, so for example: Rarely would the consultant say: 'you are angry because I was aggressive towards you'. Generally, we suggest that the anger of the group has made us aggressive. This issue is particularly sensitive when we're talking about "casualties"—when a participant becomes psychotic. In these circumstances of high anxiety, how far are we prepared to relate the psychosis not just to the projections of the members into the member-casualty, but also to the madness that the staff created?

How can the consultant make use of his/her real feelings and make them available in the quest for examining the group's unconscious? An example that could demonstrate how initiated self-disclosure when given in the right circumstances could match our ethical and professional role as group relations consultants, more than interpretations that have an authoritarian, patronizing and distant sound:

> *The attention of a large group is drawn completely to what is happening in the pairing in the inner circle. In this circle sits the person who is crowned "the dream girl" of the conference, and she is surrounded by the young and desirable men of the group. Parallel to this, it appears that all the older women of the conference sat themselves in the back rows. The feeling (that later emerges as shared by all the consultants who participated in the event)—is that what happens in the inner circle steals all the sexuality and life from the outer circle, leaving the older women with dark and ugly feelings of envy.*
>
> *One of the consultants, a veteran colleague, finding herself located in this outer circle, decides to intervene by expressing her authentic feelings. She does not interpret what is happening in the classical*

*manner, but gives a lively and painful expression to her feelings: "I feel like a stuffed animal", she says, "stuffed and dead. It's as if all the sexuality and all the desire is pouring into the center, and leaving all of us old women here past our sell-by date—and I am not prepared to let this happen. Absolutely not. I assure you that I am not prepared to let this happen..."*

*The impact of this intervention is so dramatic that a cup of coffee that is under the chair of one of the men who sits in the inner circle overturns, and a long tongue of black coffee streams straight to the chair of that consultant, accompanied by the loud laughter of all the participants in the group.*

*"At least it's no longer dry here," comments the consultant.*

*As a result of this intervention, the dynamic that ruled the group up until that point changed completely. Not only did the older women find their voices but also one of the male participants dared to express his desire and attraction for the mature female consultant.*

We are aware that there are countless technical questions that the relational approach to reality raises, but this is not the place to expand on them.

## *The self and the experience of learning from experience*

In the history of psychoanalysis, the word narcissism (Freud, 1914) has gradually been taken out of its distinct psychopathological context, and has come to be representative of a world of legitimate developmental needs in Kohut's self model (Kohut, 1971, 1977). He undid the Gordian knot that Freud created between narcissism and pathology, when he presented the investment in the self as being in opposition to the investment in the object. Only someone who loves himself can also love another, according to Kohut.

Our interest in narcissism and the need for mutual recognition, in this context as theorized by Jessica Benjamin (1990), is in relation to the question: how does the subject attain the conditions in which a feeling of self worth develops? How can one learn without losing one's faith in one's abilities? And similarly—how does the consultant work in light of his/her own needs?

The Kleinian model—which has formed the basis of several of our principles—not only does not leave enough room for the self, but also neglects attention to the narcissistic vulnerability. The Kleinian interpretations—even those given to children in analysis—seem to bypass the ego, and talk directly to its unconscious. Klein's critics would claim that they go over the ego's head, and are not really absorbed by it.

The question of how to get the "ego" acquainted with the unconscious that it wishes to know without undermining the ego experience and without damaging the self-image and self-worth in an irreparable manner, is a cardinal question for us as consultants who believe in exploring the unconscious via experience. How can we create the conditions whereby a process of development and change can exist, when learning from experience and the encounter with the unconscious occurs in group setting , and involves a constant exposure, which arouses very often feelings of shame and humiliation.

It is our observation that the meta-psychology of the group relations model, like the Kleinian and Bionian meta-psychology, lacks sufficient attention to narcissistic damage and to the average person's narcissistic desires in such a learning process, just as it lacks sensitivity to developmental needs. The Bionian ethics do not leave enough room for the possible distinction between drives and needs for example. According to this distinction, drives need boundaries, while needs require—more than anything else—recognition, holding, containment and reality mediation. Our GR conceptualization is missing, therefore, an acknowledgment of the dialectical need of the subject to obtain recognition of the other (the object) in its autonomy from it (drawing on Jessica Benjamin (1990)).

**Our main claim in this chapter is that anything, which is not conceptualized by the theory that supports the model, is pushed beyond the work space and turns it into an informal happening that could easily become a "Social Defence."**

An example would be the "ceremony" of the consultants dragging the members' suitcases—a mythological Leicester custom. This is certainly one of the strangest of ceremonies, if we examine it in light of the consultant's characteristic role-behaviour, which is usually alienated from the dependency needs of the participants, and regards them as a kind of infantile regression. Is it possible that this expresses our collective guilt feelings regarding the "sadistic" conditions of deprivation that we create for the participants? Or maybe this is an act of temptation, attracting the fly into the spider's honey trap? Or perhaps it is only the opposite of our quest to **receive** a nurturing and concerned attitude, similar to what we give the members by this act?

The problematic custom of the appearance of the director during the coffee break raises similar questions. Who and what does this serve? The director's anxiety about the participants' state? The need of the director and the whole staff for recognition, delivered via the informal encounter with the participants?

In a similar fashion, one could ask about another 'Leicesterian' custom, a custom adopted by some of the consultants who close their work with the small study group with the words: "Thanks for working with me." The question is as follows: If the consultant needs to thank the group or to recognize the work of the group—why interject this phrase at the last minute, when the group has no way of relating to this as part of its work or exploring it? If the theory had recognized the need to give or to receive recognition (and thanks), then it would make sense to change the subject into material that is central for work, commentary and intervention. In our experience, the need to recognize and to be praised by the consultant is usually interpreted as an expression of infantile dependency, and not as a legitimate "developmental" need.

And finally, the physical need for touch and physical expressions of closeness usually finds its way into the last-evening party, but very rarely serves as material for interventions in the few work spaces that remain until the end of the conference.

To complete the list of evidence that raises fears about our collective behaviour, we have to add the astonishing fact that on its own, our huge dependency on the members at the recruitment stage—a direct and concrete dependency that dictates the number of consultants and the very existence of the workshop—this dependency usually vanishes almost completely from our interventions. When was the last time that anyone heard a consultant suggesting to a group a working hypothesis like: "You may have experienced our interventions as aggressive, since we may have poured our own rage unto you, our rage for being dependent on you—during the recruitment period, a period when we had to demean ourselves as politicians before the electorate, or like street traders trying to sell their wares".

To sum up, we will say that on the whole, our language suffers from a paucity of terms that relate to developmental needs and self needs. In this spirit, we hurry to explain ignoring the consultants as attacks on them caused by envy and competition, rather than as an expression of the need for separation and autonomy. For every one of the "thirty seven words" that are available to us to describe dark impulses such as envy, hatred, competition, etc., we seem to have only few words to describe developmental needs.

In our humble opinion, this field also requires that we adapt the theory that supports the model to the changes that have happened in psychoanalysis in all that pertains to understanding developmental needs and their weight in shaping the self. These must become subjects for research within the formal work space, and not be pushed outside into the informal space and into the world of acting out.

## *Ending remark*

In this chapter we delineated some selected changes that Psychoanalysis went through and the influence it may have or should have on our work. In our GR consultant roles, we believe that enriching our way of thinking and conceptualizing will broaden and deepen our ability to give meaning to the endlessly rich phenomena of the human condition as is manifested in and by the Group Relations model, and will broaden our way of taking up the role as consultants when trying to provide members in group relations conferences opportunities but also good enough conditions for learning, development and change.

## *Note*

1. The "Motherator" of an organization?

## *References*

Aron, L. (1991). The Patient's Experience of the Analyst's Subjectivity. *Psychoanalytic Dialogues* 1: 29–51.

Aron, L. (1996). *A Meeting of Minds—Mutuality in Psychoanalysis*. London: The Analytic Press.

Benjamin, J. (1990). "Recognition and Destruction—An Outline of Intersubjectivity." In *Relational Psychoanalysis—The Emergence of a Tradition.* (Ed.), Mitchell, A.S. & Aron, L. London: The Analytic Press, 181–210.

Bion, W.R. (1959). Attacks on Linking. *International Journal of Psychoanalysis, 40*: 308–315.

Bion, W.R. (1961). *Experiences in Groups.* London: Tavistock Publications.

Freud, S. (1912). Recommendations to Physicians Practicing Psychoanalysis. *S.E.* 12, London: Hogarth Press. pp. 109–120.

Freud, S. (1914). On Narcissism: An Introduction, *S.E.* 14, London: Hogarth Press. pp. 67–104.

Freud, S. (1915). Observations on Transference Love. *S.E.* 12, London: Hogarth Press. pp. 159–171.

Freud, S. (1921). Group Psychology and the Analysis of the Ego. *S.E.* 18, London: Hogarth Press. pp. 65–143.

Freud, S. (1923). The Ego and the Id. *S.E.*19, London: Hogarth Press. pp. 1–59.

Greenberg, J.R. (1986). Theoretical Models and the Analyst's Neutrality. *Contemporary Psychoanalysis, 22*: 87–106.

Greenberg, J.R. & Mitchell, S. (1983). *Object Relations in Psychoanalytic Theory.* London: Harvard University Press.

Hartmann, H. (1939). *Ego Psychology and the Problem of Adaptation.* New York: International University Press, 1958.

Klein, M. (1935). A Contribution to the Psychogenesis of Manic-Depressive States. *The International Journal of Psychoanalysis, 16*: 145–174.

Klein, M. (1946). Notes on Some Schizoid Mechanisms. *The International Journal of Psychoanalysis, 27*: 99–110.

Klein, M. (1950). On the Criteria for the Termination of an Analysis. *The International Journal of Psychoanalysis, 31*: 204–204.

Klein, M. (1975a). *Envy and Gratitude (1946–1963).* London: Hogarth Press.

Klein, M. (1975b). *Love, Guilt and Reparation (1921–1945).* London: Hogarth Press.

Kohut, H. (1971). *The Analysis of the Self. A Systematic Approach to the Psychoanalytic Treatment of Narcissistic Personality Disorders.* N.Y.: International University Press.

Kohut, H. (1977). *The Restoration of the Self.* N.Y.: International University Press.

Kohut, H. (1982). Introspection, Empathy, and the Semi-Circle of Mental Health. *The International Journal of Psychoanalysis, 63*: 395–407.

Mahler, M. (1974). "Symbiosis and Individuation: The Psychological Birth of the Human Infant." In *The Selected Papers of Margaret S. Mahler, Vol. 2.* New York: Jason Aronson.

Miller, E.J. (1989). *The 'Leicester' Model: Experiential Study of Group and Organizational Processes.* London: Tavistock Institute of Human Relations, Occasional Papers 10.

Mitchell, S. (1993). *Hope and Dread in Psychoanalysis.* New York: Basic Books.

Mitchell, S. & Aron, L. (eds.) (1990). *Relational Psychoanalysis—The Emergence of a Tradition.* London: The Analytic Press.

Rice, A.K. (1965). *Learning for Leadership: Interpersonal and Intergroup Relations.* London: Tavistock Publication.

Winnicott, D.W. (1956). "Primary Maternal Preoccupation." In *Through Paediatrics to Psycho-analysis.* London: Hogarth Press & The Institute of Psychoanalysis, 1975, 300–305.

Winnicott, D.W. (1961). "The Theory of the Parent-Infant Relationship." In *The Maturational Processes and the Facilitating environment.* London: Karnac, 37–55.

Winnicott, D.W. (1967). The Location of Cultural Experience. *International Journal of Psychoanalysis, 48*: 368–372.

Winnicott, D.W. (1969). The Use of an Object. *International Journal of Psychoanalysts, 50*: 711–716.

Winnicott, D.W. (1971). *Playing and Reality.* London: Tavistok [1971].

Winnicott, D.W. (1975). *Through Paediatrics to Psycho-analysis.* London: Hogarth Press & The Institute of Psychoanalysis.

# SECTION II

## ADAPTATION AND INNOVATION IN DESIGN

This section brings together three chapters devoted to adaptive or innovative designs in Group Relations Conferences. Louisa Diana Brunner, Mario Perini and Elio Vera first trace the history of the Seminari di Arona, an Italian Group Relations Conference adapted from the Leicester conference model. They describe the evolution of Group Relations work in Italy and discuss the dilemmas and tensions encountered in adapting the conference model to a decidedly different culture and language. They also present some of the struggles involved in moving from dependency to collaboration with their British colleagues as the Italian conference has matured, developing its own history and traditions, as the years have passed.

Susan Long offers a discussion of an innovative new event, the Community System Event, which has been incorporated into the Group Relations Conferences sponsored by the Creative Organisational Systems Group at RMIT University, in Melbourne, Australia. She argues that the community system—a system of values, purposes and beliefs—is a system within the organization which is different from, but intersects with, all other systems, e.g., task, sentient, socio-technical systems, and that this community system can be explored, even further developed, within the conference. She describes the event itself, its evolution since its introduction in 2002, and some of the dilemmas encountered in introducing an innovative event into an otherwise familiar design.

In the third of these chapters, Zachary Gabriel Green and Mary B. McRae describe "Embracing a World of Difference", a series of conferences at New York University. The structure of these conferences has been adapted to incorporate a new event named the "World Event" which has taken the traditional exploration of role and authority into a broader sphere, with a clear focus on the multiplicity of peoples' identities and differences. In these conferences the explicit aim is to focus on a design that speaks to inter-group relations and representation and works from the individual to the organizational transformation. The authors have created a more complex, more collaborative structure, which emphasizes 'embracing' difference rather than using differences as a source of continued division.

Taken together, these chapters reflect adaptations and innovations, which allow for the expansion of Group Relations work, to include more explicitly the nature of our global, communal world and the inter-dependencies across differences to which we need to adapt. All three chapters suggest that the conference design is a critical factor in achieving the conference's purpose—primary task—and in deepening our understanding of the dynamics of the society in which we live.

CHAPTER FOUR

# Italian group relations conferences between adaptation and innovation

*Louisa Diana Brunner, Mario Perini and Elio Vera*

## *Introduction*

This paper developed from the desire to explore our experience of approximately ten years of Group Relations Conferences (GRC) in Italy. The 12th Arona Conference was held on 26 February–1 March 2009.

We would have liked to write this paper with three more people—Claudio Caffarena, Francesca Cardona and Anton Obholzer, the other founders and persons strongly involved. Still, we decided pragmatically to limit it to us, knowing that this also created some exclusions.

Our aim has been to understand the impact of adaptative and innovative processes on the development of GRC in Italy. Many definitions for adaptation and innovation can be found. For the purpose of this paper, we will use those of two actors in the Italian Conferences. According to Anton Obholzer, adaptation has a more concrete material element; it has to do with something already existing and modified in the light of experience. Innovation is a state of mind, there is no precedent; it is an idea less bounded by precedents, more adventurous and courageous. For William Halton, adaptation derives its origin from outside, the source is elsewhere, while innovation refers to a first move and it is within.

We think that some of the themes we are "putting under the microscope" will be common to Conferences in other countries.

## Methodology

We gave ourselves a structure for the purpose of this paper. We decided that Louisa would be the convener and then divided the work on the grounds of our areas of interest and expertise. Louisa did some brief interviews/conversations with the founders, Directors, and Associate Directors of the Italian Conferences: David Armstrong, Claudio Caffarena, Francesca Cardona, William Halton, Anton Obholzer, as well as Mario Perini and Elio Vera. She also interviewed Isabella Negri, who was the interpreter for some English Associate Directors. We are grateful to all the interviewees for sharing passionately their experiences with us.

This paper is the result of an integration of reflections on our experience and conceptual frameworks. The method of conceptualizing and utilizing theory and experience reflects an Italian style, which we hope to convey. The Italian university and school system, which has ancient roots in Greek and Latin cultures, has a different approach from Anglo-Saxon countries. Therefore, the structure of this paper and the method of presenting our ideas are "Italian"— possibly less rigorous, but more colloquial.

A peculiarity is that we have not particularly reflected on our experience of writing this text together, nor on the dynamics between us in terms of relationships and relatedness to the content and themes we have discussed. We have never been a group without conflicts, but the writing of this paper has been surprisingly smooth. What was the secret? The task and the desire to deliver a "good enough" paper for a sophisticated international audience were strong unifying elements. In addition, the definition of roles in the project contributed to it.

## The foundation and development of the Italian Conferences: "Seminari di Arona"

At the beginning of the 90's, Claudio Caffarena and his wife Rosanna Balbo with the Studio il Nodo "brought" Anton Obholzer to Turin where he ran some institutional analysis workshops that Mario attended, and he has been actively involved ever since.

Elio had attended for many years the Conferences directed by Gino Pagliarani of CIS, Centro Individuo Società, which utilized systemic-psychodynamic methodology for the study of organizations.

The fateful encounter was at the 1997 Leicester Conference. What appeared to be a casual meeting between the three friends, Claudio, Mario and Elio, who were enthusiastic and somewhat dazed from the force of their experience, was in reality the start of a process that brought the Group Relations Conference to Italy. Anton Obholzer, who was directing that Leicester Conference and became immediately involved, said that "there was an element of interest for a long time, various projects were going on in Italy about understanding group and institutional processes. Some had to do with the work of Eric Miller or of Harold Bridger in Italy, others with indigenous Italian influences or with the increasing development of the child sector of training of the Tavi or with the whole family therapy and group-analytical dynamics, etc. But none of them in a sense coalesced; some of them had started and then faded away."

The primary task of the founding group was to import the Leicester GRC approach to Italy. The three sponsors, CESMA Milan, the Studio il Nodo Turin, and the Tavistock and Portman NHS Trust, agreed to have a Conference in spring 1998.

One of the questions that was posed immediately was how to find the staff for the conference and how to develop a group capable of bringing about the project.

During the same time, Louisa, who was a member of OFEK (The Israel Association for the Study of Group and Organizational Processes), through which she got in contact with Elio, from then on participated actively in the Italian initiative, although she never belonged to any of the sponsors. Unlike in other countries, in Italy an association such as OFEK or AKRI has never been formed.

One feature of the Italian Conference is the location, its pleasantness, its exclusivity, the high quality of food, etc. It is a distinctive element that the founding group wanted to give, and it was emphasized in many interviews as one of the identifying aspects of the Conference's Italian style.

The first Conference took place with 22 members. Anton Obholzer was the Director and Claudio Caffarena the Administrator, the three of us were staff members and Manuela Farneti was the interpreter. It was a sort of small "family enterprise" with a clearly male-oriented management, consistent with the most typical Italian social and business culture.

**Chart 1 Conferences Directorship**

| *Edition* | *Director* | *Associate Director* |
|---|---|---|
| 1°ed. 1998 | A. Obholzer | – |
| 2°ed. 1999 | A. Obholzer | F. Cardona |
| 3°ed. 2000 | A. Obholzer | F. Cardona |
| 4°ed. 2001 | F. Cardona | E. Vera |
| 5°ed. 2002 | F. Cardona | M. Perini |
| 6°ed. 2003 | M. Perini | F. Cardona |
| 7°ed. 2004 | E. Vera | A. Obholzer |
| 8°ed. 2005 | L. Brunner | W. Halton |
| 9°ed. 2006 | M. Perini | D. Armstrong |
| 10°ed. 2007 | E. Vera | O. Khaleelee |
| 11°ed. 2008 | L. Brunner | J. Lousada |

The Conference has occurred every year (see chart 2 below showing when and the membership). From 2002 there has been an A Conference for people attending for the first time and a B Conference for those who had attended previous editions. From 2008 there will be a Training Group and the Conference will be international and bilingual in English and Italian.

**Chart 2 Membership trend**

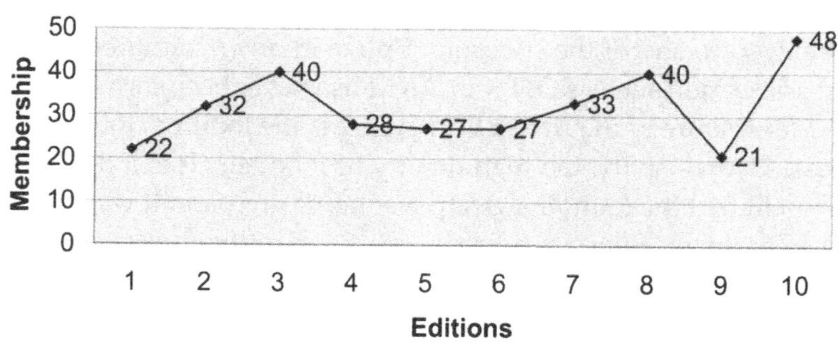

Since the second Conference Francesca Cardona—very active at the Tavistock & Portman NHS Trust and in Harold Bridger's group—was first involved as Associate Director and then as Director.

So far, in the ten Arona Conferences six other Consultants (or Associate Consultants) have been involved: Giovanni Foresti, Franca Fubini, Matilde Hernández, Paolo Izzi, Lia Ricotti, Vincenzo Villari. Two other persons have been involved as Pre-Conference Administrators, Valeria Fanelli and Salvatore De Luca. In 2003 Isabella Negri succeeded Manuela Farneti as the interpreter.

All three of us have been part of the staff at every Arona edition so far, showing such an attachment—after the early founding stage—that sometimes we wonder whether it touches on institutionalisation. These difficulties in separating from one's own organizational creatures are a typical feature of the Italian family business, where the founders' succession is often traumatic and the transition in terms of business development is often unplanned.

## *Individuation processes between dependence on tradition, desire for autonomy and anxiety of change*

### *The changes in the sponsoring organizations, developments and entrepreneurial anxieties*

Between 2002 and 2004 some significant changes took place in the sponsors. First Anton Obholzer, who still is our Scientific Supervisor, left his institutional position with the Tavistock and Portman NHS Trust, which gave way to the Tavistock Consultancy Service represented by David Armstrong and, in 2007, to the Tavistock & Portman NHS Foundation Trust with Julian Lousada. Claudio Caffarena left the IL NODO Group, which had become part of a consortium of cooperatives with Mario as the representative. Elio, who founded CESMA, is in the process of handing it over to Opera Multimedia and Marco Dragoni. The institutional framework of the Italian Conference changed. On the one hand it is a more formal and bureaucratic relationship, but on the other the trust of the new sponsors in the persons running the Conference has not had a direct impact on the Conference itself. From 2004 the partnership among CESMA, IL NODO Group and Tavistock consolidated and expanded through the creation of EMSSO (Executive Master

Specialized in Organizational Development), a programme where the Tavistock systems-psychodynamic theory and experiential events are integrated.

Probably similar to other Conferences' sponsors, there has been heavy entrepreneurial anguish: a continuous fear of low recruitment, of canceling the Conference or of running it at a heavy loss. These worries were realistic, in consideration of the uncertain and atypical entrepreneurial agreement that started the project: a "gentleman's agreement" between the CEO of Tavistock and Portman NHS Trust, the CEO of a management school (CESMA) and two freelance practitioners, a psychiatrist and a sociologist, associated with IL NODO. Profits (uncertain) and losses (though possible they actually never happened) weighed heavily on the shoulders of the two Italian sponsors, whose representatives were also members of the staff. Their double role actually added the most latent narcissistic and relational anxieties to the risk of the undertaking.

The financial anxieties gave space for particular interferences and conflicts, above all in the sphere of marketing and recruitment. The insecurity of a somewhat unknown imported product as well as the ambivalence towards the "manufacturer" brought uncertainties and contradictions in the recruitment policy—wavering between mass-selling and tailor-made products, or getting at times in uneasy situations with influential potential clients. These fears, hopefully by now overcome, of the Italian political and business habits, constrained in the grip of personal interests, favors, clienteles and nonchalant ethics, have repeatedly affected both the Italian GRC and the environment in which it had to learn how to survive and develop without revoking its mission and its inspiring values.

The subjective feeling of being a "minority" with respect to the English partner, experienced by the Italian ones, brought them put a lot of emphasis on the put a lot of emphasize to the "Leicester Model" and to the "Tavistock" logo, almost as if they entrusted the "Leicester Model" and the "Tavistock" logo for the success of their project and as guarantors of its quality. Evidence for this is the fact that, as already stated (see chart 1), in all Conferences there has been a Consultant from the "Tavistock " in the role of Director or Associate Director. Their contribution to the development of the Italian Conference has always been deeply appreciated, but at the same time some envy, splitting, "us and them" competitive feelings and domination/submission dynamics emerged. This was not only a matter of what was experienced personally, but there has always been, up to the 2007 edition, a huge (and unchanged) staff fee differential, notwithstanding the professional growth of the Italian staff, evidence of the dependency and narcissistic balances in the group, possibly a reflection of Italian culture.

### *The title of the Conference: a tension between desires of affiliation and identity crises*

In 1997 at the time of its conception, the three "Italian founding fathers" went through the dilemma between identity and belonging. They worked at length on how to call the Conference, possibly more than what would have justified promotional needs and marketing. It was like parents who choose a name for their baby—mediating between the father's and the mother's favorite names, considering taking a name of the family (that of a grandfather or uncle to keep with tradition), exploring the possibility of choosing an exotic name or inventing a new one.

The first name proposed was "*An organization that changes: innovation, transformation and resistances*"[1] Elio—who is a marketing and business communication expert—insisted on emphasizing the "change" dimension, which at the time was beginning to stir Italian society. The assumption was that the word "innovation", focusing on novelty, hope and development, was reassuring for a public that was paying heavy economic, social and emotional costs due to ongoing changes.

In November 1997, a re-thinking about "bettering communication" took place. The title was not as effective as the classic Leicester one—"*Authority, leadership and organization*", so it was integrally resumed, and "*The organization that changes*" was maintained as a subtitle. Realistic worries about a clear and appealing message for a difficult market were also a sign of the anxiety and ambivalence of the founders who, after Leicester, wanted and at the same time feared the separation from the "head company" and its lexicon.

In 1998 the subtitle was also cut: the organization didn't change any more, too scared to individualize itself. Later, upon inserting in the brochure also a short English presentation, we "noticed" that the translated title was identical to Leicester's, "*Authority, Leadership and Organization*". Anton Obholzer, the group's mentor, was contacted for advice because of copyright worries. He reassured us around the fantasies of being plagiarists and encouraged us to search an appropriate title autonomously.

After various drafts the definitive title *"Authority, Leadership and Innovation. An organization that changes."* was agreed. This title—the fruit of creative anxieties, desires of affiliation and identity crises—has remained the same until today. The subtitle was often changed and *"An organization that changes"* was soon replaced with "in groups and organizations" and/or more methodological specifications like "residential experiential Conference", etc. The reinforcement of the Conference's identity, along a line of both imitation of, and differentiation from, "Leicester", can be found in the design and programme, but also in the creation of a second name, "Seminari di Arona", from the location. Arona, a pleasant town on Lake Maggiore, has not always been the Conference location. After its second edition it went "in exile" for two years in Belgirate. Yet the "Seminari di Arona" name was maintained during the phase of de-localization.

### *Modifications to the design*

The architecture of the first Conference was largely designed on the basis of the indications of Anton Obholzer. It followed the Leicester scheme in part with an accordingly stronger emphasis on small groups (six in four days), a short inter-group event (two plenary meetings and two sessions), a couple of review groups and application groups. There was no large group event, perhaps because a shortened format of a little more than three days didn't allow the space to include it, or because it was thought that at that time the lack of experience of the staff would have made it difficult to manage. The opening plenary meeting was short (fifty minutes), and another large group meeting on the second day was a sort of large review group. Corresponding to the Leicester day off, a "two-hour" break on the third day gave a chance for more informal relations among the members, boat trips on the lake, etc.

The participants that were first-timers at the Conference turned out to become "co-founders" or at least acted as tests for the model. To them we owe many of the things that we learned and transferred into later Conferences, and some of them eventually became considerable partners or staff.

For seven editions the design did not change much. Some variation was introduced in the last two by running the organizational event. At times it was thought of having other new events, but these ideas were always ruled out.

Apparently the "Seminari di Arona" formula, changing little over time, "betrayed" the innovation element contained in the title. According to David Armstrong, the most important changes were not so much in the architecture of the Conference (that nevertheless didn't remain petrified in its original design), but rather in its organizational culture or method by which the staff and the management work before, during and after the Conference.

The anxiety to introduce new things to innovate, as mandated by the title, seemed an expression of two prevalent aspects: the first was the need for "emancipation" from the dependence on the "head company". But another unconscious stream was flowing "below the surface:" the constant, pervasive fear of confronting the unknown and the unexpected.

The anxiety of changing perspective, possibly within a relatively stable format and setting, was defensively converted into innovative pressure, while sustaining a comfortable illusion: that change is only a strategy like any other that can be introduced and made manageable and domesticated. Yet, by doing so we were denying the evidence, the disorienting and catastrophic dimension of change, a break-through that may become an opportunity but which at first we have to deal with and try to tame, like Bion's (1997) "wild thoughts".

The fear of disorientation and of the unknown triggered other specific defensive measures, like the "Pilgrim Fathers' syndrome," i.e., an idealized clinging to the spirit of the founders, a conservative tendency toward changes, sometimes a hard-line orthodoxy in the development of roles and boundaries. One piece of evidence could be some resistance to admit new people onto the staff.

## *"Seminari di Arona": between an international model, a Mediterranean atmosphere, and a national character*

### *The language and the role of the interpreter*

Since its outset the "Seminari di Arona" has been an Italian-English co-production or an interesting "franchising" experience in which adaptation to certain local characteristics was needed and hopefully enriching. In geopolitical terms Italy has always been a hinge between North and South, Europe's gate to the Mediterranean basin, the Balkans, Africa, the Middle-East, a set of cultures that have been living together for centuries without necessarily integrating, an interesting living inter-cultural laboratory.

Italy's cultural complexity has characterized the membership of the Conferences because of the differences between Northern and Southern Italian participants, which fairly accurately mirror the North-South polarity in the European scenario as well as worldwide. As was already mentioned above, the staff has never lacked an international touch with at least one UK-based Consultant and, on some occasions, even a Spanish one.

The official language is Italian and most members came from Italy, but also a few, speaking fluent Italian, came from Switzerland, Great Britain, France, Spain, and Holland.

The interpreters have had a special role, a paradigm of Italian traditional difficulties with foreign languages. By working with them and observing the interactions taking place between the interpreter and the speakers, the participants and the other staff at different levels, we realized that the function of interpreting embodied an emotionally important and alive presence, open to fantasies and projections on the part of everybody. At least in one case the interpreter was overtly attacked as a replacement target in a head-on onslaught on the Director. She somehow acted as the second-in-command described by Jaques (1953).

We hypothesize that in our Conferences the interpreter does not merely translate the words but also represents symbolically the need for a translation of the model, e.g., translating the notion of authority and leadership, which is very different in the Anglo-Saxon and Italian worlds. Just to give an example, in Italy authority is usually a formal established authority, whereas the typical concept of personal authority in Group Relations is quite uncommon.

## *Love of and ambivalence towards the foreigner*

The Arona Conference is an event with a national character—a mirror of Italian society and culture.

Italy has always had admiration for foreigners, but also distrust. The habits of having them "at home" for centuries as a conqueror, umpire, predator or liberator, has fostered (especially in the South) a mix of reverential worship and identification with the aggressor. The result is a sort of ambivalent love for all foreign things, which certainly has been present in the Arona Conference. This can be traced in the old "Italian complex", from Lansquenets through Napoleon III and the allied troops to McDonald's. The membership—and in a certain way the Italian staff—show a high respect for British culture underlying the Tavistock Model, but at the same time some people have felt vaguely annoyed with this approach, perceived as patronizing. There seems to be a fear of internalizing a protestant work ethic, a too rigid vision, with an overemphasis on duties, punctuality and responsibility. The tendency to emphasize rights and not duties, to arrive late and the cult of "being free" are very common in the Italian, mother-centered, culture.

Most opening plenaries had some empty seats, as was often true also at the first small group. In successive events, mental clocks rapidly aligned to the "Tavistock time". The impression is that, although it can be interpreted as an attack on staff authority, it can also be understood as a cultural operating model which considers the timetable as indicative and loose ("it's written 9 a.m., but it means that it begins at 9.15"), therefore a social habit more than an individual acting out.

Another feature has been the presence of "easy" and at times even loose boundaries between staff and membership, and between the Conference and the environment, represented by the hotel, its personnel and other guests. The relationships between staff and participants that during the events are defined by roles and boundaries, in the informal moments are different. After initial moments of shyness and reciprocal avoidance, as the Conference proceeds, interactions between more available staff members and participants become more frequent in the hallways, the bar and the common rooms of the hotel, brushing sometimes an amiable dimension and a confusion of roles. On some occasions, given previous contacts between a staff member and some participants, small business negotiations have been started with plans for the future, usually towards the end of the Conference. It is almost a tradition that during the last day's lunch the separation between staff tables and those of participants becomes looser or everyone eats together.

The gastronomic element is particularly well taken care of, as food is one of the Italian cultural strengths. In the hotel—with the well-wishing name of "Concorde"—food is especially good. Sometimes one eats too much. From this point of view the Arona's "Mediterranean cuisine" shows some less convincing behind-the-scenes elements, an echo of atavistic hunger and historical poverty, our archetype of the nurturing mother with ample breast, the fantasy of wanting to compensate with exquisite provisions an insufficient experiential nourishment.

### *"Dependency" and leadership*

Bion's basic assumption *"Dependency"* culture is a fairly visible Italian feature in the Conference ("tell us what we are supposed to do", "why don't group Consultants lead?", "here we have to do everything by ourselves"). This is often followed by a shift to a resentful and a bit paranoid independent attitude, which tends to organize the groups around the fantasy of challenging staff in order to make them powerless and helpless. The fate of Italian governments has followed the same script for years.

A paternalistic-charismatic leadership and an implicit followership's childish stance is one of the most popular styles in our country, in politics and business as well as in the family.

This culture is also the outcome of a thousand-year-old influence of the Catholic Church, with its hierarchical-dependent system, on Italian life. Italy is a country marked by a widespread entrepreneurship, a multitude of small and middle-sized family firms, where every entrepreneur is a leader, in a sort of illusionary independence or an unconscious defence against the dominant dependency culture.

In several Conferences we have witnessed a variety of these most traditional and typical leaderships within the membership: charismatic leadership, autocratic isolation and stiff formality or a "humane", seductive and compliant leader always open to agreements, etc.

As regards followership we have witnessed some typically "Italian" ways of relating to authority in the membership or in the staff. At first deference and obedience, with some reservations and unconscious opposition moves or isolated cases of overt rebellion. Some examples: in a plenary meeting a member turned his chair and sat with his back to the staff; once some Consultants forgot to come to a staff meeting with the management. Usually these are not real challenges against the established power, nor a coup, nor a serious self-empowerment.

### *The role of women*

The issue of women in the management and staff and in the membership of the Conferences reflects the position of women in Italian society.

All five of the women who have been Director, Associate Director or Consultant have a foreign dimension and strong international connections. None of them belongs to any Italian sponsor. It almost seems as if they partly found their authority abroad, in cultures where women have more space to work their way up, so as to achieve managerial positions at the Arona Conference. On the other hand, the Associate Consultants, the Administrator, the Pre-Conference Administrator and the Interpreters have been genuine Italian women.

Despite the strong feminist movements in the 1970s the woman stereotype of mother and/or "angel of hearth" is still very common in the Italian collective imagination. There is an ongoing debate about the few women in the government, parliament and holding top positions.

Over the years we have often seen women leaders emerging within the membership in different events. On the one hand it is, at least in part, a phenomenon mirroring dynamics in staff where more traditional male leadership was retained. On the other, something is probably changing in general among the new generations, and in the future women's leadership will be more common in Italy, too.

### *Mimetic, introjective and interpretative identifications of the "Leicester/Tavistock Model"*

In his interview David Armstrong emphasized several potential identifications with a model or an approach. On one hand there is mimetic identification, where the word 'mimetic' comes from the Greek 'mimetikè', meaning "the art of imitation". On the other, introjective identification comes from the psychoanalytic tradition. Finally, the interpretative identification introduces the interpreting dimension, a translation can be either literal or free.

Amstrong suggests that "A literal translation of a poem in some foreign tongue may capture the text's letter, but misses the spirit. To capture the spirit one has to both feel an identification and find an interpretative equivalent, from within the culture and imagery of another tongue. It is something that may emerge out of introjective identification and is then assimilated to and finds expression in one's own personal or socio-cultural frames of reference. This move, or something like it, may open up something new in something familiar. An example of such a process could be Bion's move in giving a different slant to Klein's construct of projective identification."

A stage of mimetic identification is necessary in order to acquire a model, an approach, a new language. The child cannot grow up without going through a phase of mimetic dependence. But innovation cannot occur without an introjective and interpretative identification. If a knowledge or a conceptual and experiential apparatus is not fully internalised, it is difficult to feel the emotional freedom to innovate.

If we apply these concepts to our Italian Conferences experience, we need to say that we are still midway between mimetic and introjective identifications with the "Leicester/Tavistock" model, between imitation and internalisation.

The reasons for this development may be personal, systemic or cultural, but some can also be found in the Italian cultural specificity described in this paper. The Arona Conference started as an adaptation of the Leicester model. We hypothesize that the swaying between mimetic identification and an introjective and more interpretative one can be traced perhaps in the deeply embedded ambivalence among Italians, in that oscillation between love and enchantment for foreign things and the fear of the foreigner and of the conqueror. This ambivalence can become a defence against deeper introjection of the model, lesser dependence, more autonomy or independence; it can "obstruct" or dismiss the possibility of a greater identification that could allow for a different and potentially more innovative interpretation of the model itself.

Evidence can be found in Claudio Caffarena's interview. "In these years there hasn't been enough reflection about the model and how it has been adapted in Italy in terms of what has worked and what has not ... . It is more a series of re-editions without much processing, and we have gone on without turning our experience into a model." For example, members' feedback questionnaires have not always been thoroughly scrutinized, despite some interesting remarks. A working through process about the model might be too difficult and stir up contradictions too complex to be dealt with.

## *Conclusions*

We have presented the phases and the dynamics of the development of the Italian Conferences mostly through the experiences of founders, sponsors and staff members.

We chose to emphasize how the cultural context affects the Conferences and their specificity by also presenting some cultural stereotypes of the Latin as well as of the Anglo-Saxon world. Stereotypes help simplify reality or allow for an understanding that refers to already established codes. Stereotypes can emerge with respect to environmental elements, social roles or power differences (Hilton and Von Hippel, 1996). All these dimensions played a role in our discourse.

A factor, which has gone through the entire development of the Italian Group Relations project, is the tension between task and sentient group. We use these terms according to the classic definition by Miller & Rice (1967): the sentient group "demands and receives loyalty from its members" (p. xiii). It is therefore a group that stays together not only to perform a task, but also because of the affective bonds between its members and the project's ideal.

The Italian Conferences have developed within a family-business culture, in which the sentient dimension has been strongly active and loyalty both to the group and to tradition has been deeply felt. An important contribution has been the strong motivation and passion to bring to Italy the Tavistock approach and methodology for group and organizational learning. But it is a tension "between" task and sentient group rather than an "either/or" alternative. Often the wish, expressed from time to time by some staff member, for a more task-oriented culture, further away from loyalty to tradition, a bit less idealistic or closer to market dynamics, has come up (e.g., the issue of the Consultants' fees, lower than the market ones, etc.).

We do not have an answer about how to manage such a tension, but we believe in the future of the Italian Conferences project and a constant development between tradition, adaptation and innovation.

Many thanks to Isabella Negri for the translation from Italian.

## Note

1. It is interesting to note how in these first drafts of the brochure, while the title was different from that of the Leicester Conferences, the text represented a nearly literal translation of the Leicester brochure.

## References

Bion, W.R. (1997). *Taming Wild Thoughts.* (Edited by F. Bion). London: Karnac Books.

Doglioni, M. & Rosiello, L. (Eds.). (1994). *Vocabolario della lingua italiana di Nicola Zingarelli.* Bologna: Zanichelli.

Gutmann, D. & Iarussi, O. (2003). *Psychoanalysis and Management: The Transformation.* London: Karnac.

Hilton, J.L. & Von Hippel, W. (1996). "Stereotypes". *Annual Review of Psychology*, Vol. 47, 1996.

Jaques, E. (1953). "On the dynamics of social structure: a contribution to the psychoanalytical study of social phenomena deriving from the views of Melanie Klein". *Human Relations*, 6: 3–24; and In: E. Trist & H. Murray (Eds.). *The Social Engagement of Social Science: A Tavistock Approach. Vol. 1: The Socio-Psychological Perspective.* London: Free Association Books 1990.

Miller, E. & Rice, A.K. (1967). *Systems of Organization—The Control of task and sentient boundaries*—London: Tavistock Publications.

CHAPTER FIVE

# The community system: Inter-subjective approaches to group relations

*Susan Long*

## *The community system event*

Since 2002 in Melbourne, the Creative Organisational Systems (COS) Group at RMIT University has been exploring the community system in its annual Group Relations Conferences.[1]

The 'community system' is a systemic level within the organisation, parallel to, but different from other systems such as the task, sentient, political, economic and socio-technical systems. There are systems at all levels. But the following schema may help.

```
Society
|
Broad Domain System: e.g., Health System,
Industry, Local Community
|
Specific Organisation: e.g., Corporation,
Community Group
|
Systems within the Organisation: egg, task,
sentient, political, economic, socio-technical
systems AND community system
```

The conferences we have conducted are primarily for part-time students, most of who are managers or consultants within two Masters and a Professional Doctorate program, with members of the public also invited.

The community event was conducted alongside a small study system and following an institutional system event. In the last four years it has been introduced by the conference Director in the following way.

**Primary task of the community system event**

> 'To study and further the development of the temporary learning organisation as community'
>
> This event is new. It has been conducted in the RMIT group relations workshops since 2002. It is an innovation built on the working hypothesis that organisations have many systems within which we take up and are offered roles—emotional, political, etc. These systems operate perhaps simultaneously with some more consciously evident than others, some quite unconsciously present, perhaps at different times. My working hypothesis is that there is a systemic community level in the organisation. That is, a level of interaction and relatedness affected by and affecting task (and other systems) yet different to the task system. I think it is a system of values and purposes where people within the organisation interact around values and beliefs—community or communitas.
>
> To get anything done, to work together on tasks organisation members have agreements or understandings. These may be conscious agreements or they may be unconscious—that is, collusions. There may be quite different understandings about these agreements—different ideas, roles or tasks in the mind. But a system of agreements is present and discoverable, as are some understandings of where there are disagreements.
>
> The working hypothesis is that in community, or at the community level of the organisation, agreements or disagreements are around values and purpose. These are assumed and undergird task.
>
> In this event we agree to work on the experience of this community within the temporary organisation—even though the working hypothesis may not be sustained and we may discover no such thing.

To re-iterate the event task then:

'To study and further the development of the temporary learning organisation as community.'

In 2006 and 2007 the following diagram was also provided.

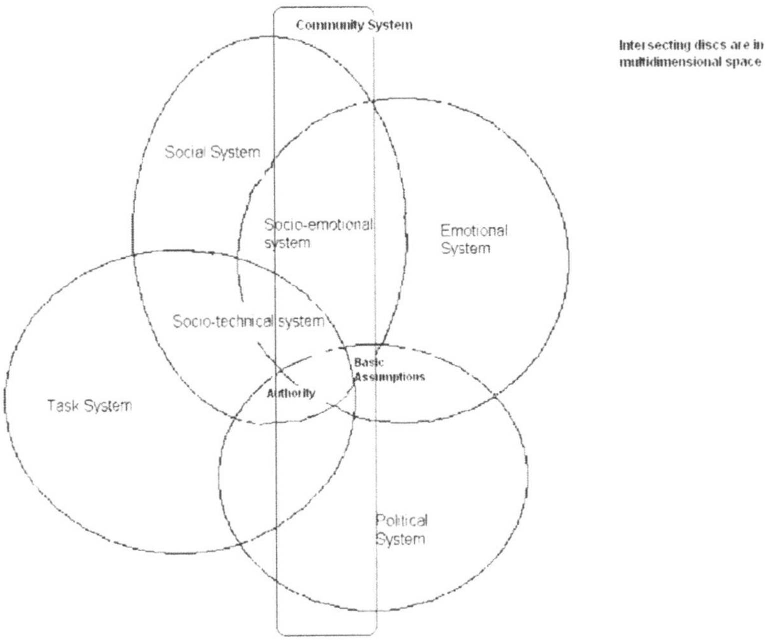


Diagram. Incomplete schematic representation of various organisational psychodynamic systems: the community system intersects these.

The community system event attempts to explore the community system in the temporary organisation of the conference. However, the event also asks members to further develop the conference community and to learn from this. The idea is not just to study what exists but to engender and study development (or not) as it occurs.

## *The staff in the event*

The staff of the conferences 2002–7 has been relatively stable. This consisted of three or four teaching staff members from the university, all experienced in group relations work, plus, since 2004, an invited colleague from the worldwide group relations network. The community event has been regarded with much interest and excitement by the staff and was the subject of extended discussion leading up to the conference each year. As Director, I had ideas about the community system and what the event might attempt within the group relations context. My ideas were new, and in relating them I found that staff had many different pre-conceptions that did not necessarily fit with mine. In discussion, we found that ideas of community were very different for different people. Often the discussion became focused on the community at large—what might be called the domain of the community. Staff members became engrossed with the communities that they had grown up in or were currently experiencing. This appeared different from the idea of the community *within* the organisation (the organisational community), but provided a necessary conversation. It was hard for us to get a collective idea of community within the organisation, so it was important to discuss differences.

More difficulty arose, however, with the nature of the event itself. Much anxiety was aroused. On the one hand, the event was new and was different to other familiar here-and-now events. On the other hand, it evoked associations to some familiar group relations events. For instance, the event requires members and staff to explore the community system whilst also simultaneously being in their task system roles as managers and members. That is, they take up roles in both task and community systems. We struggled with the idea that staff members could be both in the role of manager—a role within the task system, and community member—a role in the community system, at the same time. Fears of being uncontained came to the surface. Being in the manager role gave rise to associations about the Institutional Event. This event felt safer due to its being better known. What would it mean to be a manager in the community system?

We take up roles in different systems within the one organisation simultaneously quite naturally in everyday life, say the task and political systems. One might be an informal and powerful leader in the political system and a machine operator with little formal authority in the task system. In making a decision, an awareness of the influence of each of these systems is helpful. The question arises, even if only unconsciously or tacitly, as to which role is making *this* decision? Who am I at *this* time? What system am I representing? In the community event, we are asking ourselves and the members to take up roles as managers or members—roles given us from the task system—***and*** to take up our role within the community of the temporary institution.

The idea in the conference is primarily to explore the 'community level' of the work system. For example, is it experienced differently by managers and by members? What is the community of the organisation-in-the-mind? Inevitably in this process, the wider community with its rules, mores and assumptions enters, perhaps through the artefacts of the venue surrounding the conference.[2]

Another issue concerns the additional task to *further develop* the community system of the temporary organisation. This has implications for the development of the community system of the RMIT programs, the host body, as well as the community of each of the temporary organisations studied. Contrary to Bion's directive to eschew desire (1970), in this one aspect of the conference we are pursuing a desire for development—eros if you like. Such a desire underpins group relations work and although seemingly standing aside from such ethics in our psychoanalytic explorations, work on the community system recognizes this.

## *2002 & 2003—The large group phenomenon*

The first year evidenced typical large study group dynamics. Although members and staff were informed of the availability of other rooms, most of the time was spent in the large group. People felt 'locked into' the room. Tensions built around a woman wanting to leave and form a group elsewhere. Seemingly a simple endeavour, the process was painful: she relating it to difficulties with exercising her own personal authority and others clearly identifying with her or challenging her, provoking her to go or demanding that she stay. Eventually she left with followers. In the large group she was lauded as a kind of hero, and fantasies were explored about the exciting things that the 'break-away' group might be doing. In fact, affect became quite flat once outside 'the community'. The woman concerned did not so much discover her own authority (although her decision to leave was personally important) but more the group discovered her role as being a symbol of its illusion; viz. that the terror and deathly feelings inside the group could be escaped by going outside.

Was this demonstrating the ubiquitous 'pull' of the large group as mob? Was the community unconsciously struggling with what Chasseguet-Smirgel (1984) describes as the perverse surrender of the superego to the group's ideology, where each ego becomes its own ideal, submerged, through identification in a belief of sameness? Many authors since Freud (1921) have tried to understand why individuals surrender their own capacity for personal judgement in the face of an overwhelming group ideology or illusion. This question seems as relevant to our time as it was to those in the Nazi era or to those at the time of the Jonestown suicides. In the community described, the group who left imagined that they regained their own authority, but they were left feeling empty and depleted. Because what is authority but a phenomena that belongs to the group as a whole? The enactment seems resonant of what we experience at a community level. We may wish to leave, to escape the political struggles around values, to be outside that which we think does not or cannot represent what we truly believe. But if we do escape we are depleted. Why is that? Chasseguet-Smirgel (1984) says:

> 'We can understand that it is both dangerous and stressing not to yield to the law of the group, to be a wet blanket. If you do not always risk your life in it, at least your sources of narcissism will dry up. You become a pariah condemned to solitude, no longer entitled to your fellow men's love' (p. 64).

Damned if you stay in the community and damned if you leave!

The community event of the second year felt like an inter-group event. In session 2, men's and women's groups formed showing some hostility and aggression between groups and much camaraderie within. Discussions in the gender groups were robust and engaging and were followed by the larger community exploring the experiences around hostility and the responses of both genders to women in positions of authority (the conference Director being a woman).

In both these years the staff seemed dragged into these dynamics, unsure of the roles each had: sometimes working as if consultants, sometimes as if in a Praxis Event, with roles as ordinary members. Staff members were struggling to find their place in the community and somewhat anxious about the 'enactments' occurring. I wondered about the place of enactment and its resolution as a symbolic part of community system development.

## *2004 & 2005—Community apart and together*

In 2004 the conference moved to a different venue renovated into a modern conference facility with religious icons not obviously present as they had been at the previous venue.[3] A large space was used with smaller rooms also available. The space was organised with chairs scattered around, some in small groupings, others in pairs, others placed individually. A community notice board was introduced.

In this setting the event became more diverse. Small discussion groups formed in the large space. After about forty-five minutes, staff members began posting times and places for various activities and discussions. Members followed this lead. It was reminiscent of an 'Open Space' event (Owen, 1997a; 1997b). In 2004, the membership included a large group all from Phillip Morris, the cigarette manufacturers. Throughout the conference, allusions were made to the issue of smoking and the implied immorality of cigarette companies. The community event brought this to a head as a large number of members formed a group to discuss this issue. Members came and left, and in this process an open space was created to investigate the values of different members.

In 2005, various groups formed, for example, to draw pictures about their experience of the conference, to discuss dreams, to build a 'cubby house' (Wendy House) and to form a men's group. Often individual members would spend time alone, writing, reflecting or walking. The staff had decided that should they need to meet as management during the event they would do so. One staff member felt quite conflicted when the director called a meeting while the men's group (which he had been central in forming) was in session. Was he manager or community member first? The staff group was attempting to find its role as management within the system. There seemed little place for management except for mutual reassurance that the event was proceeding and that they could make some sense of what was occurring.

In both these years, plenary sessions occurred at the end of the event. Semi-planned, these seemed to fulfil a need for the community to share what had happened during the event and to discuss its success. It seemed that the event was being used to work on issues of the broader conference. For example, after the building of the cubby house using chairs and sheets, the builders sat inside sharing reminiscences of childhood and then discussing life issues in playful ways. Their regression might be said to be working at new ways of re-experiencing and viewing their dependencies and their authorities. The drawing groups and dream groups attempted to surface and share thoughts and feelings about the conference—perhaps a different way of working with review.

The general sense was of a community with different groups working in quite intense ways. The staff felt that they were beginning to find a useful way of working in the event.

### *2006—Retreat or transition?*

In 2006, small group activities also occurred, egg, drawing, dream sharing, discussions, story telling, group sculpture. A member described it as having 'no predetermined topics, activities or groupings. Activities emerged spasmodically like bubbles bursting through the surface.' Some parts of the community had a theatrical feel—as if they were playing at being a community. For example, a pair wandered around 'acting a part'; a human sculpture was formed. A 'campfire' was created where people sat around exchanging tales. Nonetheless, the human sculpture, drawings, dream groups and the pair were focused on experiences of the conference—many of the experiences depicted being extremely personal. Compared with previous years, although a final plenary was desired and called for, it didn't occur. Smaller groups and pairs remained, many intensely engaged, others loosely engaged until the end of the event. It was as if people were in retreat from the larger institution with its experience in-the-mind of a distanced hierarchy. There was much evidence of such an organisation-in-the-mind in the opening plenary and other events and in the drawings produced during the community system event. One hypothesis was that the members were in a psychic retreat during the event. Another was that the event provided a space for the emergence and sharing of unconscious material about the temporary organisation in multiple ways; yet another, that the event provided a space for intense creativity and worked as a transitional space.

### *Vignette: Age and succession*

About three quarters through the event, in the open space, a member of staff decided that staff should have a meeting in order to manage the event. As Director, I had previously said that I might call a meeting at any time during the event should this be needed, but I had not felt this to be necessary. This staff member, a 'younger' woman, was joined by the administrator, a 'younger' man, and they began to call staff together. The administrator came to me to invite me to the 'management meeting'. I reacted to this as a challenge to my role as Director. In open discussion, we faced the thought that the younger staff, represented by these two, felt that I had abandoned management of the event and that they should take this up. I believed there was no need to take up a more directive role in the event and that the younger staff was attempting a coup.[4] This rather tense discussion drew the attention of members, but in particular, it drew the doctoral students. Three doctoral students had been working together in the event. They were keenly aware of their position 'in between' the staff and the masters' students, struggling with their place in the academic hierarchy and the projections that they were receiving in this place. They had doubts about their presumed greater knowledge and fears about the envy this aroused. Although a dynamic set well within RMIT, through one of them being a visiting doctoral student from Europe it also represented a wider issue.

This incident had reverberations throughout the conference but also in RMIT after the conference. For example, staff in the program began more directly to face issues of succession and training. Students in the program raised issues of succession and age difference in their workplaces. The doctoral students as a whole worked on their authority and the nature of their role, becoming less dependent on staff and more interdependent with each other and staff.

### *Vignette: Drawings done in the community system event*

The community system provided a space for members to find ways of depicting their experience rather than in traditional study or discussion groups. From the drawings done, it seems the institution was experienced by some as quite violent—certainly the theme of cutting or chopping is present. One told a tale of a family dispute and leaving home. Below is a sample of the drawings.

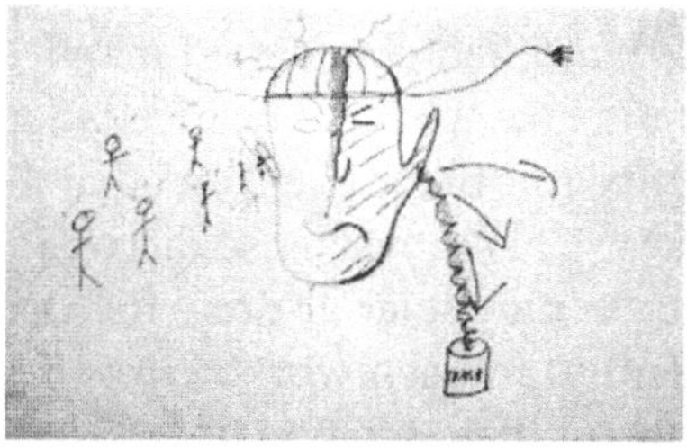

Some few drawings were not violent and depicted a peaceful gathering, a self-portrait and an aboriginal tribal setting. These seemed to represent a hoped for community of sharing and finding self identity. Yet, many held the element of violence. I believe that was how the task system was experienced. The picture of a distant mother with her foot over the child's train track exemplifies an image of malevolent authority. The control depicted in the split electrified mind resonates with the idea of authority as controlling and denying the capacity for integration. The community event allowed a mutual surfacing and exploration of this. It provided a transitional space where dynamics in the task system could be surfaced and processed.

### *2007—The community as home*

In the 2007 conference, there was a strong push to have an ongoing 'community group' in the large room. This became a place for swapping stories and collecting information about the smaller groups that had formed. Each of the smaller groups worked on aspects of members' experience in the conference. However, a lassitude and lack of energy seemed to dominate in the second session. I noted that both staff and members were becoming complacent, evidenced in a flight from the task of exploring community. The large group in the big room had become lethargic and the small groups disengaged from it and each other.

I found myself thinking about this overnight and prepared a speech to give to the community from my roles of Director and community member. I spoke about the flight from task and gave my evidence. I spoke about the nature of authority and the ways that I was seeing it taken up or avoided in the conference. I urged the group to examine the ethics of retreat from the community. I felt that I was mobilised into my leadership role as Director and that this mobilisation was as a fight leader—fighting the tendency toward flight. Many members said they felt inspired by my speech. Perhaps this was also evidence of the transference of student to professor, or of the pairing impulses from the membership to the Director. Certainly we were in the midst of some powerful basic assumptions. Nonetheless, in this I was also mobilised to think carefully, to develop working hypotheses, to give evidence from observation and to promote learning, all tools of the group relations methodology. Following this, some of the unspoken issues in the community began to surface.

### *What has the event given us?*

How successful have we been in working in these events? Several questions arise. Have we simply recreated other group relations events in a different guise- the Large Group? the Inter-Group? the Praxis Event? Open space? Is it that the Community Event is 'time-off' from the more challenging here and now events that work directly with authority relations? Alternatively, have we been working with a task that readily enables us to see some broader societal values, purposes and dynamics at play through their enactment and interpretation in the community of the temporary institution? Is there an ethics of community that arises in this event?

### *Some theory*

A series of hypotheses about systems within group relations conferences will be used to explore the nature of the event. The first suggests that group relations theory about the task system acts as a container for anxiety in the conference. The second suggests that the community system is a system of values and purpose (ethics and eros or thanatos) supporting or directing the task. The third suggests that defences occur in the community system when subjectivity is threatened.

### *The group relations conference and the task system*

> **Hypothesis 1:** The theory of task, role and authority is a central container for the exploration of learning from experience in the Group Relations Conference. It allows individuals to maintain a stance of thinking and learning from experience in the face of unconscious anxieties and the unconscious violent mob.

We have come to understand social systems in terms of task versus sentience systems. Now we are finding a greater complexity. There are the multiple systems of task, power, emotions, social, socio-technical, financial, intellectual. Each system is related to the others but acts in quasi-independent ways and each has roles available. Often members take up or are offered roles in different systems that bring about internal and/or external role conflicts. Role analysis (Newton, Long and Sievers, 2006) has often to work with these multiple roles.

Group relations conferences evidence the operation of all these systems with their infinitely multiple roles. They have a major focus on the task system, or the enterprise system, to use Eric Miller's words. The focus is on how it operates and how it is consciously and unconsciously resisted or corrupted (Chapman, 1999 provides an analysis within this tradition). Tasks are established by conference management and agreed by members entering the conference. The tasks are for the institution of the conference as a whole. This is critical, even though it may be stressed that individual members are responsible for their own learning. The tasks established for each of the conference events are consistent with the primary task of the conference, which is consistent with the basic philosophy of learning through experience, in the here-and-now of the conference.

The consultant staff works toward understanding their own experience and the dynamics occurring and makes this understanding available in the form of interpretations or queries. Staff has available collectively its own theories of group dynamics, predominantly within psychoanalytic object relations applications to groups and organisations, to help explore, shape and contain experiences. A central shared theoretical device or tool is the theory of *task, role and authority*. Unconscious psychodynamics are framed and understood through this. Importantly, the retention of sanity and a capacity to think within the conference depends on the containment provided by this theory as put into practice. When thinking is attacked by the unconscious mob, or the lassitude or sloth of the group,[5] the rule—almost mantra—of 'stay *with* task and *in* role' provides a central bedrock in the maelstrom. This is for staff and members alike. The capacity to stay with the task of learning from experience is critical for the work of the conference, as is the capacity to stay in role as consultant, manager or member.

Like most aspects of a working social system, roles and their authority become regular, institutionalised and entrenched. This is so because they provide a solution to the anxiety and chaos attendant upon the loss of differentiation into the mob, or, at a less regressed level, a solution to interpersonal disputes and anxieties aroused by the tasks and responsibilities of the system. This is all described in theories of social defences against anxiety. The utility of a particular division of labour with its attendant authorities may long be outmoded and recognised as such, but an entrenched and internalised system may be sustained because of its defensive power.

Individuals learn about this in the Group Relations Conference. Experience is reconceptualised and toxic systems more easily survived. Yet, years of exposing, recognising and interpreting such phenomena have not necessarily led to widespread change (Long, 2006). We can often see social defences operating in destructive ways, but finding alternatives is not easily accomplished. *If we have come to see and articulate the problem, we have not yet found long-term solutions.*

## *Inter-subjectivity and community*

> **Hypothesis 2:** In community, or at the community level of the organisation, agreements or disagreements are around values, purpose and ethics. These are often assumed and under-gird task. The community within the organisation is linked through these to the wider society.

An inter-subjective approach has a history through authors such as Hegel and Winnicott and finds more recent expression in the work of Benjamin(1988). A major motif of the inter-subjective or relational position is the possibility of equality of relationship between subjectivities. Here equality refers to the mutual existence, assertion and recognition of subjectivities. This includes the recognition of the need for an existing 'other' subjectivity in order that our own subjectivity might exist and be asserted. The other is more than an 'object' to be internalised into a world of inner objects for solipsistic use, but is required to be really 'other' for subjectivity to develop. In Winnicott's famous terms 'there is no baby without a mother'. That is, the roles require each other. In Hegel's terms, the Master needs the Slave to be a Master. Without the recognition of his mastery by the Slave, then he cannot be the Master. For this recognition to occur, the Slave retains some aspect of his freedom: his capacity and authority to bestow recognition on the Master's subjectivity. Perhaps this is the essence of freedom.

For most relational theorists, subjectivity is regarded as developed through the relationships engaged throughout life. Although intra-psychic tensions and conflicts exist in response to developmental phenomena, these are shaped through the relationships in which that development is embedded. Change is brought about through recognition of 'enactments' of past relational patterns in the here and now.

This paper argues a step further. Recognition of system and role is important. Subjectivity is not synonymous with individuality but a position within a system (Lacan, 1977) in relation to other subjectivities. In everyday terms this means that for each role we take up there are role counterparts. For a doctor there must be a patient (and perhaps a hospital administrator, or a government health provider, depending on the system); for a teacher, a student, educational bureaucrats, parents and so on. Each player in these systems enacts patterns from past experience, some of which are due to personal histories and some of which are culturally shared.

While this is true for work ***task*** systems, it is equally true for political systems, economic systems, symbolic systems, socio-emotional systems and community systems within organizations. Our subjectivities are discovered through our *subjection to roles* in these systems. Role mediates organisational life and allows the person to find ***a place or identity in relation to others***. It incorporates the person who is part of many different systems within the organisation. Role is a very lively concept, and through taking up the authorities and accountabilities that different roles offer, we learn to become effective social beings. Understanding our roles allows for a better understanding of the systems we are in (the organisations and systems in our experience) and hence, the frameworks from which we interact with others.

In the organizational community system, we take up the role of community member somewhat akin to 'citizen' of the broader organisation, although without the implications of an organised civic state. The community system has the flavour of a system where roles are focused around inter-subjective equalities. Here relationship is as important as relatedness.[6] This may seem just another expression of the sentient system, but it is more than just the emotional and friendship bonds formed in the organisation. It is a system of institutional and social values at a communal level. Perhaps it is the level where a common symbolism is formed.

A key point is that inter-subjectivity amongst interacting members of a community system provides a social 'glue' as does a common task, and as does a common culture. The connectedness of people through the task system is through task, authority and role. My working hypothesis is that the organization *per se* encompasses a system of positions in the task system (and the political, social, fiscal etc., systems) *plus* a system of roles that engages subjectivities at the community system level of experience.

> **Hypothesis 3:** Social defences may threaten subjectivity and community.

According to the Menzies-Lyth study (1970), a culture developed whereby the student nurse role was infantalised and nurses were psychologically distanced from their patients. Menzies-Lyth suggested that this was due to the operation of a social defense against the anxieties of working closely with the patients. Primitive libidinal anxieties were aroused alongside anxieties about death and dying. However, the system was then unable to provide the recognition needed by the nurse (as with the paradox of the Master-Slave relation), who also cannot assert her authority for task, because of the infantalisation of her role in the defense system. The task system operated, beds got made, temperatures were taken but many student nurses dropped out because the social defense system was, it is hypothesized here, an assault on their capacity to further develop their role and their personal subjectivity within role.

Many nurses did not have personal defence systems congruent with the social defence system of the institution. They were unable to develop their place within the community level of the hospital as well as to take up the nursing task. Menzies-Lyth found that the social defense system worked insofar as it at times minimised the direct experience of aspects of the task that most directly aroused unconscious phantasies about sexual intimacy and death. But in addition, I suspect the hospital training system had no way of directly helping student nurses to surface and face their fears. There was no real subjective 'other' for the student nurse to encounter. The task system became objectified, and student nurses were not encouraged to look at the values and purposes underlying the work, perhaps because there was no real leadership available or developed for this process.

I am suggesting here that our institutionalised defences against anxiety fail when they do not support subjectivity within the community of the organization, even when the task is protected. In such a situation individual voices are not heard, communion is stunted and people feel empty. The social defence no longer successfully contains anxiety, but deadens the community that supports and gives meaning to the task system.

## *Place of the community system event in the conference*

The local staff who have worked in the community system event over the past six years have come increasingly to regard the event as a transitional space within the conference. Here the values underlying task and organisation can be visited. It is a conference event in evolution, beginning now to take on a practical shape from out of its conceptual beginnings. For many, both staff and members, it provides a place where rite-of-passage within the learning of the conference occurs: a seeming 'time out' that allows a free floating state for exploration of underlying values and ethics. The idea of 'communitas' is important with its implications of transition and liminality. In community, hierarchical roles in other systems are suspended. There is a moment of true democracy.

The practical heritage of the event lies with group relations events, systems psychodynamic technologies and associated methodologies such as the praxis event, the large group, social dreaming, psycho-drama, work drawings, open space technology and dialogue groups. Many of these are visited in the COS Group programs and it is not surprising that they are taken up by participants in the community event of the group relations conference. Its conceptual heritage comes from group relations, both the Leicester model of task and authority and Harold Bridger's ideas of double task, together with Winnicott's ideas of transitional space. Its political heritage is in ideas in workplace democracy, where having a voice and identity comes as much from one's place in the organisational community as from one's role in the task system.

But beyond being a time out or reflective transitional space, the event has a positive role in building community. It is an event that is 'other' to the task level analysis of the other conference events. Perhaps large organisations and corporations such as those from which many of the members come are increasingly experienced as at some level perverse or corrupt (Bakan, 2004; Long, 2008), where authority is abused. The community level of organisation provides a system where values and ethics can be visited, questioned and reforged. The enterprise is primarily about task, but this should not be at the cost of basic values. This may be the hardest work.

## Notes

1. I wish to acknowledge here the work of staff and members in the development of this event. I cannot name all the members here, most are current and past students in the COS Group programs. Staff who have worked with me on the event and who have provided many ideas in discussion are (in alphabetical order): Eduardo

Acuna, Mary Burgess, Jane Chapman, Paul Dunstone, Michael Faris, Amy Fraher, Wendy Harding, Paul Hoggett, James Krantz, Janelle Morgan, John Newton, Brigid Nossal and Himadri Potter. Wendy Harding has been particularly helpful in discussing ideas about inter-subjectivity.

2. See Schien's (1992) ideas on organisational culture.
3. Such venues are relatively cheap compared to large corporate venues and thus enable our group relations work to proceed. Through this, the change in the Church, with lesser members and a need to raise revenues, impacts on group relations work.
4. The vignette about age and succession highlights the difficulty of working with multiple roles in multiple systems. The administrator raised this with me after the conference. I quote from an e-mail sent me by Himadri Potter, September 2006.

> The role offered ... *staff* ... was member of the community or 'citizen' in a system in which hierarchy is suspended and our task was 'to study and further the development of the temporary learning organisation as community'. It could be argued that a meeting was called by one or two citizens in a system of suspended hierarchy for the purpose of the task ... Acting from out of the role of citizens our behaviour could be argued as an initiative valid and useful as any other initiative that came from other 'citizens' that day ... but ... .it seems the citizen role was used to take an action that had meaning and motivation in the management role and the political system. The request to remain in the management role—that involves the experience in being in a hierarchy of authority—while exploring the citizen role—which involves being in a system in which hierarchy is suspended—is problematic is it not?

It was clear at the time that the meeting had been called as a management meeting, not a community members meeting, and was a challenge to the director. The management of the event was noted as the reason for the meeting. A political act to challenge the existing hierarchy was thus germinated within the community system. He then asked the question whether people can act or interact in an organisation from the role of citizen 'that is not experienced as undermining of the task and associated differentiated authority system. Such a basis for relations seems to have a particular political agenda and upsets the status quo.' I feel, however, that we must be able to work within both systems without one undermining the other; our survival and sustainability depends on it. Perhaps thinking within one system *about* the other is what is required. I am indebted to Himadri for a stimulating debate around these matters.

5. See Long (2008).
6. For a discussion of this in terms of the Large Group see Harding (2006).

## References

Bakan, J. (2004). *The Corporation: the pathological pursuit of profit and power* London, Constable.

Benjamin, J. (1988). *The Bonds of Love: Psychoanalysis, feminism and the problem of domination* New York, Pantheon Books.

Bion, W.R. (1961). *Experiences in Groups* London, Tavistock publications.

Bion, W.R. (1970). *Attention and Interpretation* London, Tavistock Publications.

Brown, N.O. (1959). *Life Against Death: The psychoanalytic meaning of history* Wesleyan University Press: Middletown, Conn.

Chapman, J. 'Hatred and Corruption of Task' Socio-Analysis: *the Journal of the Australian Institute of Socio-Analysis*, 1(2), 127–150.

Chasseguet-Smirgel (1984). *Creativity and Perversion* London: Free Association Books.

Freud, S. (1921). *Group Psychology and the Analysis of the Ego* London: Hogarth Press and the Institute of Psychoanalysis (1949).

Harding, W. (2006). *Intersubjectivity and Large groups: A systems psychodynamic perspective* Unpublished PhD RMIT University, Melbourne.

Klein, M. (1975). Envy and Gratitude and other works 1946–1963 NY: Dell Publishing Co.

Krantz, J. & Maltz, M. (1997). 'Framework for Consulting to Organizational Role' *Consulting Psychology Journal: Practice and Research*, 49(2), 137–151.

Lacan, J. (1977). *Ecrits* London, Tavistock Publications.

Long, S.D. (2001). 'Destructivity and the Perverse State of Mind' *Organisational and Social Dynamics*.

Long, S.D. (2006). 'Organisational Defenses Against Anxiety: What has happened since the 1955 Jaques paper?' *International Journal of Applied Psychoanalysis*.

Long, S.D. (2008). *The Perverse Organisation and its Deadly Sins* London: Karnac.

Menzies-Lyth, I.E.P. (1970). *The Functioning of Social Systems as a Defence against Anxiety* Tavistock Institute of Human Relations Pamphlet No. 3.

Miller, E.J. (1999). 'Dependency, Alienation or Partnership? The changing relatedness of the individual to the enterprise' in R. French and R. Vince (Eds.). *Group Relations Management and Organization* Oxford: Oxford University Press.

Newton, J. Long, S. & Sievers, B. (Eds.). (2006). *Coaching in Depth: The organisational role analysis approach* London: Karnac.

Owen, H. *Open Space Technology: A User's Guide* (3rd Edition) (1997a) Berrett-Koehler.

Owen, H. (1997b). *Expanding Our Now: The Story of Open Space Technology* (Berrett-Koehler).

Prins, S. (2002). *"Who's in charge here?!" Leadership Dynamics in Multiparty Collaboration.* Paper presented at the Symposium of the International Society for the Psychoanalytic Study of Organizations, June 20–22, Melbourne, Australia.

Schien, H. (1992). *Organizational Culture and Leadership* San Francisco, Jossey Bass.

Schoeck, H. (1966). *Envy: A theory of social behaviour* NY: Harcourt, Brace and World.

Turquet, P. (1974). 'Leadership: The individual and the group' in G. Gibbard, J.

*CHAPTER SIX*

# A world of difference: Lessons and innovations on the study of race, authority and identity

*Mary B. McRae and Zachary Gabriel Green*

All over the world issues of difference confront us in almost every society. Many parts of the world currently experience ethnic, religious, socio-economic, racial, tribal, political and other difference with violence and hostility. Making it more urgent to address difference, all kinds of difference, more effectively; the challenge that confronts each of us, our offspring, and those in our varied subgroups is to find different ways to transform our conversations and actions on difference. At New York University we have done a series of Group Relations conferences that have focused on working with difference. Since 1999 the conferences have moved from a focus on issues confronting subgroups in the United States to more global issues, reflecting the broader context that we exist in and the various connections across racial, cultural, ethnic, socio-economic, and religious groups in the present day smaller world that we live in. After September 11, 2001, the citizens of the United States realized how much a part we are of the larger world that our protective status from bombing and war inside of our boundaries was no longer a reality.

Working with difference in groups and organizations involves recognizing the existence of various identities and what they represent as a part of the whole, boundaries (historical, psychological, physical) that exist between groups, issues of leadership, authority and authorization that relate to the roles that various group members are given and take up. The ability to embrace the complexity of the coexistence of multiple identities and difference *and* the ways in which they impact the functioning of the group and/or organization is primary in today's world.

In this chapter we discuss a conference design that evolved from our work individually, as a pair and with groups. It began with Mary McRae, the first author's interest in adapting the group relations model to focus on working with difference in a series of conferences at New York University (NYU). She then collaborated with Zachary Green who developed the innovative design we describe. In these conferences our explicit aim was a design that spoke to intergroup relations and representation. The focus was on personal transformation as a route to organizational transformation. In this thinking, differences are embraced rather than used as a source of our continued division. We begin with our personal narratives on difference, then trace the roots of our innovations in the literature, provide some lessons from the series of conferences done prior to the development of the new design, introduce the design, and end with a brief summary.

## *Personal narratives*

Our personal narratives are quite different, though on face we are both African American. As such the meaning and experience of how authority works within, between, and through us could fill this chapter. We used our relative locations to learn from one another and create the "Embracing a World of Difference" conference series at NYU.

### *Mary*

I am a sharecropper's daughter, born in the segregated south, in a house with a pump outside the kitchen door for water and a toilet in a little wooden shack. I am the sixth of seven children born in such a house, with the local midwife there to catch us as we entered the world. We lived in the rural south, a segregated world. My family moved to New York when I was a teenager, holding on to southern traditions, struggling to make a living doing factory and domestic work. Being one of the younger children provided me with more educational opportunities and being a child of the 60's and 70's was very timely. I am now a tenured professor who has made group relations theory and practice the focus of my work. Zachary has been instrumental in helping me to own my disparate parts; he is forever challenging me, while holding me in such a caring way, like nurturing the earth for a blooming flower.

### *Zachary*

My father was a professional athlete who leveraged his sports career into a successful, highly lucrative business and my mother was a teacher. My brothers were a Wharton MBA and a Ph.D./JD respectively and I am a Ph.D. psychologist. I am privileged, in fact, by all measures we were an American success story. For many years I was not comfortable owning this privileged aspect of my life. It is not to say that I did not experience prejudice and oppression in my life. I was once hit with a baseball bat by marauding white youths because of the colour of my skin. I was subjected to racist's jokes designed to make me feel less than less and I witnessed subtle denigration of my young parents who found themselves unexpectedly in the role of integration pioneers.

As may be evident, our narratives illustrate distinct difference between us, which we had to learn to embrace in order for us to forge the collaboration and innovations that followed. We have worked from the premise that we all operate with multiple identities about which we have little consciousness. Beyond social identities such as race, gender and sexual orientation viewed from a group "diversity" perspective where meaning can be obscured by politically correct analysis, we sought to explore the role and boundaries of authority within and between identities. This approach sharply challenged such notions as "the black experience" or "gay and lesbian coalitions" or "whiteness" to invite exploration of differentiation within these groups as well as differences in how authority came to be expressed in role.

### *Roots in group relations literature*

The Group Relations model offers a framework to work experientially to understand and develop innovative ways of working with difference among groups. A. K. Rice described the group relations conference as providing opportunities to learn and to study behaviours as it happens (Rice, 1965). He stated:

> "In short, the basic conference method is to construct situations in which the conventional defense against recognizing or acting on interpretations and intergroup hostilities and rivalries are either removed or at least reduced. This permits examination of the forces at work. The method consists therefore of lowering the barriers to the expression of feeling, both friendly and hostile; providing opportunities for the continuous check on one's own feelings, and for comparing them with those of others, about given situations. Or, to put it another way, it is to check fantasy against reality" (p. 73).

The staff designs a program and helps members to create an institution in which they feel safe enough to experiment, to examine old behaviours that surface in their interactions and to explore new behaviours and ways of interacting. We believe that Rice in his seminal paper, "Learning for Leadership" (1965) provided a basic framework for working with group and intergroup difference. While a few authors have written about diversity in group relations conferences (McRae, Arora, & Short, 2007; Reed & Noumair, 2000; Noumair, Fenichel, & Fleming, 1992), little has been done to further the conference design and method to adapt to what might be described as the new world order. By the new world order, we refer to the shifting power relations between groups who in the past had less or no power and authority.

The fact that the group relations model is geared to the study of authority and leadership in groups and organizations makes the study of social identity difference and the multiple identities held by each individual even more pressing. What is the relationship between who has authority, who takes up leadership roles and the racial, ethnic, and other difference that define reference groups? Miller (1980) warned that every transaction across boundaries of political identity has the potential for disaster. He purported that there is a fantasized boundary between how a person sees "me" and "not me" that may not stand the test of reality. Each time there is an interface between two people from different backgrounds there is a risk of being forced to re-introject the bad bits that have been projected to the other and to surrender the good parts that have been introjected. According to Miller the differences between individuals from various groups are not properties of the system, but are constantly being negotiated. Intergroup relations involve a constant process of patterns of power and coercion on the one hand and bargaining and cooperation on the other.

### *Identity, representation, boundary, and leadership*

According to embedded intergroup relations theory, the group is an entity representing various identity groups (Alderfer, 1991). An individual reflects a uniquely related set of roles representative of an intergroup. Each individual belongs to multiple identity groups including the ones they were born into such as race and gender, as well as to other groups that they choose to belong to such as professional, work and social groups. In embedded group theory "every transaction between two or more people depends upon (1) the unique personalities of the individuals, (2) the messages the individuals receive and internalize from their own group, and (3) the present and historical relationships between the groups that the individuals represent" (Alderfer, 1994, p. 221).

Embedded intergroup relations theory also proposes that one identity group may be more salient than another at certain times. Individuals who represent identity groups meet at the boundary that separates them from other groups. These boundaries can be impermeable or permeable, depending on historical relationships, hidden agendas, stereotypes, belief systems, values, etc. Intolerance of difference, ambiguity, paradox, and multiple realities locks groups in paranoid-schizoid relations and make it difficult to work across boundaries (Skolnick & Green, 2004). From work on race at group relations conferences, Wells (1990) suggests the notion of "black authority" as an oxymoron. His work raised questions about the real financial value placed on race and skin privilege. Connolly & Noumair, (1997) suggests that working across boundaries create a level of risks to a group member's security in his or her own subgroup. Holding and expressing multiple [salient] identities and working within "multiple realities" carries risk and political implications for the exercise of authority (Skolnick & Green, 1998). Berg and Smith (1990) purport that holding the ambiguity of affirming the primacy of the group while at the same time seeking acknowledgement as an individual creates a paradox, a tension that can be threatening both to the individual and the group. They warn of the temptation to focus on one side of the contradiction and lose perspective of a natural and central aspect of group existence.

Representation, leadership, authorization of leadership, holding on to membership in ones' constituent group, while taking up an integral role in the new group of representatives is the work of managing intergroup relations in the new world order that we exist in today. We believe that the group relations model has much to offer in providing a framework to study and explore intergroup relatedness and ways of working more effectively in representative groups.

## *Embracing a world of difference conference design*

The goal of the design was to move beyond "honouring diversity." Our concern at the time was that "diversity" had slipped into becoming a cliché term and increasingly passé approach to working with human difference. Key to this thinking was an emerging recognition that conferences were tending to make certain identities essential. As such, there was a corresponding absence of capacity to recognize or hold the multiplicity of identities present in any person or group. As such "embracing a world of difference" presented the challenge and possibility that staff and members could work consciously and unconsciously on more than what could be easily seen or expressed as identity. In other words for a member to speak of being a "gay, black, male," while an important and necessary first step of exploration, could no longer be seen as providing more than a cursory understanding of the individual, the groups with which the member identifies, or some presumed known process that accompanies this cluster of identities.

## *Conference events*

The way that each of the events in the conference were termed was changed to reflect systemic and conceptual frame of the theme of the conference design. Thus the plenary events reflected more directly the applied learning that took place and that all, members and staff were to attend. The small study group provided a lens in which members could explore the system and understand their role in it. The large study group was a matrix to compare the realities of the individual with those of the larger group; to locate one's self in the context of the whole. The role analysis groups were set up as a time to explore personal narratives, to compare behavioural patterns observed in the temporary institution to those taken up in the outside world. The intergroup and institutional event was a place to explore intergroup relations and representation as they exist in the world, but with the key shift that members were encouraged to take leadership of their own representative forum. The events became known as the "WE ALL SEE MORE NOW" model, with the events paralleling the traditional ones:

**WE** World Event/*Intergroup & Institutional Event*

- An opportunity for members to experience development of their own representative forum that holds nested authority for learning in parallel to staff management.

**ALL** Applied Learning Lectures/*Plenary Events*

- A variant on the traditional conference plenary where music, narratives, meditation, and movement may be introduced to enhance learning and foster reflection.

**SEE** System Exploration Event/*Small Study Group*

- A process where consultants work close to the boundary of the experience of members and invite exploration within and beyond more commonly held ways of seeing authority and one another.

**MORE** Matrix of Realities Event/*Large Study Group*

- A large group experience where the emphasis is on holding concurrent realities in mind while expanding the "here-and-now" to include the full life of the event.

**NOW** Narratives of Ongoing Work/*Role Analysis Group*

- An approach to review and application that helps members to look at their known story anew and use the conference experience to begin the process of transformation.

The emphasis on the study of unconscious processes, authority and leadership remained in this design, but with more attention given to how this study could be shared authentically with the members. Our aim was explicit in seeking to unmask familiar narratives that explained things in terms of gender, race, orientation, and nationality. We were determined to see how these and other such categories actually illuminated one corner of a dynamic but were perhaps being used in a basic assumption way to foreclose the exploration of other elements, leaving them in darkness. We learned from previous conferences that seduction of the illusion was a powerful and highly desired defense against learning. The illusion usually took the form of offering our experienced yet facile understanding of the familiar narratives associated with social identity groups. The seduction was in the implicit suggestion that we actually knew a lot about the individual or group, thus giving us permission to enter these worlds with our definitive interpretations. While this approach served to pre-empt exploration of difference at a deeper level, it was attractive because of the way it helped make sense of a world that is otherwise too dynamic. We have learned that the belief that something could be "known" in identity analysis helped bind anxiety for staff and members alike, leaving the terror of how little we really know about each other far from discovery.

Paradoxically, the purpose of the entire "Embracing" approach was to allow for more potential points of connection to be named, explored and worked. The challenge of such a way of conducting group relations work or any other such exploration is that known narratives that have served people for life become challenged and often altered. Once this has occurred, there is no possibility of returning to the familiar story without denying the shift in consciousness. No other event in the "Embracing" approach made these challenges and opportunities more available than the World Event.

## *The World Event*

The World Event is specifically designed to turn over an element of authority to the members to exercise in parallel to the staff, rather than merely state that the members also have authority. This stance moves conference life from a well-known social hierarchical approach to one in which nested, interdependent authority relations are exercised and placed into practice.

### *Primary task of the World Event (WE)*

Akin to the traditional Institutional Event in group relations conferences, the primary task of the World Event remains to study the relationships between and among groups, including a Conference Management that works in public session. The difference comes in how the World Event invites members to study issues of leadership and representation through the formation of the World Forum. This designated body, composed of ambassadors from each group or constituent community, works as a complementary and/or parallel structure with the Conference Management. While Conference Management retains authority and responsibility for the overall conference boundary, the World Forum once formed assumes primary authority for the World Event.

Conceptually, the World Event sets out to simulate the opportunities and tensions present in the nested authority relationships commonplace in the post-modern world. Parallels may be seen in how individual governments of sovereign nations relate to entities such as a United Nations or European Union. Each nation has its own relationship to the world while having representation in a world or continental body. In both realms, there are efforts to influence the nature of global discourse through laws, resolutions, policies, treaties, and accords. Tensions arise when the direction of world bodies clashes with those of a given nation, especially those with strong economic, military, natural resource and/or political power.

The World Forum is authorized to set policies for the World Event in accordance with the primary task of the conference. They may also offer hypotheses about the nature and meaning of the emerging conference institution. With control over the resource of the plenary room, they also have the authority to convene groups and negotiate use of the space for groups who seek to convene themselves in "neutral" territory. In these ways the members of the groups gradually recognize over time that they have given over a significant degree of authority to the World Forum, The need for linkage to and communication from the individual ambassadors of groups becomes palpable, often resulting in threats of recall. Such issues often challenge the World Forum and its ability to function continuously as a representative body.

Members have the opportunity to form their own groups/communities of similar or mixed social identities such as race, ethnicity, gender, religion, sexual orientation, or other grouping. As a representative leadership forum of members that leads and manages member's work in the World Event, the World Forum puts into place an organizational structure that gives meaning to the experience. When functioning optimally, the leadership of the World Forum promotes a spirit of inquiry into the myths and realities of group and intergroup experience in the World Event. How they communicate with the groups in their process of forming, framing and testing working hypotheses (those of the groups and that of the World Forum) influences the depth of learning and potential for transformation.

The staff works in three different, nested role structures to facilitate the work of members in the World Event. Unlike how such relatedness is often presented in the traditional institutional event, great emphasis is placed on how each staff role in the World Event is an extension of delegation from Conference Management. The structures are:

- A Conference Institution Management Team—made up of the Conference Directorate.
- An Advisor to the World Forum appointed by the Conference Institution Management Team.
- A Consultant Team, appointed by the Conference Institution Management Team.

In this model, the first task of the Consultant Team is to consult to the assigned territories and to consult to the designation of ambassadors for the World Forum.

*Creating the groups/communities*

Members are free to create groups, also called constituent communities in the World Event to place an emphasis on the issues of representation, on themes of their own choosing. While asked to keep in mind the theme of the conference and issues of salient identity, members are not required or restricted to these considerations. This approach allows themes that are "here-and-now" in the consciousness of members to emerge in the World Event. Representation in the World Forum, however, is limited to groups where two or more members gather in a space assigned by Conference Management.

Through the help of the consultants, the groups affirm the group/community's name, focus of work and location. They are encouraged to share this information with the Conference Management Team, other World Event groups/communities, and the World Forum. This more directive approach to the beginning of the event is to promote greater boundary permeability and launch a more robust exploration of mutual and nested relatedness in the emerging system. As such ambassadors are able to enter the World Forum with an idea of the core of what they are representing. Similarly, the World Forum is better equipped to begin its work of managing the event and developing hypotheses with a sense of what the overall system is saying at this genesis.

Structurally, the World Forum consists of: a maximum number of ambassadors, not to exceed the number of assigned authorized spaces for the World Event. Among the first tasks of the World Forum is to designate a chair. The Chair of World Forum, unless otherwise designated becomes the primary voice of the group and, through work with the World Forum Advisor, establishes a direct link to the Conference Director to begin the work of negotiating the nature of the relatedness between the World Forum and Conference Management.

Like the Conference Management, the work of the World Forum is conducted in public. The term of each ambassador is for the duration of the World Event, though subject to the policies of their respective communities. While the term of an ambassador may be limited or terminated by one of the constituent community, and such ambassador no longer represents their group, they retain the title of ambassador. Ideally the World Forum also operates continuously for the scheduled sessions of the World Event to provide constituent communities optimal opportunities for interaction.

### *Nested authority and the staff*

The World Event relies on clarity of communication at all levels of the event. Accordingly, in the three parallel systems of the staff that function concurrently, periodic meetings of the Advisor to the World Forum, Convener of the Consultants, and/or a representative from the Management team are essential. While important to note the potential for competition and more destructive rivalry between the systems, in terms of the primary task, the staff system operates with its own nested authority structure within the World Event. The quality of the study of intergroup relations and the capacity of the World Forum to take up its own authority for the event is strongly influenced by the clarity with which the staff is able to work and communicate with nested authority.

### *Implications*

The study of difference has created the conditions for important innovations to the group relations model. While continuing the

Original design Zachary Green/Mary McRae at NYU and Bruce Irvine, Grubb Institute

tradition of attending to unconscious processes, basic assumptions, leadership, and authority central to conference life, we are learning how the focus on difference reveals a nested layer of experience that also requires exploration. It is becoming our experience that authority and identity are integrally linked. Through the lens of difference we see the tenacity with which familiar patterns, at the interpersonal and the systemic levels, are used to limit learning and continue rote and routine enactments of known narratives.

By putting into practice our espoused theory that the members also have authority through efforts like the World Event, we expand the range and deepen the connection of group relations work to the lived experience of people in their day-to-day life. As we learn that race, gender, orientation, class, and nationality are only a layer of what makes us human, we enter a realm of freedom to explore authority with more authenticity and the possibility for personal and organization transformation. Fundamental to this kind of practice will be the continued courage of consultants in group relations life to move beyond traditional psychoanalytically based interpretation and facile identity analysis discourse to see more dimensions to dynamics we purport to reveal. The continued relevance of our work may hinge on how well we deal with embracing difference within the world of group relations so that we may begin individually, collectively and systemically to see the world that is emerging before us anew.

## *References*

Alderfer, C.P. (1991). Embedded intergroup relations and racial identity development theory. In: C.E. Thompson & R.T. Carter (Eds.). *Racial Identity Theory: Applications to Individual, Group, and Organizational Interventions* (pp. 237–263). Malwah, NJ: Lawrence Erlbaum Associates.

Alderfer, C.P. (1994). A white man's perspective of the unconscious processes within black-white relations in the united states. In: E.J. Trickett, R.J. Watts, & D. Birman (Eds.). Human diversity: Perspectives on people in context (pp. 201–229). San Francisco: Jossey Bass.

Berg, D. & Smith, K. (1990). Paradox and groups. In: J. Gillette, & M. McCollom (Eds.). Groups in context. A new perspective on group dynamics (pp. 106–132). New York: University Press of America, Inc.

Bion, W.R. (1961). *Experiences in groups.* London: Tavistock.

Connolly, M.L. & Noumair, D.A. (1997). The white girl in me, the colored girl in you, and the lesbian in us: crossing boundaries. In: M. Fine, L. Weis, L.C. Powell, & L.M. Wong (Eds.). *Off White: Readings on race, power, and society* (pp. 322–332). NY: Routledge.

McRae, Patel & Hsu, (Unpublished Manuscript). There is Power in Numbers.

McRae, M.B., Kwong, A. & Short, E.L. (2007). Racial dialogue among women: A group relations theory analysis. *Organizational & social dynamics, 7*(2) 211–234.

Miller, E.J. (1979). Open systems revisited: A proposition about development and change. In: W.G. Lawrence, (Ed.). *Exploring Individual and Organizational Boundaries: A Tavistock Open Systems Approach,* London: Wiley.

Noumair, D.A., Fenichel, A. & Fleming, J.L. (1992). Clarence Thomas, Anita Hill, and us: A group relations perspective. *Journal of Applied Behavioral Science, 28,* 377–387.

Reed, G.M. & Noumair, D.A. (2000). The tiller of authority in a sea of diversity: Empowerment, disempowerment, and the politics of identity. In: E.B. Klien, F. Gabelnick, & P. Herr (Eds.). *Dynamic Consultation in a Changing Workplace,* (pp. 51–81). Madison, CT: Psychological Press.

Rice, A.K. (1965). *Learning For Leadership.* London: Tavistock.

Rice, A.K. (1969). Individual, group and intergroup processes. *Human Relations,* 22(6), 565–584.

Skolnick, M.R., & Green, Z. (2004). The denigrated other: Diversity and group relations. In: S. Cytrynbaum & D.A. Noumair (Eds.). *Group dynamics, organizational irrationality, and social complexity: Group relations reader 3* (pp. 117–130). Jupiter, FL: A. K. Rice Institute.

Turquet, P.M. (1985). Leadership: The individual and the group. In: A.D. Colman & M.H. Geller (Eds.). *Group Relations Reader 2,* Washington, DC: A.K. Rice Institute, pp. 71–89.

Turquet, P.M. (1975). Threats to Identity in the Large Group. *In Large Group Dynamics and Therapy,* L. Kreeger (Ed.). London: Constable.

Wells, L. (1990). The group as a whole: A systematic socioanalytic perspective on interpersonal and group relations. In: J. Gillette & M. McCollom (Eds.). *Groups in Context: A New Perspective on Group Dynamics.* New York: Addison-Wesley.

# SECTION III

## ADAPTATION AND INNOVATION IN ROLE TAKING AND APPLICATION

The four chapters in this section consist of hands-on, pragmatic illustrations of the ongoing relevance and applicability of the Group Relations Conference model.

In the first of these four, Charla Hayden takes a close look at the AKRI's training programme for group relations consultants. Hayden brings together a range of theoretical positions, including those of Rice, Bion, Schon and Wheelis, to stress the quality of 'wonder', which she sees as key to the capacity to consult ethically in a GR context.

The second chapter, by Willem de Jager and Mannie Sher, provides a fascinating account of a Group Relations intervention in the Banking context. The writers account the Group Relations workshop for the bank's internal HR consultants, which they designed and delivered as part of a broader organizational change programme with the bank. It is not often that money and psychoanalysis are discussed side by side, but this chapter evaluates the workshop from both a psychoanalytic insight into the leadership development and the financial contribution to the change process perspectives.

The third chapter, by Yoram Lahav, is a poignant attempt to extend the tools and theory of GR to examine the dynamics of belonging and identity in and between groups. Lahav does this by reflecting in-depth on the first international conference on Jewish Identity, which took place in Israel and which he directed.

The fourth chapter in this section, by Rosemary Viswanath, is a touching account of a group relations conference for the Dalits in India, who are ranked as 'untouchables' at the bottom of India's caste system. Viswanath movingly explores the application of group relations insights to the empowerment of Dalits, including tough questioning of attitude to authority within the context of deeply embedded cultural values that haven't been abolished despite changes to the country's constitution in 1955.

Taken together, these chapters offer a unique contribution to the relevance and applicability of Group Relations Conferences to the exploration and understanding of social, personal or professional identities as reflected in a people's history, culture, professional sector or geographical location.

CHAPTER SEVEN

# Learning to consult with wonder: One approach to preparing group relations consultants

*Charla Hayden*

## *Part I: Discovering the power of the role*

On November 11, 1972, I first attended a 3-day group relations conference in Berkeley, California, at a freestanding graduate institute for social-clinical psychologists. By the third session of the Small Study Group I had become so infuriated with the behaviour of the Small Study Group Consultant that I decided to get up and leave the room, and persuaded four other people to leave with me. We sat in the library of the institute for two hours, celebrating our superior intelligence and our courage in escaping the tyranny of this misguided, ill-prepared consultant. I remember we considered reporting her to the conference director as an incompetent in the midst of the otherwise accomplished staff!

When our congratulatory revels waned, however, we began to wonder what we might be missing. As we contemplated returning to the Study Group room, we speculated that the consultant might be angry with us for our rebellion. There was a copy of Freud's ***Ego and Group Psychology*** on the library shelf, and we decided that I, as the ringleader of the rebellion, should be the one to express the group's contrition and give the consultant this book as a peacemaking token. After this had been agreed, we climbed the stairs and entered our group's room. In stunning contrast to what we had expected, our chairs had been shoved out of the circle—by other participants! It was they who refused to allow us to re-enter, not our consultant! She did persist, however, in making oblique comments on what was happening during the period of our grovelling and humiliation. After we had negotiated our way back in as group participants, and I had the opportunity to kneel in front of her to offer our token of contrition, she said nothing, and made no gesture to receive it. I placed it on her lap.

It was my first experience in a sequence of many over the years, which have highlighted the positional power in the roles people take as group relations conference consultants. In my viscera, I can still recall how heavy I felt when I pushed up out of my chair to leave that room, and similarly, how profound an act it was for me to kneel in an offering to a stranger in a role I didn't understand but whom I deeply needed to allow me back into the circle.

Let me offer another example from personal experience that illustrated the power of the consulting role for me during the years when I was just discovering the nature of what we can learn from it—whether we are enacting the role ourselves or receiving consultation from another person. Not long after I had attended a sequence of several residential and non-residential conferences as a participant, I was invited to join the staff of a 5-day residential conference as a Small Study Group consultant. Although I thought myself ready to consult, I was to be given another lesson in humility. Once I found myself in the first Small Study Group session, during which one chair for a participant was left empty the entire time, I realized how little I knew about finding the role and finding myself in it. I panicked—I was quiet, I was loquacious, I was dazzling, I stuttered—all in the course of an hour and a half! I developed an erotic interest in one of the members there, which I had no idea how to work with. When the ending time for the session came, I could barely keep from running to the door. As I twisted the doorknob, it was simultaneously being turned from the other side. As the door opened and I briefly considered whether the director had somehow found me out and come to deliver my dismissal slip, I saw ***myself*** on the other side of the doorway! A young woman of my same colouring, size and age stood there, just as amazed as I was with the encounter. She turned out to be the absent participant who had been late and confused about when and how to find her way to the Study Group. Seeing my image in the doorway—unprepared, shocked, and inept—was the jolt I needed to locate a legitimate "place" I could work from. Although I can hardly claim the consultation my Small Study Group received during the rest of our sessions was noteworthy, I did manage to claim novice status inside myself and with the group members, and to hold the consulting role with openness to see what I could contribute to their learning—and mine.

With those two stories about how I discovered the role of group relations consultant from the outside and from the inside, I want to launch into the focus of this chapter: ***Learning to Consult with Wonder: One Approach to Preparing Group Relations Consultants.*** In particular, I plan to emphasize two very important aspects of the role of group relations consultant, and describe the training and certification process the A.K. Rice Institute has implemented to prepare people who want to do this kind of conference consultation.

The experiences I've described mark the beginning of my journey of *wonder* in group relations conference work. *Wonder* has multiple meanings: when a *noun* it describes something that causes astonishment or a feeling of surprise from perceiving something unexpected. As a *verb* it means to feel wonder, sometimes mixed with doubt, or to have curiosity or doubt about something (as defined in the O.E.D, 1971, p. 3810). I hope that as we move together through these thoughts you will be considering how your own history with group relations work, including the beginnings, has been held in you over time, and whether the strange, awesome and painful *wonder* of this work is still alive in you.

## *Part II: How do we understand the essence of the consulting role?*

From my perspective, Kenneth Rice said it best:

> *The skill of the consultant lies in his capacity to analyze—on a barely conscious intellectual framework—his feelings, and to express them in*

> *ways that will help the members of the group to understand their own feelings as they are experiencing them. But this does not mean that either the feelings, or the understanding of them, are necessarily conscious. Much of the communication and hence much of the learning take place at the unconscious and experiential level ... . Hence the consultant's behaviour is as important for learning as what he says; perhaps more so, since the words he uses to describe his feelings are symbols, of greater or less abstraction, of the behavior they represent (1975, p. 74).*

A few paragraphs earlier in Rice's description of *The Basic Staff Role* in ***Learning for Leadership***, he describes the challenges the consultant faces in being present and effective in his role in the "here and now" of group life:

> *[a consultant] uses his own feelings to sense what is happening. He cannot observe with a detached objectivity that relieves him of the responsibility of taking account of what he is feeling himself. If he finds himself becoming embarrassed, anxious, angry, hurt, or pleased, he can ask himself why he is feeling what he is feeling, and can attempt to sort out what comes from within himself and what is being projected onto him by conference members. So far as he is* ***sure*** *that some of the feeling is being projected onto him and not the result of some idiosyncrasy of his own personality, he can use himself as a measuring instrument—however rough and ready—to give him information about the meaning of behavior, both consciously and unconsciously motivated. If he can then find an explanation of the projection in terms of the specific task set for that event, he can make an 'interpretation' about the behavior of those present, including himself (ibid, p. 73).*

The capacities necessary to contain, examine and interpret one's personal anxiety as one goes about working in the consulting role are described later in the segment of ***Learning for Leadership*** in which Rice treats *Learning about the Anxiety of Making Decisions. Since one cannot learn about anxiety without becoming anxious, members of staff who are not anxious at some points in a conference are unlikely to be in close enough touch with what is happening in it to fill their own roles appropriately. What is important is that staff demonstrate that they can contain and understand their own anxieties and use them to further conference experience for the members; that is, that they can learn themselves*

> *from their own anxiety and through this provide opportunities for others to learn as well (ibid, p. 89).*
>
> *Furthermore, the staff must be able to cope with the kinds of situations they help to create. Even though they provide only opportunities for learning, and members must take their own responsibility for how much they learn, the provision of the opportunity itself implies that it is safe for members to take it (ibid, p. 89).*

The role we set for ourselves when we consult then, if we're working from the frameworks established by Rice and by Bion, is made possible by a set of complex boundaries which require mindful self-scrutiny and a capacity to confront unsettling emotions at the very time we are working to offer expressions of our feelings in ways that are useful to members' learning, and do all of this *without memory or desire a la* Bion! (Bion in Symington, 1996)

### *Wondering about oneself as requisite*

The part of wondering in which we take dives into our own inner worlds is one of the most significant aspects of practice in group relations consultation. For further exploration, I would like to take us to the work of Donald A. Schon on ***The Reflective Practitioner*** (1983) and ***Educating the Reflective Practitioner*** (1987) because I believe Schon's thinking helps illuminate the dilemmas we face, and leads us toward understanding the approach the A.K. Rice Institute has taken to preparing its conference consultants based on a competency-based model for learning.

### *Schon's ideas on reflective practice*

Let's first be clear that the professional roles Schon, and his close colleague, Chris Argyris, are aiming to prepare professionals for are action-oriented. These are not roles in which a practitioner is merely offering the learner an opportunity to learn and later decide whether to act on that learning or not, which is what they term *applicable* learning. Rather, the roles they refer to are designed to provide *actionable* learning based on the assumption that if the learner or consultee does not act, something is either awry in the nature of professional consultation s/he has received, or the learner has proven unwilling to assume responsibility for taking action. (It would be an interesting discussion, but a different one, for us explore which type of learning, *applicable* or *actionable*, each of us believes we're providing in group relations conferences.)

The first book Argyris and Schon published on this subject was ***Theory in Practice: Increasing Professional Effectiveness*** (1974). In it they hypothesized, based on their first 20 years of research, that most professionals apply what Argyris and Schon call "Model I" or "Single Loop Learning" in which a *theory-of-practice-in-use* is assumed by both consultant and consultee to be valid and unquestionable. This underlying assumption leads consultants to react defensively when their *theory-of-practice-in-use* is questioned for its accuracy and utility. Argyris and Schon also posited "Model II" or "Double Loop Learning" in which a dialectic about the methods being applied takes place *within* the practitioner, and a dialectic *between* the consultant and the consultee also occurs. Model II provides for the continual examination of assumptions, methods, and effectiveness. Schon believes much of the process of professional training—which has traditionally been based on a "normative professional curriculum"—has perpetuated Single Loop, or Model I, Learning. In contrast to typical professional training, Schon's proposal is that what we "identify as practice knowledge consists in largely tacit knowing-in-action and in the ***capacity of practitioners to respond to surprise in the midst of action through a process of on-the-spot reflection and experimentation***" which Schon calls "reflection-in-action". (1974, p. xix) (For a more thorough discussion see Schon's Educating the Reflective Practitioner, 1987, pp. 26–31.)

As I see it, Schon's ideas about how to prepare "professionals" for their practices is much akin to Bion's early formulations about his role when he worked with groups in a military psychiatric hospital and to Rice's descriptions of effective practices for group relations consultants, reviewed above.

### *So, what does all this have to do with wonder, and with double loop learning?*

Dr. Wesley Carr used to like to use the word 'provisional' with regard to the approach we use when we consult in group relations conferences. I take that way of looking at it as extremely useful, especially the more often I read Bion's and Rice's descriptions of what they were striving to do.

Schon's formulation is that double loop or Model II work happens in the moment of surprise, which requires reflection-in-action and experimentation from us rather than an application of what "we already know". The capacity to treat our own methods as always provisional, always questionable, always within our capacity to reflect on in the moment, and to invent *beyond* those methods—is a major aspect of what I mean by *wonder.*

## *Wonder which can lead to terror*

I would like to turn now to another aspect of *wonder* in group relations work—one which I find terrifying when I allow myself the full experience of it. Some time ago a friend gave me a copy of American psychoanalyst Allen Wheelis' new book, ***The Way We Are***. Wheelis' book is an impressionistic journey through the conclusions he has reached about the nature of the human species, based on his decades of work as an analyst. He exhorts us to face the reality of *what* we are squarely—a species mired in illusions of our own making. These "fleshy" aspects of social construction, as he calls them, function to hide us from ourselves, and our unconscious construction of reality makes our real nature, as well as the fact of our inevitable deaths, more bearable to us. Wheelis talks about the difference between the *way things are* and the *scheme of things*. The *scheme of things* redeems *the way things are*, by giving us an infrastructure of meaning—often through religion or forms of philosophy—that rescue us from seeing the underlying truth of *who* we are and what our lives are, both individually and in the collective. When we do group relations work, I think we are attempting to see the way things are. We are looking at ourselves from an unexpected angle and at an unusual depth. I don't think we are about improvement of the species—we leave that for the examination of those who come to conferences, and for ourselves, beyond the boundaries of conference work. As Mark Twain and countless other wits, often our European friends, have observed, we Americans seem to have unending zeal for perfecting individuals and society. As an American born and bred, I find it a constant challenge not to want members who attend conferences to conclude they must act on what they "see" in conference life. But I do not understand that to be our conferences' purpose. I believe, to use Wheelis' framework again, conferences are about seeing beyond the scheme of things, which includes even our own investigatory methods.

I'm not sure that everyone who does group relations conference consultation, or who attends group relations conferences, would go as far as Wheelis does in describing the unnerving reality underneath the social constructions and various cultural norms that guide our taken-for-granted behaviour in groups and organizations. However, I believe what we have in common with Wheelis is the motivation to take an unrelenting look at the shadow side of what happens in the connection between individuals and the groups of which we're members. What various ones of us conclude from engaging in the endeavour to *see* more fully under the cover of social assumptions and conventions is another subject. But I believe that we, like Wheelis, are seeking to see fully, without illusion, what work and life in human groups is—in particular how we deal with the dynamics of power and authority. This is another form of *wonder*—and perhaps another play on the meaning of the word, as in, *I wonder what this group is really doing while discussing how glorious the food served in the conference dining room is in front of the conference director in the Large Study Group?*

Let me offer an example of some moments of terror in a Large Study Group and how it was managed by the group, though not resolved. The conference took place on a weekend in Autumn, 2005, at Columbia University Teachers' College in New York City. There were 91 members, mostly drawn from undergraduate and graduate programs at Teachers' College, including a contingent of approximately 20 men and women graduate students from West Point Academy's Officer Training Program. (This is the U.S. Army's premier program for preparing its officers.) There were three of us consulting to the Large Study Group in a room which could hardly provide seating space for 94 people. There were two doors to the room from the hallway outside, one on either end, but barely any space through which anyone not sitting very near a door could make his/her way without colliding with several other people. We were on the fourth floor, so egress through the windows was out. In the last session of the Large Study Group, a debate between one of the older West Point graduate students and a young, gay, Puerto Rican student broke out. The subject of the debate was about whether any meaning at all was being derived from the conference, especially from the Large Study Group. Someone called for a stand-up vote of the members on this question. The pressure in the room to choose sides increased—it seemed a passionate division was about to be acted out. After a group of less than half the members stood up to vote yes on the question of whether there was meaning in the Large Group exercise, two of the other West Point officers stood up and gradually calmed the group by making overtures across the fight boundary. The potential eruption of violence across several aspects of identity, as well as political perspective, was managed by the group in this way. A major fracture in the Large Group, with its palpable potential for physical violence, had been avoided. After a long silence just before the session ended, a male voice rose from one corner of the room: "What if this is all there is?" A pause, and another male voice from the other corner responded, "Then we're fucked." That is how the Large Study Group ended—a group which I had found frightening since the first session. This episode's richness as an enactment of the conflict over whether the war in Iraq has meaning or not was not even accessible to me to consider until later—the visceral experience itself was too powerful.

When we try to chart the surprising and painful terrain of the unconscious life of groups, reflecting on *how* we are feeling and *how we are thinking* about our feeling is essential. Otherwise, how can we know *which* need we serve: revelation or diversion? We must cultivate a tenacious commitment to self-reflection. And then we must have the courage to see beyond the gates we open, in either direction.

## Part III: The A.K. Rice institute's program for preparing group relations conference consultants

At the A.K. Rice Institute's national scientific meeting in 1991, Wesley Carr and I presented a paper called, *"Responsibility, Accountability and Ethics in Organizations: the Evaluation of Group Relations Conference Consultants"* , which grew out of our experiences as the staff for the Training Group at the 1990 national conference at Vassar. This initial attempt at explicating the requisite capacities for people who do group relations conference consulting, of which there were eight competencies at the time, was greeted uneasily. Many of those who attended the session were attracted to the ideas; others ridiculed the ideas and us. In fact, at the plenary session which closed the conference, five colleagues who were/are influential members of the Institute went on stage and recited a ditty they had composed which ended with the refrain, "But don't tell Charla and Wesley Carr!". This induced much merriment all around. We experienced it as both playful and derisive, directed at our temerity in putting forward a framework for examining the quality of conference consultation work. But it also seemed an expression of fear on behalf of the Institute's membership. I have felt this fear myself, ever since June of 1990 when Wesley and I took on the obligation to explain to the two people involved why we were holding them back from matriculating to practice consultation in the larger conference. To make an explicit, criteria-based assessment of another's work in conference consultation seemed to rock the ground underneath us.

This began a long, thoughtful journey of exploration, joined by many others along the way, which culminated in the A.K. Rice Institute implementing a required training and certification program for those aspiring to do group relations conference consulting. The program opened for enrolment in October, 2002. Let me describe some of the work and the dynamics which have characterized this journey—I believe it has been replete with overt and covert tensions between what Argyris and Schon would call Model 1, or a Single-Loop Learning approach, and a Model II, or Double-Loop Learning approach. The most amazing, and I think salutary, aspect of this tension is that it has been held by everyone involved during these years—just as much in those who, like myself, have mainly carried the effort forward as in those who have acted to quash it. In other words, this has been a culture-shaking innovation that has challenged thoughtful people from all perspectives.

After the Hayden/Carr paper was presented in 1991, the movement toward establishing a training process made slim progress for a few years. In 1995, after a series of business meetings and retreats, the AKRI Board decided to establish a formal effort to pioneer a training and certification process under the capable leadership of Dr. Debra Noumair from New York. It was to take six years and two sets of committee members to bring these ideas to fruition.

Throughout the process, the Board offered us support, funding, and ample feedback.

### *What were the challenges to implementation?*

The Board had set a major task for us; namely, to bring them a design and implementation plan for a formal, required process to train and certify anyone who wanted to consult at an AKRI-sponsored group relations conference.

On the surface, the expressed resistance to the idea of having specific requirements to qualify to consult in conferences came largely from the eight Centers affiliated with the A.K. Rice Institute which were located around the continental United States. Since the time the A.K. Rice Institute was actually chartered in 1975, and even before, every Center was free to create, or not, its own criteria to qualify those who wished to consult in the conferences that Center sponsored. The Institute's establishment of a set of *right to work* criteria in 1996 elicited great controversy. Consistent implementation of the "right to work" criteria took at least two years to take hold. The Administrator for the Institute at that time, Anne-Marie Kirkpatrick, reported that the amount of energy required of her to pursue this issue with the Centers and those who were directing conferences, was enormous. And the AKRI Board member who was charged with implementing a related initiative to "grandparent" those who had been consulting at conferences and did not wish to comply with the *right-to-work* criteria, described his assignment later as tantamount to a kind of organizational *hara-kiri*.

In 1999, those of us serving on the second Training and Certification Committee decided that we needed to take our ideas about competencies and a mentored training process "on the road": we visited all the affiliated Centers to explain why we had come to believe that having an explicit training process to prepare group relations conference consultants within AKRI was a logical development to assure quality and integrity in conference work. We also made a presentation of the design at the national scientific meeting in New York in 2000. We were greeted with challenges having to do mostly with the Centers' historic resentment of the national organization, and the continuing theme of the loss of autonomy of Centers. Many seemed to appreciate the criteria, or competencies, as we had begun calling them, which we felt characterized the capabilities of effective consultants. But the idea of having an obligatory training process required by the national organization was repugnant to others.

Late in the summer of 2001 the Board of AKRI voted to implement the training and certification process effective October 1, 2002. Those who did not want to use the new training process were given time to qualify under the existing "right-to-work" criteria. Since October, 2002, 45 people have enrolled in the program, 7 have been certified, 29 are actively pursuing certification, 2 are awaiting a mentor, and 7 have dropped out. We have 22 experienced consultants acting as mentors.

## *Core competencies in the A.K. Rice training and certification program*

I'd like to turn now to the approach to competency assessment and development used in the A.K. Rice Institute's training program. Below you will see the current competencies, organized in 3 stages for the training process, which are the focus for learning of those who have enrolled in the Institute's training program. Please consider for yourselves whether these competencies provide a framework for self-scrutiny and for confrontation with what is under the surface of group life. When I look at them now, six years since I've "put my hands on" them for rework, I feel they move us in those directions, but they also pull for some social reconstruction of what is likely to be a more real experience in group relations conference work. They may require further revision.

## *Group relations consultant competencies*

### *Pre-requisite competencies for candidacy in the training program*

- The ability to be reflective and self-examining.
- An understanding that the task of the consultant is to further the study of authority relations.
- The embodiment of genuine curiosity about what is happening in the group as a whole.
- An acceptance that the experience of others is as valid as one's own.

- The capacity to be vulnerable in the service of one's own learning and the learning of the group.
- The capacity to work collaboratively with the experiences of others in understanding the group or conference as a whole.

*Stage 1 Competencies for certification as a consultant candidate*

- The capacity to maintain task and role boundaries in the face of positive or negative responses from others.
- An understanding that taking up authority may include tolerating loneliness, derision, or being misunderstood.
- The ability to reflect on and express one's internal experience rather than acting on it.
- A respectful and curious stance toward others' learning and experience.
- The courage to speak what is felt to be unspeakable in the particular work context as long as it relates to the task of the group at hand.
- The ability to recognize that individuals "carry" or express some aspect of the experience of the group as a whole, e.g. scapegoating and rescuing.
- An appreciation of the range and complexity of unconscious activity.
- The capacity to adapt role behaviour to suit the task of the group.
- An understanding that the exercise of leadership and representation affects, and is affected by, group and intergroup dynamics.
- An understanding of how organizational dynamics reflects the larger socio-political context.
- The ability to shift one's attention to consider intrapsychic, interpersonal, group, and intergroup perspectives in order to understand what is happening in the group as a whole.
- An understanding of how elements of one's own identity and history affect one's work as well as calling forth particular fantasies and projections from others in the context of groups.

- An understanding of how one's own experience in role relates to the working environment as a whole.

*Stage 2 Competencies for certification as an AKRI group relations consultant*

- The ability to formulate group-level unconscious processes as they are occurring using words, images, analogies, and metaphors.
- The capacity for self-containment and the ability to "hold still" emotionally long enough to identify and feel along the boundary between what resides in the group and the environment and what resides in one's self.
- The ability to be reflective and self-examining in role and to own mistakes in front of members and other staff.
- The ability to regain the consultant role after it has been lost.
- The capacity to work on the task of providing learning opportunities about authority relations rather than meeting personal needs.
- The ability to make group-level interpretations and to intervene managerially, if necessary, based on the understanding that individuals "carry" or express some aspect of the experience of the group as a whole.
- The ability to work effectively within a task team as well as across a boundary with other task teams.
- The ability to report on events in a manner that supports colleagues' work.
- The capacity to follow those in leadership roles and to express differences in a manner that supports the work.
- A commitment to examine conference methods as the technology and theory evolve.
- The ability to examine how the dynamics of the staff group affect the conference as a whole and how member group and staff group experiences influence each other.
- A recognition of the interrelatedness of subgroups in the organization as a whole.
- The ability to understand how conference dynamics reflect the larger socio-political context.
- The capacity to examine and speak to the dynamics of the system as a whole.

- An ability to facilitate members' application of conference learning to their experiences in other contexts.

The three stages here refer first to the pre-enrolment stage in which 6 competencies are required to be assessed by the applicant and two people who know him/her before s/he can start the program. The second stage refers to 13 competencies which constitute the focus for work between the trainee and his/her mentor prior to qualifying to serve as a consultant candidate in actual conference work. And the third stage, which has 15 competencies as its focus, is related to the practices the trainee is working on during actual conference consulting work. In each of these stages the mentor is required to participate in assessing the trainee's readiness to move forward in the process, joined with the trainee's own assessment. During the last stage of training, the directors of the conferences in which the trainee works also submit assessments of competencies attained by the trainee to the mentor. The Training and Certification Committee, through its boundary work, manages the process and provides approval at each stage, including certification, through the review of documentation submitted to illustrate the trainee's progress and dialogue when there is uncertainty about progress. A nominal fee is required at each step of the process. This funds the administrative work involved and provides a small honorarium for the mentor when the trainee achieves certification.

The AKRI competencies support Double-Loop Learning in the main. And they provide for consultation that functions to assist in seeing into the heart of what is happening in a group. I think both Schon and Wheelis might approve of these competencies, though they do, of course, constitute a kind of professional orthodoxy in their own right and as such do require being taken "provisionally" all the time themselves.

The words we've used to describe the competencies always strike me as clumsy and inept—very much related to Rice's reference to how the words cannot speak for the actual experience. They are only an approximation of what is meant. It has been very challenging over the years to capture in thought and language just what the skills "inventory" of effective group relations conference consultants is. I hope that you will review the competencies with *wonder* yourselves to see whether these articulate something important about doing consultation in our conferences or not, and whether you think this approach has value.

## Conclusion

There are times when I regard what we do at group relations conferences with a different kind of *wonder*, as in, *What segment of our species would actually choose to sit around in circles for days on end talking about what is happening inside us as individuals and among us in groups, suffering much at times, catching glimpses of elusive other layers of our connectedness to each other, and often going away puzzled and full of dismay?!* And, sometimes, but perhaps less often, catching a glimpse of the loving and noble aspects of human groups. Of course, there is the joy of having those glimpses, and there is the sense of having joined with others at least temporarily in some perceptual field that deepens a sense of what is more real than everyday experience allows. I always have the wonder though about whether it's worth it and whether I am personally useful to the endeavour. I'm glad that I wonder. For me that is the heart of learning to consult with wonder—to always question what we are doing in conferences—and whether it is more valuable to *see than not to see* what members of human groups do together—and how we are doing it. Are we open to the surprise of what emerges in the group and can we move toward wondering what it means in the particular context rather than consulting from our prior assumptions?

The competency learning sequence developed by the A.K. Rice Institute is arguably not *the* answer to deepening consulting effectiveness. After all, there are so many variables at work. However, from my viewpoint we have an obligation to practice as well as we can understand how to. Committing to consult from a position of continuing wonder, and having a framework to apply to reflecting on my own work is useful for me. What about you?

## References

Bion, W. in The Clinical Thinking of Wilfred Bion, Symington, N & Symington J. London: Routledge.

Hayden, C. & Wesley Carr, A. (1993). Responsibility, Accountability and Ethics in Organizations, in Transformations in Global and Organizational Systems: Changing Boundaries in the 90's, A.K. Rice Institute.

O.E.D., (1971). Compact Edition, Oxford University Press, p. 3810.

Rice, A.K. (1975). In Selections from Learning for Leadership by A.K. Rice, *Group Relations Reader 1*, ed. Colman and Bexton, A.K. Rice Institute.

Schon, Argyris, Chris, and Donald, A. (1974). Theory in Practice: Increasing Professional Effectiveness, Jossey-Bass Publishers, San Francisco:. CA.

CHAPTER EIGHT

# Knowing the price of everything and the value of nothing: The application of group relations to organizational development and change with a financial institution

*Willem de Jager and Mannie Sher*

## *Introduction*

In order to understand the structure, functioning and dynamics of an organisation, its 'products' need to be understood. The 'products' of financial institutions are money, i.e. it borrows money to lend money to make money, to lend more money to make more money in ever widening circles. From the perspective of a financial institution the psychological meaning of making money from money is rarely understood, except in the bald expression of status symbols that come with rank such as shares, profit sharing, etc. Money is therefore a convenient way to facilitate exchange and acknowledge debt.

Money is also associated with the twin aspects of guilt and wealth. One side of money is called 'heads' and it usually has on it a head, the part of us that enjoys pleasures such as eating, smelling, hearing and looking. It represents wealth, the good side of money. The other side is 'tails' and it has on it symbols of death, guilt and destruction, tombs of dead people and birds of prey. These images represent guilt, the bad side of money. Whenever money is passed along, both heads and tails are circulated, good and bad, food and poison, life and death (Bornemann, 1976; deMause, 1988).

Ever since Freud pointed out the anal origins of money and its link to experiences in early childhood in the anal phase of psychosexual development (Freud, 1905), money unconsciously reflects ambivalent attitudes toward body products, the rich are "so rich they stink", and debtors are "up to their necks in shit." In early civilizations the Aztecs called gold "the shit of gods," while the Babylonians called it "the shit of hell." The valued and devalued have always been acknowledged to be combined in money (Bornemann, 1976; deMause, 1988).

Financial institutions that produce money have to deal with the anal aspects of money. These are split off and become the "shadow side" or feared role of the organisation that spoils the fun by calling in overdrafts, raising interest, forcing bankruptcy and making people feel guilty about their needs. Bad feelings from wanting and greed can be projected (Klein, 1952) into financial institutions that become "containers of poison" (deMause, 1988). Rage, guilt, despair and need for love, which are too dangerous to experience consciously, are projected into money and institutions of money. When too much pleasure stirs up the punitive superego, feelings of polluted sinfulness are directed at leaders of financial institutions who can reduce pleasure through the destruction of goods. Modern societies accomplish this through recessions and wars (Greider, 1988).

As organisations use leaders unconsciously for their purposes, so societies unconsciously use organisations for their purposes. Leaders in financial institutions are therefore the modern sacrificial priests who handle poison money and destroy goods when prosperity becomes threatening and guilt becomes great. Instead of investing in productive enterprises, speculation in inflated stock markets happens, poison money is send to Third World elites who waste it and tax codes are changed to favour the rich since they only can 'digest' its pollution. Money supplies are multiplied as more and more 'containers of poison' are required to contain growing guilt. This is where bankers are called upon to take their most serious roles, "to take away the punch bowl when the party gets going" (Greider, 1987). Financial institutions have a haunting fear that someone somewhere may be happy.

## *The organisational transformational change context*

Group relations consultation from a systems psychodynamic paradigm (Miller, 1989; Neumann, Kellner & Dawson-Shepherd, 1997; Obholzer & Roberts, 1994; Stapley, 1996) was applied to a transformation and change programme in a national financial institution. The organisation was South Africa's largest financial institution which had to transform and change in relation to two major influencing forces, firstly, high performance drivers towards globalisation, (Magretta, 1999; Moon & Bonny, 2001) requiring vigorous performance management (Welch, 2001), talent management and reward, information technology (Magretta, 1999; Moon & Bonny, 2001) and democratisation of the workplace (Ackoff, 1981; 1994; Gibson, 1998); and secondly, South Africa's legislative transformational change (Employment Equity Act, No. 55, 1998) to redistribute power consequent upon changes in the country's social, economic and political landscapes.

Global competitiveness compelled the organisation to re-organise its operating business model in all its 45 segmented product business units, demanding that leadership in the business units work interdependently across organisational boundaries in a matrix structure in order to enhance cross-business collaboration (Hirschhorn & Barnett, 1999).

Qualitative in-house research was conducted to understand social dynamics during this transformation and change phase. The research aim was to inform a Leadership Development Programme (LDP) on how to accelerate transformation and change.

## *Research method*

Non-probability and non-random samples are normally used in qualitative research, as sample sizes are rarely determined in advance. In this research, convenient and purposive selection was used (Guba & Lincoln, 1989; Huysamen, 1994; Mouton & Marais, 1992; Neuman, 2003) to select two hundred and twenty five leaders representative of race and gender. The leaders were conveniently available in the organisation for the research. Twenty focus groups were facilitated with the following themes; "How do you experience leadership of the organisation's new operating model?" "How do you experience cultural transformational change?" Audio-recorded focus groups were transcribed verbatim for processing. Grounded theory using open, axial, and selective coding was used (Durig, 1999; Strauss & Corbin, 1990; White, Chalip & Marshal, 1998) relying on inductive and deductive reasoning to identify social dynamics. A summary of the results are described below with excerpts from the focus groups (De Jager, 2003).

## *Research results*

### *The impact of re-organisation on the organisation's new operating model*

Employees expressed anxiety, fear and lack of trust in the organisational holding environment (Stapley, 1996) in the new matrix structure:

> *"With all the changes, everyone is scared of everyone—you even pick it up with clients—all our comfort zones are gone."*

Resistance to change resulted in less visible socially structured defense mechanisms (Menzies, 1988; 1989; 1993). Depersonalisation, categorisation and denial of the significance of the individual were evident:

> *"If you don't adapt to change, the system will spit you out—we do as we are told."*

Elimination of decisions by ritual task performance was evident in regressions back to autocratic policies and procedures:

> *"We are managing nonsense—one doesn't need checkers and checkers of checkers—there is just more and more control."*

Idealisation and underestimation of personal development opportunities were expressed:

> *"Some young people aren't trainable you know, the changing demands are at God's mercy—you have to understand accountancy, different industries, clients and the hierarchy."*

Leaders held onto the old structure in the mind (Armstrong, 2005; Neumann, Kellner & Dawson-Shepherd, 1997) and resisted transformational change towards the new matrix structure:

*"We are faced with a dilemma of living in two different worlds—the real working world and the new world we need to accept."*

Middle management split off and project onto top leadership responsibility to transform, while top leadership split off and project irresponsibility onto middle management through strict policies and procedures:

*"Middle management is like a 'stamp'—they are printing us the way they want us to be. We are often asked for our inputs by top management, but we know that they have already made their decisions."*

Purposeful obscurity in the formal distribution of responsibility was evident as the matrix structure failed to define roles fully:

*"Some clients don't receive the service they require, the service offering is not defined in performance contracts, and business units are working against each other. There is poor communication on what is required to be done."*

Conscious and unconscious efforts of individuals and groups to defend their interests and expand influence over individual and group boundaries were part of instinctual interactions in sentience groups (Miller & Rice, 1967; Kernberg, 1998):

*"There are so many rumors about retrenchments that nobody knows what is going on—everyone runs with the grapevine that some operations are closing down."*

Basic assumption groups (Bion, 1991; 1994; Lawrence, Bain & Gould, 1996). The least durable and visible defense mechanisms against change were evident. Dependency, flight/fight, pairing, oneness and me-ness were expressed:

*"We need someone to say we will do things this way—leadership must inform us of what is happening and tell us where we are moving to."*

*"What's the use of ordering communications materials if no one knows what they will be used for—I am not managing information for Head Office—it makes people on the ground scared of what is coming? If I cannot change, I should leave and join another organisation."*

*"Some business units' work together in order to have more power over other business units."*

*"Integrated delivery services will make more money than the different business units have ever been able to."*

*"Our business unit will do its own thing, we don't need change management—we also don't require the services of a delivery channel."*

Regressions in leadership styles as a result of regressive group processes (Hirschhorn & Barnett, 1999; Colman & Geller, 1980; Kernberg, 1980a; 1980b) were evident and indicated a breakdown in work effectiveness that stemmed from organisational change. Authoritarian personality and organisational structure, schizoid, obsessive, paranoid and narcissistic personality features were evident:

*"It is management by fear; do as you are told or leave."*

*"You definitely don't want to take them on—finding and nailing—that's the old style."*

*"We don't know who rules what in the matrix—there are too many bosses—who do I report to?"*

*"It is all work according to technology control systems, policies and procedures and Head Office control."*

*"Head Office knows the big picture, why don't they share it?"*

*"My business unit is the most profitable, I will do what I think is best, I am not interested in other business units and their struggles."*

The organisation was making a transition from a hierarchy to an integrated matrix with segmented products. Role ambiguity affected leadership authority (Colman & Bexton, 1975; Hirschhorn & Barnett, 1999; Obholzer & Roberts, 1994) in the taking of leadership roles:

*"There is no right or wrong being a leader today—this is quite confusing"*

*"I don't get time to practice leadership, all I am doing is communicating."*

### *Transformational change towards the Employment Equity Act*

South Africa's Employment Equity Act require that race and gender distributions in organisations' are representative of national race and gender distributions. In the Bank, however, socially structured defense mechanisms (Menzies, 1988; 1989; 1993) emerged to sustain the power of white males who were in competition with black male and white female leaders:

> *"We (white males) should not apologise for this phenomenon. Historically, we have been the heads of our families—we provided leadership in the past. It is not going to change easily."*

In the competition for positional power by minority groups, white male leaders were continuously pushed forward as "idealised" leaders in groups as a defense against change. A black male leader and white female leader expressed the following, while black female leaders were silent:

> *"Who said I (black male) should speak to be a leader; I listen and then share the information with my group."*

> *"There is nothing wrong with white male domination in leadership roles (white female), it has always been like that and they have always led successfully."*

Depersonalisation, categorisation and denial of the significance of the individual were evident in organisational language used by white leaders when speaking about black leaders:

> *"I have eight employment equity candidate's, I am on target with the 'amount' I should have, but I am not sure if they are all going to make it."*

White leaders project incompetence into black leaders by limiting black promotions:

> *"We (black male) receive the same development over and over. All new black leaders are assigned to mentors and coaches. This is not the case for new white leaders?"*

Projection of responsibility and irresponsibility that affected trustworthiness between white and black leaders was evident:

> *"When a black teller's figures are short, a disciplinary hearing and dismissal follow; white teller shortages are overseen by white supervisors—we (black female) have a fear of being labeled as thieves."*

White leaders envy black leaders as a result of black leaders being sought in organisations to meet Employment Equity targets:

> *"They only stay with the organisation for a few months and then leave; they are earning more than us, with less experience and qualification."*

Black leaders are set up for failure as a result of attractive career opportunities in organisations to meet Employment Equity targets:

> *"New black leaders never receive the same orientation as white leaders when entering the organisation. We are not shown the 'kitchen and the utensils', of course we are going to fail."*

The socially structured defense mechanisms against Employment Equity legislation transformation described above, operate as a collusive system of inferiority and superiority projections between white and black male leaders, and white and black female leaders for positional power in South Africa (De Jager, 2003).

### *Intervention delivery method*

Two major workshops were designed as part of the Bank's Leadership Development Programme to address the challenge of transformations using an integrated organisation development (Cummings & Huse, 1989) and group relations model (Miller, 1989). Both workshops relied on the use of an 'institution-in-the-mind' conceptualisation. Workshop delegates were consultants from the Bank's human resources department (HRCs) whose task was to consult to transformational and change processes that would lead towards a matrix structure of the Bank. Business Unit Heads (BUHs) were encouraged and facilitated to implement cross-business collaboration initiatives in order to optimise the integrated functioning of products and segments in the matrix. Both workshops were consulted to by the authors from a systems psychodynamic consultancy stance as described by Miller, (1989); Neumann, Kellner & Dawson-Shepherd, (1997); Obholzer & Roberts, (1994); Stapley, (1996), within an experiential learning context (Miller, 1989).

## *A three-day group relations workshop for the HR consultants: "Taking transformational change consultation roles"*

### *The aim of the workshop*

The 3-day workshop aimed to provide opportunities for internal consultants from HR to develop more effective consultation skills to assist in the Bank's transitions. We anticipated that the HR consultants would become targets for scapegoating (Colman, 1995)—a usual position for 'outsiders' and likely dynamic in consulting to cross-boundary collaboration initiatives. Reflection can become problematic if it is facilitated by an 'inside' person, as facilitators may get caught up in the 'power dynamics', and may, therefore, collude with their BUH consultees to retain the status quo (Jaques, 1955; 1989; Menzies, 1988; 1989; 1993). The consultants would need to interpret defenses and identify collusive practices, especially between and against race and gender minority groups.

Role clarification and authorisation of the BUHs would be important aspects of the consultants work (Hirschhorn, 1998). Developing their leadership *and followership* skills would be important part of their work. Emphasis on collaboration and integration meant that business units could no longer operate in silos and new behaviours were required.

Business Unit Heads challenged the consultants' abilities to take up transformational change consultation roles. We regarded these challenges as expressions of anxiety and resistance towards individual and collective learning. The fact was that the BUHs needed the HR consultants, but did not wish to acknowledge their dependency on them, so they developed destabilising behaviours on the one hand, and an unrealistic inflation of their own sense of competence on the other, including convictions, bordering on the delusional, that they could solve their organisational and leadership problems alone. The BUHs undermined the aims of collaborative working practices at individual, business, intra-organisational and inter-organisational levels.

### *Workshop design criteria and philosophy*

The workshop was designed to simulate the Bank's structures in order to examine the organisational dynamics that hindered cross-business collaboration in the matrix. Identifying and understanding these dynamics, we believed, would assist the HR consultants to take up their roles more effectively. Workshop participants received the research results discussed above as pre-workshop reading.

### *Workshop design*

The following is a summary of the workshop design over three days:

(i) **Opening and closing plenaries.** The primary task of the plenaries was to further the process of crossing boundaries and learning about workshop dynamics as a mirror of the transformational changes taking place in the Bank.

(ii) **HR transformational change consultation syndicates.** Members organised themselves into groups based on criteria of race, gender and membership of the Bank's businesses. The primary task of the consultation syndicates was for the HR consultants to develop their consultation skills in dealing with conflict in their work with the BUHs.

(iii) **Large study group.** The large study group assisted in understanding how the HR consultants would intervene in the various large cross-business collaboration initiatives.

(iv) **Institutional event.** The institutional event studied relationships between different HR sub-systems as these formed in the workshop—their beliefs and ideas about leadership and authority during transitions.

(v) **Review and application groups.** The review and application groups helped apply workshop learning to the Bank's transitions.

Six months later the second major two-day intervention took place to prepare the Business Unit Heads for the Bank's transformations. This workshop too used a group relations model. Four consultants worked with 45 Business Unit Heads.

## *Two-day institutional event workshop for business unit heads: 'Cross business collaboration in the matrix'*

### *The aim of the workshop*

Pre-workshop telephone interviews were conducted with all the Bank's Executive Committee and Business Heads in which the following questions were asked: "How do you rate the effectiveness of current cross-business collaboration between the BUHs?", "What specific initiatives are required to improve the Executive Committee's and BUHs transformation capability in cross-business collaboration?", "Can you describe the main problem, as you experience it, in the Bank's social and political environments", "What do you expect as possible outcomes of the workshop in the short and long term?".

The content of the interviews were transcribed and communicated to the interviewees for content validation (Siu-Leung, 2006). The content of the transcribed interviews was then grouped into sixty topics. With further filtering, sixteen themes emerged that were then grouped into four categories for the workshop to consider. An integrated report based on the telephone interviews, including the sixteen business themes within four main categories, was sent to all the BUHs for pre-workshop reading.

### *Sixteen identified aspirational themes in four main categories*

(i) **Learning and development.** Develop the Bank as a learning organisation, including mentoring and executive coaching; review training needs; develop matrix management skills; and provide training in conflict resolution. Establish a programme of work reviews; learn to differentiate and work with internal and external competition; improve understanding of top-line growth strategy.

(ii) **Roles.** Review the role, function, size and leadership of the Group Operating Committee (GOC); develop performance and leadership evaluation capability; examine relationships between the Executive Committee, the GOC, and the Leadership Councils (LCs); focus on the Executive Committee's role in re-organising the businesses into logical clusters with clear leadership.

(iii) **Leadership.** Refine leadership's purpose and values; measure leadership against performance criteria; improve implementation capability; manage tension between group participation and individual accountability; set agenda for Leadership Councils; resolve issues raised by succession.

(iv) **Structure.** Examine race, gender and other group affiliations and their impact on business performance; address and improve levels of trust; review reward and incentive systems; develop reflective skills that support collaboration; review the new operating model and its matrix structure.

### *Two-day workshop design*

(i) **Small work group—exploration of business issues.** The 4 small work groups reviewed, debated and evaluated its four chosen topics, and prepared recommendations for presentation to the whole system meeting. By the end of the workshop all sixteen topics had been thoroughly debated. Allocation to the small work groups were done prior to the workshop on the basis of the BUH's interest in topics, including selection of colleagues with whom they wished to work.

(ii) **Consultation syndicates.** The consultation syndicates' task was to integrate, on behalf of all the BUHs the outputs of the four small work groups, and to devise ways for those outputs to be moved into the Bank. This workshop design and its approximation to actual structures in the Bank led to more effective cross-business collaboration and improved, faster means of decision-making.

(iii) **Staff meetings.** Staff meetings, held in public, reviewed the work at the end of each day, i.e. in the presence of the BUHs, sharing their thoughts and experiences, discussing the opportunities taken and missed by staff and BUHs alike; commenting on the dynamic processes of the workshop with the aim that these would be helpful to the BUHs understanding of their own roles, tasks, boundary and authority issues. Sharing thoughts publicly served as a model of leadership and aimed to help BUHs think about how to take leadership roles inside their businesses and to help them take their authority in other sub-systems.

(iv) **Plenary.** In the opening plenary BUHs voiced expectations, opinions, hopes and fears about the workshop's purpose in relation to the broader aims of the Bank, such as enhancing cross-business collaboration. The final plenary reviewed the workshop outputs and considered how to take the work forward into the Bank's structures.

## *Organisational outcomes*

Serious problems in cross-business collaboration were identified as a major blockage to transform the Bank from a national to a global competitor. Three Leadership Councils that met monthly thereafter, formed to improve the chances of enhanced cross-business collaboration. The creation of Leadership Councils, together with consultancy interventions by the HR consultants and executive coaching were important ways of helping the BUHs take broad authorised leadership roles across the organisation.

Key leadership issues were successfully addressed like managing stability and consolidation during succession of the CEO. The Bank's "core philosophy" was reclaimed of moving away from individual business ownership of the customer to corporate shared ownership. Tensions between business segments and products in the matrix were successfully resolved through consultancy interventions. The "ghosts" of previously failed businesses were laid to rest, and the Business Units could organise themselves on a leaner basis with fewer bloated committees. Anxiety of BUHs about losing their power bases in a matrix structure largely disappeared.

Relying on Lawrence's (1994) conceptualization of the politics of salvation and revelation, two striking transformational change leadership styles were identified as a result of the workshop:

***Salvationist leadership*** that relied on a "find-and-fix" approach, solution driven, and action oriented, valued tangibles over "soft" issues, disregarded the value of dialogue and social relationship building, and relied on bullying and hyper-critical behaviour towards self and others. Salvationist leadership did not promote good team playing, produced low frustration tolerance levels, was opinionated, and believed there was only one truth and was contemptuous of the views of others. On the positive side, this type of leadership style was rational in its thinking, highly visible and articulate, unafraid, offered certainty and was intellectually intelligent.

***Revelationist leadership,*** on the other hand, searched for meaning in roles, was inclusive, reflective and willing to learn from experience, evaluated, took action, reviewed, planned, implemented, re-evaluated and re-implemented. It was able to tolerate repetitive business cycles, spent time attempting to understand problems before settling on solutions, and acknowledged that knowledge came from several sources, and was comfortable with dichotomies, paradoxes and ambiguities. On the negative side, this type of leadership was perceived as too open-ended with low implementation capability.

The two group relations-type workshops held 4 months apart, helped in avoiding premature "jumping-to-solutions" leadership types in favour of more collaborative inclusive leadership types. The abiding organisational "myth" that one business unit would bring down the Bank was also resolved. A dependency culture, characterised by a "keep quiet and follow me" attitude, was also successfully challenged

As a result of these two group relations workshops, the share value of the Bank increased by 40% in nine months. As with any change intervention, there were numerous overt and covert responses to the changes. Although the Leadership Councils provided a structure for business heads to collaborate overtly, natural resistances required frequent revisiting of issues to ensure successful cross-business collaboration.

## *Conclusion and new challenges for the organisation*

As a result of the work done in the two workshops, the perceived threat to the matrix structure (also experienced as a threat to self, role, status, power, and authority of the Business Unit Heads) disappeared. A change in leadership capacity was facilitated by increasing understanding of systems psychodynamics among the Bank's change leaders (Obholzer & Roberts, 1994). The organisation won "The Best

Company to Work For" national awards for two consecutive years following the Leadership Development Programme. Key financial fundamentals in the Bank following the Leadership Development Programme's success, led to a successful bid by a UK-based international financial institution to purchase a controlling share that gave the Bank an international reach.

## *References*

Ackoff, R. (1981). *Creating the corporate future.* New York: Johan Wiley & Sons.

Armstrong, D. (2005). *Organisation in the mind. Psychoanalysis, group relations, and organisational consultancy.* London: Karnac Publishers.

Bion, W.R. (1991). *Learning from experience.* London: Tavistock.

Bion, W.R. (1994). *Experiences in groups.* London: Routledge.

Bornemann, E. (1976). *The psychoanalysis of money.* New York: Urizen Books.

Colman, D.C. (1995). *Up for scapegoating. Awakening consciousness in groups.* Illinois: Chiron Publishing.

Colman, D. & Bexton, H. (1975). *Group relations reader 1.* An A.K. Rice Institute Series. Jupiter: AK Rice Institute.

Colman, D. & Geller, M.H. (1985). *Group relations reader 2.* An A.K. Rice Institute Series. Jupiter: A.K. Rice Institute.

Cummings, T.G. & Huse, E.T. (1989). *Organisation development and change.* London: Routledge.

De Jager, W. (2003). *Leadership development from a systems psychodynamic stance.* Unpublished PhD Thesis. University of Johannesburg: Johannesburg.

deMause, L. (1988). Heads and tails: Money as poison center. *The Journal of Psychohistory,* 16 (1).

Durig, A. (1999). *Qualitative models.* (Online). Available: http://www.indiana.edu/~socpsy/papers/QualEncyclo.html

Freud, S. (1905). Three essays on the theory of sexuality. In: SE (1953). Vol. 7. London: Hogarth Press.

Gibson, R. (1998). *Rethinking the future. Rethinking business principles, competition, control and complexity, leadership, markets and the world.* London: Nicholas Brealey.

Greider, W. (1988). *The shadow debate on the American Economy*. Rolling Stone, July, (14–28).

Greider, W. (1987). *Secrets of the Temple: How the Federal Reserve Runs the Country*. New York: Simon and Schuster, p. 65.

Guba, E.G. & Lincoln, Y.S. (1998). *Fourth generation evaluation*. London: Sage Publications.

Hirschhorn, L. (1998). *Reworking authority. Leading and following in the post-modern organisation*. Cambridge: MIT Press.

Hirschhorn, L. & Barnett, C.K. (1999). *The psychodynamics of organisations*. Philidelphia: Temple University.

Huysamen, G.K. (1994). *Methodology for social and behavioural sciences*. Pretoria: Southern.

Jaques, E. (1955). Social systems as a defence against persecutory and depressive anxiety. In: M. Klein, P Heimamann & R. Money-Kyrle (Eds.), *New Directions in Psychoanalysis*. London: Tavistock Publications.

Jaques, E. (1989). *The requisite organisation*. (2nd ed.). New York: Cason Hall & Company.

Kernberg, O.F. (1980a). *Internal world and external reality: Object relations theory applied*. New York: Jason Aronson.

Kernberg, O.F. (1980b). Regression in groups: Some clinical and theoretical implications. *Journal of Personality and Society*, 2: 51–75.

Kernberg, O.F. (1998). *Ideology, conflict and leadership in groups and organisations*. London: Yale University.

Klein, M. (1952). Notes on some Schzoid mechanisms. In: J. Riviere (Ed.), *Developments in Psycho-Analysis*. London: The Hogarth Press.

Lawrence, W.G. (1994). *What makes consultancy work–understanding the dynamics*. London: University of South Bank Press.

Lawrence, W.G. Bain, A. & Gould, L. (1996). The fifth basic assumption. *Free Association*. Vol. 6, 1.37: 28–55.

Magretta, J. (1999). *Managing in the new economy*. Boston: Harvard Business School.

Menzies, I.E.P. (1988). *Containing anxiety in institutions: Selected essays*, Vol. 1. London: Free Association.

Menzies, I.E.P. (1989). *The dynamics of the social: Selected essays*, Vol. 2. London: Free Association.

Menzies, I.E.P. (1993). *The functioning of the social systems as a defence against anxiety*. London: The Tavistock Institute of Human Relations.

Miller, E.J. (1989). *The "Leicester" Model: Experiential study of group and organisational processes.* Occasional paper no.10. London: Tavistock Institute of Human Relations.

Miller, E.J. & Rice, A.K. (1967). *Systems of organisation.* London: Tavistock Publications.

Moon, C. & Bonny, C. (2001). *Business ethics.* London: Profile Books.

Mouton, J. & Marais, H.C. (1992). *Basic concepts in methodology of the social sciences.* Pretoria: HSRC.

Neuman, L. (2003). *Social research methods. Qualitative and quantitative approaches.* Boston: Pearson Education.

Neumann, J.E, Kellner, k. & Dawson-Shepherd, A. (1997). *Developing organisational consultancy.* London: Routledge.

Obholzer, A. & Roberts, V.Z. (1994). *The unconscious at work.* London: Routledge.

Siu-Leung, E. (2006). *Face validity.* (Online). Available: http://repositry.ust.hk/dspace/handle/1783.1/130

Strauss, A. & Corbin, J. (1990). *Basics of qualitative research: Grounded theory. Procedures and techniques.* Newbury Park: Sage.

Stapley, L.F. (1996). *The personality of the organisation: A psychodynamic explanation of culture and change.* London: Free Association.

Welsh, J. (2001). *What I've learned leading a great company and great people.* London: Headline Publishing.

White, G. Chalip, L. & Marshall, S. (1998). *Grounded theory and qualitative analysis.* (Online). Available: http://www2.aucland.ac.nz/mch//hrmas/qual2d.html.

CHAPTER NINE

# Exploring Jewish identity, belonging and leadership through the lens of group relations: Reflections and challenges

*Yoram Lahav*

*"Let us search and examine our ways, and turn back to the Lord..."*
Book of Lamentations 3:40

## *Background*

This paper describes a theoretical and practical attempt to extend the tools of understanding and work within the world of group relations to examine processes of identity and belonging in and between groups. Every group has identity characteristics, mechanisms of belonging and links between its sub-groups.

The Jewish experience is complex. The historical experience marks the Jews as a group that dispersed and returned to its homeland. The link between Israel and the Diaspora affects and is affected by contemporary aspirations to define Jewish identity, yet Jews in Israel and in the Diaspora cope with different issues relating to their Judaism. The State of Israel exists within threatened, vulnerable borders. As a Jewish, democratic state, Israel exists under diverse structural contradictions. Internally, the state was established as a Jewish state and the state of the Jewish people, but it has not yet fully defined whether Judaism is a religion, nationality, historical heritage or political entity, nor has it determined the status of the minority of non-Jews who live in Israel. Life in the Diaspora, on the other hand, requires a different definition of Jewish identity. The majority of Jews dispersed in the Diaspora are at risk for recurrent expressions of anti-Semitism in Europe and accused of supporting or failing to stand by Israel; a process of assimilation affects 50% or more (Becker, 1998). The leadership question for our generation is who should control issues of identity and belonging under such changing circumstances? Does the theoretical and practical field of group relations offer tools that can assist in understanding these complex questions? Can the Jewish experience teach us something about the nature of conscious and unconscious processes concerning social identity, belonging and leadership in other groups?

On the backdrop of these questions and these times, the first international conference organized by OFEK, the Israel Association for the Study of Group and Organizational Processes, was held in May 2005, at Kfar Blum, Israel. This experimental conference, entitled "Jewish Identity, Belonging and Leadership: Israel—the Diaspora," was the first of its kind. It was attended by 18 participants and 6 staff members, men and women from Israel and the Diaspora, from the fields of education, welfare and community work, media, academia and religion. The conference was conducted over five days during which attendees received accommodation and full board. The conference's primary task was "*to provide opportunities to participants to explore and examine questions relating to Jewish identity, belonging and leadership in the context of Israel-Diaspora relations, through an investigation of the intra-personal and inter-personal relations, intra-group, intergroup and systemic relations as they occur.*"

The conference was structured as a learning setting that used the Tavistock tradition adapted to the exploration of Jewish identity, belonging and leadership in the context of Israel and Diaspora relations. The conference focused on several main points:

a. The conference focused on the examination of identity, belonging and leadership as an extension of the concepts of authority and leadership that generally function as the focus of group relations conferences.
b. All staff members identified themselves as Jewish.

c. The conference offered an opportunity to explore processes relating to the geographically dispersed members of a national, religious and ethnic group.
d. The staff examined the question of Jewish identity over the entire work process.
e. The various events typical of the Tavistock model were adapted to the primary task, as illustrated below. The work spirit in the conference is illustrated by a section of a dream presented by one of the participants in the "large group/social dreaming" session. This session, which took place at the beginning of the conference, contained a concentration of the main conference themes: Jewish identity, belonging and leadership in the context of Israel-Diaspora relations.

"I am staying with my mother at a hotel. The sewage is blocked and the filth is overflowing. I ride my bicycle in Amsterdam to seek out a professional handyman. People on the street tell me that the hotel and not I, should be taking care of a plumber." *The dreamer saw the filth in her dream as an expression of the terror and violence in Israel as well as her own repressed and unconscious material. Her desire to be with her mother in a hotel was interpreted as the need to bring her own Jewish identity and Jewish democratic tradition to Europe after the Holocaust.*

Below we illustrate how the conference themes were examined in terms of program and processes. Although the main concepts were present at many conference events, from the preparatory stages to its completion, they are highlighted here separately.

## *Examination of Jewish identity*

Membership in various groups honed issues of personal and group identity that touched upon the similarities and differences between the individual and others. Engagement in group identity immediately reveals the difficulty concerning the "paradox of identity": according to its lexical definition, identity is "individual" and all that makes an individual unique, but it also represents similarities and commonalities between the individual and others (Miller, 1999). Group members structure the elements of their social identity in different ways. We can identify a typology of 4 modes of interpretation of the relations between social identities: an approach that defuses the connection between these identities; an approach which prioritizes identities; an approach which limits their importance; and an approach which powerfully connects these identities (neutralizing, ordering, restricting and containing) (Lahav, 2005). Containment of all elements of one's identity involves increasing difficulties in view of the toll of social belonging or rejection. Exposure to multi-culturalism, increasing opportunities of territorial mobility, and the potential for establishing organizations and families with worldwide branches expand the individual's cast of identities and requires the individual to manage these identities without losing oneself within one's family, job or society. This situation requires a change in a strategy based on splitting these identity components between these elements, in an attempt to make open-ended and extensive use of these components to enrich the individual and the organization (Berg, 2002). Menachem Mendel of Kotzk has long noted this challenge, and he offered an interesting method for managing identities: "If I am I, because I am I, and you are you because you are you, then I am I and you are you. But if I am I because you are you, and you are you because I am I, then I am not I and you are not you" (Buber, 1979, p. 438). The tension between I and you creates a problem for identity management, especially when the individual is threatened. For example, Jewish identity can be split from the remaining identity elements, or it can be brought to the fore in a comprehensive manner as necessary.

## *Issues of Jewish identity at the conference*

At the conference, the difficulties in containing the various elements of identity were discussed around several key questions: professional Jewish identities and their impact on efficacy; Jewish identity based on an experience of "otherness;" and understanding the stereotype elements projected onto Jewish identity and their connection to hatred directed at Jews.

In the task definition stage, the staff addressed two main issues: the feasibility of applying the group relations model to the study of identity, and the definition of suitable participants for the conference. *The staff wondered whether it was possible to apply a group relations model to the study of identity, belonging and leadership, and specifically, what would result from the encounter of the psychoanalytical language of this model and issues of Jewish identity compared to other conferences; what was the significance of the primary task of this conference, and how can theoretical themes be transformed into concepts that can be understood through process-oriented study. The staff was also concerned that the conference might attract several different types of participants such as: "know-it-alls" who use the knowledge they gain in order to avoid internal exploration; "captivated infants," those students of the Tavistock "temple" who will see it as yet another site for pilgrimage; and the "terrorists" who may view a Jewish conference as yet another target of physical or symbolic terror. Staff members wondered if and how the participation of each group would affect conference learning. These concerns led to the question of whether the conference was intended exclusively for Jews. The staff's decision not to conduct any "selection" of the registrants had numerous implications as illustrated below.*

### *Staff members' Jewish identity*

At the conference director's discretion, the conference staff was comprised exclusively of members who were Jews. As early as the invitation and confirmation stage, some wondered whether they were "good enough Jews" or "too Jewish" to assume a role in the conference. *The staff wondered whether the identity of a conference consultant could be compatible with his or her identity as a consultant in group relations conferences. Staff members apparently sensed anxiety, weakness and a sense of being trapped due to entry into this new field and as a result of the conceptual and applicative change in the staff's roles.*

### *The question of the participants' Jewish identity*

Participants wondered what defines them as Jewish. They expressed a fear of stagnation that would render their Jewish identity devoid of all content; they expressed a fear of identifying themselves through the stereotypes that are projected onto Jews, and they explored the role of faith in defining their Jewish identity. Conference participants addressed the issue of their Jewish identity based on painful personal stories that centered on several identity markers: *the relationship to the previous generation: identity that stems from parents, their being the offspring of Holocaust victims, the children and grandchildren of rabbis, and the return to Hebrew/Jewish names. Identity was defined in the context of the* ***tension between stagnation and renewal****. Failure to resolve this tension led to the fear that their Jewish identity would be emptied of all content. Jewish tradition, especially Orthodox tradition, was repeatedly attacked during the conference, community lives were perceived as empty and boring by some participants, and contemporary Judaism was seen as petrified and something that could become irrelevant. One participant dreamed of "adolescents' unmoving heads" in stagnation, and the absence of a subsequent generation was discussed. One of the consultants noted that the cemetery is the point of encounter for Jews, and participants also noted that to be buried as a Jew, the individual must be part of a community. This conflict can be seen as representing confusion between "renewal" and "sanctity." Identity was examined from the perspective of the* ***stereotypical trap of Judaism and impulses****, that is, the definition of Jews as greedy, victims or attackers. The question arose as to whether a Jew could be strong without being considered an aggressor. The theme of Jews as aggressors was discussed, and images of the Good Jew and the Bad Jew were discussed. Participants raised the issue of Jews and victims, and their own contribution to this image; participants discussed the fear of directing aggression inward, as* stated **in Isaiah 49:17 "thy destroyers and they that made thee waste shall go forth of thee."** *One thought that was suggested was that strong Jews become aggressive, and the question was raised as to how the Nazis transformed Jews into victims by training them to be aggressive. The risk of utilizing Jewish suffering as a calling card or brand was discussed, as was the risk of transforming suffering into a "worn-out slogan." On the positive side, participants asked whether Jews were permitted to be hedonistic and egotistical and how these are connected to Jewish values such as mutual responsibility.*

*One of the definitions of Jewish identity at the conference was the* ***definition of Jewish identity through the "other."*** *The participation of a non-Jew in the conference was a significant event. In various sessions, the group found it difficult to work on questions of identity and "otherness" through him.* The conference offered an opportunity for an encounter between OFEK as a permanent organization and the conference as a "temporary learning organization" reflecting similar organizational culture and methods. The encounter positioned two "extreme images" of two types of "others" in the conference: on one hand, a conference on implementing psychoanalytical insights was directed by someone who, unlike most of OFEK's conference directors in the past, was not a psychoanalyst, the "other" in terms of the parent organization; and on the other hand, a non-Jew participated in the conference in which the majority of participants were Jews occupied with their Judaism. This researcher of theology was perceived as the "other" in the temporary organization, "the Jew" of the conference.

The final area that I will mention concerned Jewish identity and the relationship with God. *Participants and the staff suggested contents relating to faith, based on their feeling that the loss of faith empties Jewish identity of all content.* Two important hypotheses were proposed in the course of the staff's work: *One hypothesis was that part of the hatred toward Jews is related to Jewish ambivalence towards God. Jews should be hated for having God, for being the first ones who adopted God and assumed a covenant with God, or otherwise be hated for losing their connection with God and consequently losing the right to exist.* The second hypothesis *concerned the "dance of death" between Christians and Jews who fight over the true "Abrahamic" faith in one God. According to this hypothesis, the Jews' failure to accept Jesus as the messiah, and their role in his crucifixion, justifies abusing the Jews. It is possible that the Jews' aspiration to preserve their unique identity contributes to anti-Semitic ideologies relating to "blood purity" and is re-projected onto the Jews as a license to harm them.*

### *Belonging*

Belonging defines the relationship between an individual and a group in terms of intimacy and alienation. When crossing the border into and out of the group, the individual loses his or her sense of belonging. A group cannot exist in empty space, and its boundaries must be open to the environment (Miller & Rice, 1967). The issue of borders provides an opportunity to explore unconscious parts relating to the other, the parts inside and outside the self, and it brings the group to meet the "alien" and the "enemy." The other is on, near or beyond the group/social boundary, such as foreign workers, ethnic minorities or holders of other faiths, the group leader or the analyst in a therapeutic situation. "... as individuals who are naturally "on the border," they become the natural target for projections of hatred and animosity as well as other contents" (Erlich, 2001, p. 28).

## *Belonging, Jews and others*

Jewish experience is replete with the experience of otherhood, both in the Diaspora and in the sovereign Jewish state. I believe that two main sources of this "otherhood" are related to the borders of group belonging and the group's primary task. Judaism maintains strict codes of admission boundaries in order to prevent any "poisoning of the wells" in service of its mission to "repair the world" and its role as a "light to all nations." This attitude evokes a broad range of feelings and projections toward its members. Living amidst other nations requires the selection of a single pattern of relationship with others to manage the tension between the individual and the universal. This selection has far-reaching implications on the potential of living in peace with other groups based on the Midrashic patterns of Abraham, Sarah, Solomon and Jethro (discussed by Rozenak, 2000). The "Abraham and Sarah" pattern represents people of faith who withstand their trials and, despite their being Jews, are on the other side Vis a Vis the rest of the world, and they continue to engage with the others. In this pattern, group identity and individual identity do not efface universality. The "Jethro and Solomon" pattern represents a complex paradigm that symbolizes the universal polar of Judaism. The universal pattern alludes that universal wisdom can be consistent with the Torah. Another option is to perceive animosity as a destiny based on the Midrashic pattern of "Esau the enemy of Jacob," who represented two hostile worlds despite the fact that they were twins; this mutual hatred is a historical principle that Jews must frequently experience.

## *Jewish belonging in the conference*

Belonging in the conference was defined along several key issues: common territory, family cohesion, shared roles and boundaries of belonging that "qualify" a Jew to be "one of us."

Israel is perceived as an unsafe and problematic territory, as a closed "refuge for paranoids" that is used as a shelter in times of trouble but also evokes a desire to escape from it due to its changing nature.

Throughout the conference, many indicators infused the conference with a sense of a family convention. Participants discussed the importance of preserving some "family secrets" in an attempt to guarantee continuity (such as family ties in the staff, concealed ties between staff members and participants, and fantasies concerning relations inside "the family" and group pressure that called for family belonging by "Israelizing" names and customs of those from the Diaspora).

Belonging to the Jewish nation appeared to be related to the need to fulfil the role of "the chosen nation" and a shared assumption of the hatred relating to this role. Engaging in the covert universal aspiration "to be selected/chosen," especially by "the parents," was experienced in the conference in the strong desire for belonging and being elected to a group, especially to the administrative group that was perceived as the "group of gods," the "ideal others," who had the power to grant or withhold their favour. This disguised aspiration also functioned as an "actuating theme" based on a second significance relating to the concept of "the chosen people" as a type of "marker and signifier," and revealed it to be a foundational concept for the desire to belong and the toll involved in belonging.

The issue of assimilation resulting from life in a non-Jewish culture was present at the conference, which frequently gave the appearance of a "conversion conference." Many questions relating to the "kashrut" of the conference were raised. One staff member shared the following dream: My wife is conducting a very seductive and provocative conversation with a principal (whose name is identical to the name of the conference director) of some school. In one of the scenes, the man places his hand on my wife's lips with a clearly sexual connotation, but the dream "knows that this act is kosher."

## *Leadership*

Authority and leadership relations stand at the center of the study of the group relations model.

The Sages, who acknowledged the dangers of assuming positions of power and their potential for diverting the individual from the path of righteousness, cautioned those who assumed leadership tasks as follows: "Love work and despise positions of power" (Avot, 10:1). The power granted to the spiritual authority to help the group realize its goals is reflected in the following Hasidic adage: "If one thousand faithful Hasidim gather around a log, it too will perform wonders." This expresses the frequent dynamics that evolve among a group of Hasidim in a rabbi's courtyard, as well as among participants in group relations conferences. Participants felt they belonged to a closed group that is performing sacred work and holds a truth and a tradition that must be preserved. Although it is impossible to identify a single leadership style for all Hasidic leaders, the dialectics are clearly reflected in the leader-group dependency.

### *The issue of leadership in the conference*

The issue of leadership was reflected in the conference in the structure of the events and the style of staff work, the manner in which staff hierarchy formed, the manner of competition and collaboration between leaders from Israel and the Diaspora, the effect of the issue of Jewish and professional identity on leadership capabilities, and the affect of the moral elements in the fields of mutual responsibility and the gender-based perception of leadership. Engagement in issues of Jewish identity allowed the staff to rely on, yet renew, refine and adapt the group relations model to a different type of investigation.

The assessment and implementation group focused not only on the world of work in the context of Jewish leadership and the use of Jewish identity in work, but in additional references of belonging such as the family, the community, Israel and the Diaspora.

Experiences in the conference reflected shared leadership of Israel and the Diaspora from an approach of flexible hierarchy: the conference director and associate director were from Israel and the Diaspora, and in their roles they represented the parent organizations (OFEK and the Tavistock Institute) and the shared history of these two organizations. (The British organization provided considerable assistance to OFEK during its establishment stage.) In the course of the discussion between the director and associate director on the latter's attitude to experiences under such circumstances, the associate director replied: "For the Torah will go forth from Zion, and the word of the Lord from Jerusalem." The competition between staff members, the organizations they represent and the truth of each organization, raised the question of "Why two Jews need three synagogues?" Staff members began their work out of a sense of diminished professional efficacy, expressed in a sense of their being "heavy of mouth and heavy of tongue" when reporting from the groups, because they feared that they were defiling the sanctity of the Tavistock approach and therefore needed to shift from a reductive divisive approach to an integrated approach that requires full capacity, an approach that relies on internal authority that combined both sources of their identities. Their sense of individual efficacy was also affected by their ability to operate outside their "natural territory"; people of the Diaspora continue to maintain the role of the "Wandering Jew" (an image that appeared that same morning in the associate director's dream of losing a suitcase) as a leader who works outside his familiar environment, and feels debilitated by the encounter with Israel's physical, cultural and organizational climate.

### *Leadership among the participants*

Participants expressed an unconventional attitude toward competition, motivation for leadership, gender-based leadership, the role of orthodoxy and the ease of assuming responsibility for others versus assuming personal responsibility. It appears that defiance toward authority in the conference was "softer" than typically seen in conferences of this kind. Participants also fled from a clear definition of representational values that emphasized competition among themselves. Motivation for assuming leadership was related to the need to ensure continuity of generations among second-generation Holocaust survivors caring for both parents and children. Much was said about the accepted structure of Jewish orthodox hierarchy, passed down from generation to generation, and the need to develop alternative leadership patterns. This was especially conspicuous regarding women's leadership and Judaism. The large number and powerful presence of female participants who assumed leadership roles in the conference points to the potential in this field and the need to grant an opportunity for female leadership in the current point on the continuum of Jewish history.

### *Israel-Diaspora relations*

"Israel" is the name of the state, while "Zion" is the place that is in the collective Jewish memory and which every Jew swears never to forget. The term "Diaspora" exists "in the mind" (Armstrong,

1998). The issue of relations between Israel and the Diaspora reveals the significance attributed to the Jewish Diaspora and life in the Diaspora, and this affects the connection between Israel and the Diaspora. Two main approaches lead this insight: According to the first approach, the Jewish Diaspora is punishment for the sins of the Jewish nation. This approach is based on statements of the prophets including "And I scattered them among the heathen, and they were dispersed through the countries: according to their way and according to their doings I judged them" (Ezekiel 26:19). The opposite approach sees the destiny of the Jewish Diaspora as a spiritual mission and the expansion of Judaism throughout the world. "And I will sow her unto Me in the land" (Hosea 2:25) (cited in Orbach, 1983 presenting the explanation of Rabbi Elazar).

### *Israel and the Diaspora in the conference*

Consistent with the above, the conference also raised the issue of the goal of the state and of Diaspora Jews and the mutual connection between them as well as the role of the nations in this complex relationship. Participants expressed the need to maintain this connection, and they discussed the difficulty in maintaining this relationship due to love, hatred and suspicion, revealing inter-group competition.

Surrounding the issue of Israel-Diaspora relations, emotional and turbulent issues were raised, ranging from despair and embarrassment to pride and hope. Shame and pain over the price of living in the Diaspora were expressed, including the need to collaborate with the Nazis in order to survive. One poet from Israel dreamed of a night of forbidden love that gave birth to princes and kings, possibly expressing a sub-conscious group wish to return to the days of the united kingdom before its divisions and destruction, illustrating the subconscious aspiration for "pairing" (to use Bion's term) that generates a new kingdom. Such love-hate-suspicion relations in the encounter between Israel and the Diaspora were symbolized in one participant's dream, a dream in which he receives a loving embrace from a stranger, on the beach in Tel Aviv, who then stabs him in the back with a knife. The suspicion between Jews in Israel and the Diaspora, alongside their mutual need for each other and fear of harm, led to the projection of extensive hostility on the conference's non-Jewish participant, based on the feeling that the family party would have been perfect without his presence. This theme resonated with the role of others among Jews, including the Israeli-Palestinian conflict that helps groups in Israel and in the Diaspora refrain from battling each other. Participants discussed how Jews living in the Diaspora experienced difficulties in presenting a "Jewish facade" as well as the issue of the double loyalty they feel. In the inter-group event, representatives of the Diaspora group went to check whether the Israel group still existed, and declared "Am Yisrael Hai!" On the other hand, members of the Israel group were accused of being inhospitable to guests. Participants were doubtful whether the State of Israel could meet the Diaspora Jews' need for protection and whether Israelis would treat them hospitably. On the other hand, several participants perceived Europe as the country of death, whose ground is saturated with the blood of Holocaust victims, and where Jews are once again the Wandering Jews who seek new places of existence.

### *Summary and conclusions*

Experiences in the conference open a window to a more extensive application of the theoretical and applicative model of group relations. The conference shifted from a process of learning on leadership to a study of identity and belonging. Various parts of identity and their connections were explored by a group that is positioned in an identity matrix comprised of religion, nationality, historical memory and heritage, territory and shared destiny. The largely homogeneous nature of the staff and the participants functioned as a laboratory that hones the connection between identity, belonging and leadership.

The encounter between the group relations world and issues of Jewish identity invited a dialogue between two types of distinct discourse and was therefore replete with tension and risks. The resonance of this dialogue was evident in the absence of legitimacy, blame and shame that were present in the conference and in the fear that if the distance between these two loci of identity is stretched to the brink of tolerance, the result may be assimilation and/or alienation. The conference demonstrated that defining identity can stem from an experience of otherness, difference and adversity, but it could also become a definition that stems from belonging and from liberty.

The conference experience indicates the potential of investigating group relations from a culturally sensitive stance and a dualistic—in contrast to an integrative—approach to ethnic identity, specifically. It was clear from the experience that work on Jewish identity is not possible from the basis of an individualistic Western approach that emphasizes mainly power, achievements and competition. Jewish identity by definition contains a collective moral dimension that includes values of mutual responsibility and collaboration.

It is possible that the conference brought together "extreme images" and enabled an encounter based on authentic, liberating reflection, an investigation such as that which occurs in "no-man's land" and permits osmosis and rejuvenation. The conference, which gave a focal expression to otherness (by themes and structural characteristics), was also required to address the theme of the absolute other, the god as a crucial and inescapable center of gravity.

The space of defining Jewish identity is limited both by Jewish tradition and by the stereotypic attribution of traits to Jews. This dual approach requires one of two difficult options: being a victim or being an aggressor. An integrated approach proposes that life should be based on an awareness of past suffering without transforming the suffering into a worn slogan. Thus, the conference demonstrated the difficulty and the necessity to fill roles as directors and consultants in order to make Jewish identity a valuable professional resource, but also as a source for projections that use the term "Jew" as a stereotype.

It may emerge that the concept of shared destiny may promote staff development based on a model that does not obliterate hierarchy, on the one hand, and reinforces collegiality on the other hand. Furthermore, subordinating Jewish identity to the stereotypes that have adhered to Jews over history, diminishes the position of the inter and intra-personal leadership and undermines its legitimacy.

This conference was the first experimental conference of its kind. At the same time, it presents a challenge to extend our perspective from a study of authority and leadership to the use of a temporary learning organization as a tool for a more comprehensive social study targeting leadership, identity and belonging.

## References

Armstrong, D. (1998). *The 'Institution in the Mind': Reflections on the Relation of Psyco-Analysis to Work with Institutions*. London: Free Association Books.

Backer, A. (1998). Israel and the Diaspora. In: Aharoni, S. & Aharoni, M. (Eds.), *Men and Activities in Israel*, Tel Aviv: Miksam Publishers. (Hebrew).

Berg, D. (2002). Bringing one's self to work. A Jew reflects. *The Journal of Applied Social Sciences*, *38*(4): 397–415.

Buber, M. (1979). Or Haganuz, Hasidic Tales. Tel Aviv: Schocken Publishing House. (Hebrew).

Erlich, S. (2001). Otherness, boundaries and dialogue: Thoughts. In: Haim Deutsh & Menachem Ben Sason (Eds.), The Other. 19–36. Tel Aviv: Yedioth Books. (Hebrew).

Lahav, T. (2005). Female principals of Mizrahi background in Israel: The interplay of social identity and professional perceptions. PhD. Thesis, Leicester University. U.K.

Menachem Ben Sason, (Eds.), The Other. 37–51. Tel Aviv: Yedioth Books. (Hebrew).

Miller, E. (1999). Dependency, Alienation, or Partnership? The changing relatedness of the individual and the enterprise. In: French, R. and Vince, R. (Eds.), *Group Relations, Management and Organization*, Oxford University Press.

Miller, E.J. & Rice, A.K. (1967). Systems of Organization. Tavistock Publication.

Rice, A.K. (1965). *Learning for Leadership*. London: Tavistock Publications.

Rozenak, M. (2004). Jews, sameness and strangers: Three Midradhic types. In: Shahar Arzy, Michal Fechler & Baruch Kahana (Eds.), *Life as a Midrash, Prespectives in Jewish Psychology*, Tel Aviv: Yedioth Publishers. (Hebrew).

Urbach, E.E. (1982). *The Sages. Their concepts and beliefs*. Jerusalem: The Magness Press, the Hebrew University (Hebrew).

*CHAPTER TEN*

# Identity, leadership, and authority: Experiences in application of group relations concepts for dalit empowerment in India

*Rosemary Viswanath*

> The right to touch and to be touched[1]—the application of group relations insights to dalit empowerment.
>
> Rosemary Viswanath, Learning Network, India


## *Executive summary*

*This paper explores the relevance of group relations concepts to work on surfacing the deep-seated unconscious assumptions in the dalit psyche. In her work with a collective of bodies working on dalit rights the author argues that unless dalits understand the dynamics, both conscious and unconscious, that perpetuate systems of caste discrimination, they would possibly be playing into these dynamics themselves and self sabotaging their efforts to counter these societal processes. In order to transform themselves and their struggles, dalit leaders needed to look deep within themselves—to have the courage to uncover shadows that would in turn help uncover fault lines and shadows in society that have been unconsciously allowed to perpetuate in a bizarre and inhuman collusion.*

*The author had a series of interview-conversations with dalit members of group relations conferences to uncover what the meaning and benefits of attending these conferences were to them and how they linked these experiences to their struggles. The learning's were at the level of individual as well as the institution. Drawing parallels between the ideological basis of group relations concepts and that of human liberation and empowerment and in particular dalit liberation the author argues that the group relations concepts themselves provided a powerful metaphor and framework to situate such self discovery and insights. The paper concludes with the question "Can and should ways of thinking and acting in this framework (group relations) be making a more overt an active contribution to social change at work, community, national and international level"?*

I attended my first group relations conference as a member in 1989, and first worked with a non-profit organisation (in India these are more popularly referred to as non-governmental organisations or NGOs) working with dalit communities as consultant nearly 10 years later in 1997. The engagements ran as parallel streams for a while, but they were destined to meet. As my immersion both with group relations work and with the struggles of dalits for their rights intensified, I realised that, for me, one was incomplete without the other.

## *Who are the dalits?*

Some 167 million people in India (and approximately 220 in South Asia) live a precarious existence shunned by much of society because of their rank as untouchables at the bottom of India's caste system. Dalits[2] as they have chosen to call themselves (the word literally means broken people) are discriminated against, denied access to land and education, forced to work in degrading conditions, and routinely abused and even killed by higher caste groups that enjoy state (police, judiciary and bureaucracy) impunity and even protection. Dalit women are frequent victims of sexual abuse, usually the first victims to face the brunt of anger against the community. In what has been called India's hidden apartheid, entire villages in most Indian states remain completely segregated by caste. National legislation and constitutional protections serve mostly to mask the social realities of discrimination and violence faced by those living below the pollution line.[3]

The concept of untouchability is one of the most difficult for non-Indians to understand (and for Indians to acknowledge) particularly in the context of modernity. There are still groups of people who are by birth permanently impure, not to be touched, forced to do work that is polluting, relegated to the margins of society and yet necessary for the maintenance of society. This concept bears some relation to racial and ethnic divisions and prejudice in other parts of the world,[4] but is systematised and deeply entrenched in the Indian culture. The caste system as groups of graded inequality and strict stratification has existed for over 2000 years. With Brahmans as most ritually pure at the top and the untouchables as the most polluted as the outcastes—so impure that they are not even included in the system of caste.[5] The practise of untouchability was abolished in the constitution of India and made punishable by law in 1955. However more than 60 years later, the practice flourishes, and in most cases the discrimination and violence when the untouchables assert their rights is even more pronounced.[6] The prevalent images of a modern shining India in the international media, makes it even more difficult to believe that caste discrimination continues to be a systematised and deeply entrenched aspect of contemporary Indian culture and ethos.

## *Why group relations?*

Examining the different categories of interventions both societal and systemic that have been attempted by Dalit rights activists, political formations and movements it is clear that most have had fallen back on legislative provisions, institutions to safeguard rights, human rights bodies and political struggles for entitlement and movements for self respect. My professional engagement with a large network-collective of dalit organisations initially in South India and later on a national platform as a consultant working on change processes—mostly focussed on leadership and capacity building, internal processes, aligning vision, objectives and processes and helping greater role clarity, gave me a privileged opportunity to examine the institutionalising of caste. As our work progressed, with the particular focus on leadership and capacity building, it became clear that we could go no further unless we began surfacing the deep-seated unconscious assumptions in the dalit psyche.

The work of breaking from the bonds of caste based thinking also needs a search within.[7] The internalised oppression had to be acknowledged in order to leverage the interventions in other areas. Like patriarchy, colour, religious intolerance, and any other form of wide social discrimination, the caste struggle depends not only on individual change, but on the ability of the oppressed to understand and leverage the struggle at the level of collective consciousness. As we worked on processes of capacitation for leadership ... why were we coming up against an invisible wall? Each time I returned from a workshop I fell ill as I had introjected the pain of the injustice and the inhumanity—each time I asked myself: Why had the dalits allowed this? How could they accept a discourse of "lesser than"? In order to transform themselves and their struggles dalit leaders needed to look deep within themselves—to have the courage to uncover shadows that would in turn help uncover fault lines and shadows in society that have been unconsciously allowed to perpetuate in a bizarre and inhuman collusion.

Also unless we understood the dynamics, both conscious and unconscious, that perpetuated systems of caste discrimination, we would possibly be playing into these dynamics ourselves and self sabotaging our own efforts to counter these societal processes.[8]

### *Models and interventions for dalit empowerment*

From the 14th century onwards there have been many dalit protest and resistance movements ranging from those within the structure of Hinduist reforms, to mass conversions to other religions. The demand for social and political reform and rights began pre-independence with the prominent struggles being spearheaded by Dr BR Ambedkar.[9] Later movements like the dalit Panthers integrated a class analysis along with class. From the 80's both political parties and dalit NGO's have been engaged at different spectrums of the struggle for dalit emancipation. The most prominent threads of the discourse have been

1. **Ambedkarism**—the teachings of Dr BR Ambedkar—iconised in his lifetime and even more so after. Dr Ambedkar worked for reclaiming the identity of the dalits and felt that once they were a political force they could not be ignored. His strategies

focussed on self-respect and the reclaiming of their culture. The mainstream brahminical culture dominated and dalits needed to find (rediscover) their own roots and their own culture, which would be a source of pride, and self respect. Ambedkar lay the foundations also for the demand that the state and its institutions were responsible for the upliftment of the dalits through constitutional provisions and protective legislations. *Ambedkar's exhortation: "My final words of advice to you are educate, agitate and organize; have faith in yourself. With justice on our side I do not see how we can lose our battle. The battle to me is a matter of joy. The battle is in the fullest sense spiritual. There is nothing material or social in it. For ours is a battle not for wealth or for power. It is battle for freedom. It is the battle of reclamation of human personality... ." has been a source of inspiration for millions of Dalits.*

2. **Marxian** class analysis integrated into a class perspective informed some political struggles—particularly the more radical struggles in western and southern India.
3. **Dalit theology**—which was inspired by liberation theology and the recognition that the church had failed to take a position on discrimination and justice within its structures and the fact that a large percentage of Christians in India were dalits[10] (having converted to escape from the oppression of a case bound Hindu religion).
4. NGO's in the last 10–15 years also adopted a **human rights perspective** to their struggles. The National Campaign on Dalit Human Rights' (NCDHR[11]) landmark interventions in the World Conference against Racism in Durban in 2001 with their slogan "dalit rights are human rights" and subsequently in the UNCERD[12] drew international attention and solidarity to the dalit question—forcing the Indian state to present a rather weak defence of its inaction.

In the model below, interventions that work for dalit empowerment are both societal-systemic and personal.

Societal-systemic interventions aim to address both the ideologies that justify inequality and discrimination as well as to change institutions and structures that reinforce inequality and discrimination. At the individual and personal level what is attempted to be changed is the access to resources. What is worked less on is the change in mindsets—the internalised oppression both of the oppressor and

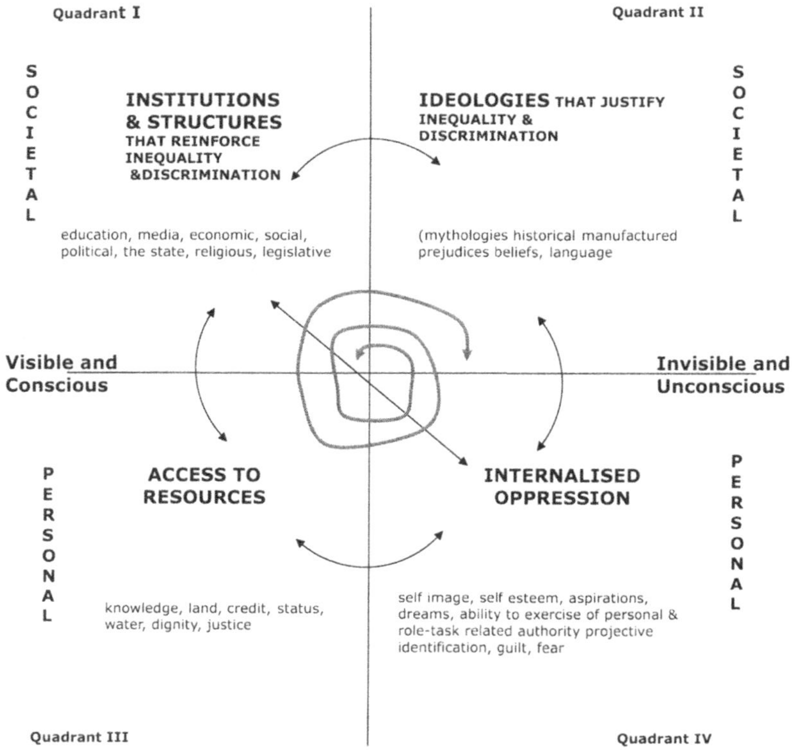


the oppressed. What was assumed perhaps was that pressures to change in quadrants I, II and II would change quadrant IV. What we are now suggesting is that simultaneous work in IV through frameworks such as what group relations offers will in turn change and render more effective interventions in I, II and III.

The model[13] suggests that most of the recognised interventions work in the arena of quadrants I, II, and III. However all of them tend to neglect quadrant IV—the internalised oppression. It seemed critical that work needed to be done in that area as well in order to, in turn, leverage the strategies and possibilities in the other quadrants. The fact that in spite of strides in the other quadrants, caste based prejudices ran deep indicated that the battle had to also be fought at the level of the mind—and the mind not just of the oppressor but the mind of the oppressed. While the black arrows all lead to increased internalised oppression that held the dalits in a vicious clutch, the red spiral also indicates that each of these areas informs the other. It seemed to suggest that work in quadrant IV would be the lever to convert a vicious spiral into a virtuous one.

## *Engaging with group relations in Dappu*

The author's association with Dappu (a network-cum-collective of dalit organisations in the south Indian state of Andhra Pradesh) in the course of its formation and capacity building dates back to 1998. A series of interventions with the first and second rung leadership focussed on building dalit leadership and on working on institutional processes systems and roles to build a network. Very soon it became evident that it is not enough to work on systems and processes at a macro level. It was necessary to help individuals access conscious and unconscious material related to the exercise of their own personal authority, a process which is a prerequisite to the exercise of one's leadership. A few key leaders were encouraged to attend a Group Relations Conference in July 2002 which was sponsored by the Eastern Institute for Integrated Learning in Management, Kolkata. They found this a fascinating experience, came back with many personal learning's and were keen that such a learning opportunity available to a wider section of dalit leaders. This led, in March 2003, to what seems in hindsight a landmark event. Dappu and Learning Network jointly sponsored a public Group Relations Conference titled Identity, ***Authority, Leadership: Resistance, Self Empowerment and Transformation in Organisational and Social Systems***. The brochure[14] of the conference placed (perhaps for the first time) caste quite clearly as an issue to be grappled with.

In hindsight again, the more powerful act was of a dalit organisation actually sponsoring and inviting others to a learning space to explore identity and caste in its unconscious dynamics—it was a powerful symbolic act of self-assertion which has had ripples in the spawning of many other such spaces within Dappu as well as others. The conference was an exciting and vibrant learning space for the members and the staff. Many of the personal learning's enumerated below are actual quotes from members of the dalit collective who were GRC members and the GRC became a trademark term (as well as the material of many stories and jokes!) within the leadership of the collective. A follow-up workshop to help take the conceptual framework and application of learning's further was organised. Members of the Dappu collective as well as others from the National Campaign on Dalit Human Rights used opportunities to attend other group relations conferences and workshops in India, and at the Grubb Institute and the Tavistock, and have also been on the staff of conferences as well. A workshop on Gender and Authority was offered jointly by Chindu and Australian centre for Socio-Analysis in August 2005, and the framework and concepts have been used in consultations and workshops with both Dappu and NCDHR. More recently in August 2007 some of them also participated in Exercising Leadership in a gendered world—a group relations conference that focused on authority and gender.

In the span of a few years this group of dalit NGO networks and platforms has engaged quite consistently with the GRC and its framework in a variety of creative ways. Members have also attributed directly to GRC's their transformation in terms of leadership which in turn contributed to the cause of dalit empowerment. The question is why did they engage with such vigour? Did the GRC framework contribute not just to personal and organisational effectiveness but also provide a vehicle or piece of the jigsaw to work on the wider cause of dalit empowerment?

## Learnings

*The author interviewed personally or telephonically several dalit members of groups relations conferences to ask what the benefits of participating in these conferences were. While the interviews and conversations were open ended many of them veered to how these conferences literally created a space to face and work on the internalised oppressor. Listed[15] below are some of the key learning's categorised at the personal and systems level*

### Learnings at the personal level

- Recognising patterns of behaviour in oneself and (unconscious) psychological roles
- Focussing on oneself instead of externalising
- Dealing with and accessing personal authority-Dealing with the notion of ones own personal authority and that of others

- Recognising when one is abdicating role—managing self in role, and linking role to task
- Recognising and dealing with anxieties
- Learning how to say no, particularly to those in positions of authority
- Ability to approach those in authority and engage with them in assertive manner
- Working with the notion of boundaries as related to task
- Recognising the notion of a primary task
- Able to express anger
- Release of blocked energy and transformed the way one involved in issues
- Realising that the unconscious was a factor and a layer driving all transactions—being alert and open to this whole new layer
- Being open to diversity

While these may seem like a simple and obvious list, it must be contextualised within the reality of systematic and systemic oppression of the dalits—the ability to express anger in functional ways, the experience of exercising of personal authority were revolutionary and extremely liberating.

### *Learnings at the organisational level*

A large proportion of those from the dalit networks who attended the GRCs, struggled to go beyond their curiosity and actively engage with the challenges and issues. These were the dalit leaders who were able to apply their learning's quite significantly in their roles. The 2003 Dappu—Learning Network conference for instance was in itself an intervention for Dappu. It was a time when a significant amount of energy of the network was legitimately and consciously focussed on issues of vision, values, leadership and capacity building. The conferences gave a framework and language to this search and exploration. It gave the network a language to engage in a new manner with their task—the ability to unselfconsciously take on leadership for the cause (and not fear that it would be seen as a selfish personal act and lacking Christian values of humility—therefore shirk from the risk of exercising leadership).

The idea of working with a primary task and the concept of pictures in the mind and institutions in the mind were also worked with powerfully.[16] In the non-profit sector (the spectrum of NGO's, not only those working on dalit issues), organizations are particularly prone to erosion and even non-definitions of boundaries, as they work in macro spaces. The battles they take on are large scale and defy notions of tasks achievable within manageable time frames (even one's lifetime). For example: eliminating caste based discrimination. As an unconscious defence against the anxiety related to taking on such mammoth and "impossible" tasks, NGO leaders often take on and act out unconscious fantasies of omnipotence. This leads to lack of accountability to their organisations and constituencies, organisation systems that do not work with notions of boundaries, and unilateral, inefficient and even autocratic ways of functioning.

The idea of looking within and around oneself for parallel processes—going beyond what one is aware of and also being open to someone else pointing it out without this being seen as an affront or received with shock or defensiveness were tried out. "Undiscussables" came to the table with greater legitimacy and ease—this included the power dynamics, the shadows, and even issues of sexuality which was until then like a forbidden four letter word. The workshops and conference on Gender and authority for instance provided an important space to confront themselves, to look at why the network had "neglected" dalit women's leadership. When it was able to battle discrimination on the basis of caste why had it sabotaged work on discrimination based on gender?

Being more attentive to institutional processes and the idea of management was also fascinating. The concept of boundaries as liberating and not constraining, the ideas of time, task and territory as being a valuable framework was experienced and then applied with vigour. Many members spoke of their sense of "freedom" to work with building institutions to work on vision, instead of seeing institution as a constraint.

## *Contributing to the larger dynamics of Dalit empowerment*

Alan Schaffer in his paper (2006) on Group Relations and the Politics of Engagement[17] asks the question "Can and should ways of thinking and acting in this framework (group relations) be making a more overt an active contribution to social change at work, community, national and international level? I was delighted to read this question and his paper as this has been a question that has seized me ever since I began to more actively use the group relations framework. It seemed to me that such a powerful framework was underutilising its own potential by not addressing the larger social and political issues of our times. To be staff on series of conferences where individual members certainly engaged and learnt was a satisfying experience. But it seemed not to go too far or far enough.

The sociological/political/cultural element of caste and the dalit experience had been researched and articulated initially through Dalit literature and later through Dalit studies. The GRC framework offered an opportunity to articulate the dalit experience from a psychosocial and psycho cultural and psychodynamic perspective.

The 2003 GRC was the first time that a dalit group was not just participating but hosting sponsoring such a learning opportunity. This was certainly a role reversal and perhaps was seen as an example of dalit audacity. That the conference employed a state of the art tool like GRC[18] to look at caste and discrimination openly was itself valuable. The issue of caste was so suppressed that visibilising it and understanding the dalit psyche from the point of view of the experience of caste discrimination was invaluable. That issues of—caste and authority—particularly accessing personal authority—did not get merged with other issues or pushed under the carpet required courage. It also implied that staff were also willing to examine and face their own values and deep-rooted prejudices of caste and discrimination in order to create a container in which such work could be done.

The tools that the dalit networks had used for their struggles were primarily based on the self respect and political identity aspects of Ambedkarism. Marxian analysis of dialectic materialism, Christian theology and human rights perspectives were also added layers.

All these tools had a focus on the outside—the powerful external factors either inimical or benevolent that were linked to the emancipation of the dalits. If the caste system had demonised the dalits these tools did not help them to see how they had internalised this demonised self. Group relations helped them to turn this inside out—to look at these processes from within. To face the question—how and why have we swallowed these images of ourselves? How could this be pushed into us? Working with the concepts of projection, introjection and unconscious dynamics of the system they asked themselves: why can I not take the personal authority to not swallow?

Dr Ambedkar while relentless in fighting the caste system was perceptive enough to say that the phenomenon of brahminism could exist in all the castes including the untouchables, for that was the essence of casteism. But the enemy was externalised completely and dalits worked almost exclusively with the practise of fighting and blaming the dominant caste for their plight. The GRC offered the rather stark opportunity (If one was not too shocked by oneself) to face the residue of "dominant caste shit within oneself". This was rather dramatically exemplified in the Dappu—Learning Network 2003 conference when a member who had rather peremptorily in the opening plenary (coming in late and occupying defiantly the empty chair facing the conference directors) declared the conference to be a farce as the staff was corporate and brahminical. The same member a few days into the conference reported that he was struggling to face the Brahmin within. This was quite a revolutionary admittance from someone who headed a political movement based dalit network. He has subsequently attended a few more conferences and participated actively in them.

The notion of caste systemically and structurally denies the idea that the dalits should and could exercise personal authority. Its very definition and implementation for two millennia disallowed this. The group relations work challenged this concept in a clear and unequivocal manner—it seemed to the dalit members that here was an ally—a mainstream framework that understood dalit oppression and attacked its roots frontally.

The notion of learning from one's own experience itself is a power act of self validation particularly to the dalits who have been told that her/his experience is of no value. Further, the use of the idea and terminology of hypothesis rather that personal conviction or dogma came as a revelation and a great relief. (due to the process of having unfortunately iconised Ambedkar—even political ideology was often experienced or presented as dogma). The ability to hypothesise opened up spaces for working with experiences, rather than of proving loyalties to persons or ideologies.

It is important to understand why these series of interventions was so effective and impactful. They spoke to a community and spoke to their struggle. It was thus a powerful lever. Group relations framework was a mainstream idea that defended staunchly and actually gave a framework and language to the hitherto difficult to articulate struggle of the dalit at the collective psychological level—it was thus a powerful and liberating tool.

Like caste, patriarchy, colour, religious intolerance, and any other form of wide social discrimination, the struggle depends not only on individual change but on the ability of the oppressed to understand and leverage the struggle at the level of collective consciousness—change is possible only then. Any serious attempt at empowerment and transformation in society and in organizations would necessarily need to address the dynamics of privilege and disprivilege, access to justice, resources and opportunity, and the distribution and use of authority and power.

The transformation of any system poses threat to all its stakeholders and unless the conscious and unconscious resistances are surfaced and worked with transformation will at best slide back to status quo or even have the backlash of punishing those who dare to transform. Further, empowerment and transformation of society and organizations cannot happen unless individuals, who bring life to organizations, are willing to empower and transform themselves and become aware of their own unconscious resistance to such transformation. This will also imply working on individual and collective identities and what is held and sometimes imprisoned within these identities that may itself be a unacknowledged resistance to transformation. The Group Relations framework provides an opportunity to work on these issues, provided of course, we choose to take the steps towards this transformation.

## *Notes*

1. My friend and colleague Paul Divakar, currently Convenor National Campaign on Dalit Human Rights described to me the struggle and demand of the dalits in these moving terms.
2. The term dalit came into currency in the 1970 as a part of political struggles for assertion of their rights. Dalit—oppressed crushed people is a name that the untouchables have given themselves with pride as a political act of assertion.
3. Broken People: Caste violence against India's untouchables, Human Rights Watch, New York.

4. Caste and analogous systems of social hierarchy operate across the world, particularly in Asia and Africa, subjecting millions to inhuman treatment on the basis of being born into a certain caste or similar social group. Though the communities themselves may be indistinguishable in appearance from others, unlike with race or ethnicity, socio-economic disparities are glaring, as are the peculiar forms of discrimination practised against them. It is approximated that around 250–300 million people across the world suffer from caste, or work and descent based discrimination, a form of discrimination that impinges on their civil, political, religious, socio-economic and cultural rights, and their right to freedom of choice to develop as individuals and as a community with dignity. Common features seen in caste and analogous systems across the world include the following:

    - Physical segregation
    - Social segregation, including prohibition on inter-marriages between caste groups Assignment of traditional occupations, often being occupations associated with death or filth, coupled with restrictions on occupational mobility
    - Pervasive debt bondage due to poor remuneration for lower-caste occupations
    - High levels of illiteracy, poverty and landlessness as compared to so-called higher castes
    - Impunity for perpetrators of crimes against low-caste communities
    - Use of degrading language to describe low-caste communities, based on notions of purity and pollution, filth and cleanliness
    - Double or triple discrimination against and exploitation of women of low castes on the basis of sex, class and caste.

    Black paper National Campaign on Dalit Human Rights 2001.
5. The four fold system of organising society into varna—Brahman (priests), kshatriya (warriers), vysya (traders) and sudras (other work) which was occupation based stratification, later mutated into caste. Caste is determined by birth, is on a principle of graded purity—pollution and does not permit intermarriage. While the caste system is broadly organised in these 4 categories—the rules vary from geographical region to another and there are thousands of subcastes. I have not gone into the origins and the corruption of the system and a detailed account and related hypothesis can be read

in Chattopadhyay "Hierarchy Guilt and Projective Identification" Free Association 2006.

6. Black Paper: National Campaign on dalit Human rights 2001. www.dalits.org
7. My history being drawn into work on Dalit rights has its roots in personal experience of being a Kerala Christian woman marrying a Tamil Hindu Brahmin man. Vish and I met at management school and fell in love in 1984. Having been brought up in a rather liberal urban setting I was naïve about the consequences of an inter-religious—but more importantly—inter-caste marriage. The experience of being discriminated on these grounds by my in—laws was first of disbelief and shock and later bewilderment and anger. It took me many years to confront and challenge this issue in the family. This resulted in a rather painfully learnt lessons—about how deep rooted caste was within Indian society, how difficult it was to summon the personal authority to confront it, and that the personal was indeed political. It took me many more years to learn the necessity to access compassion and generosity while engaged in struggle—but that is another story! This intense personal experience of being discriminated on the basis of caste however led to my long term engagement and deep friendships with outstanding activists struggling for dalit rights in India.
8. I am not in anyway underrating the need and importance for the oppressor in turn to explore and examine the nature of his oppression (and his own victimhood in a sense). This paper focuses on the impact and links that group relations work had on the oppressed—and may in some ways unconsciously reflect the author's own bias towards working for and with the oppressed—in political and ideological terms—as a social justice issue.
9. Dr BR Ambedkar, 1891–1956 (called Babsaheb) is the undisputed and revered leader of the politically awakened dalits. Scholar, politician and constitutionalist, Dr Ambedkar, a dalit himself, is modern India towering symbol of protest against age old and yet contemporary forms of oppression and exploitation.
10. A majority of Christians in India are from lower—backward castes or dalits as religious conversion was the hope of escaping the social ostracism and stranglehold of caste. This however has mostly proved to be a chimera as the social norms were simply imported into Christianity, Islam and Sikhism. In that sense caste proved to be undefeated by the boundaries of religion, even if its origins were in Hinduism, and ironically belief in caste is one of the things that binds the highly diverse Indian society!

11. The NCDHR received the prestigious Norwegeien RAFTO prize in 2007 in recognition of its work and of the struggle to end discrimination and human rights violations against India's 167 million Dalits.
12. United Nations Convention on the Elimination of all forms of Racial Discrimination.
13. An earlier version of this model was presented by the author in the Gender and Authority workshop 13–16 August 2005, at Hyderabad. It has also been greatly influenced by the model of institutional change "What are we trying to change?" formulated by Aruna Rao and David Kelleher of Gender at Work in" ***Is there life after Gender mainstreaming?*** Gender and development Volume 13 No 2 July 2005.
14. Extract from the brochure describing the conference context:

    > Against the backdrop of a catch-all term globalization, is the evidence of many interconnected issues and struggles. Key among them is the iniquitous power relationships between developed and developing nations, the march of neocolonialism and the rule of corporations, the alarming rise of violence and armed conflict, and the unthinking destruction of the environment. Within our own country these have been compounded by shrinking democratic spaces, the edging out of the poor from the global marketplace, the growing rightist intolerance and religious fundamentalism. Embedded, or perhaps cementing this complex web of issues, is the system of social stratification based on both class and caste.

15. This paper owes its existence to experiences and reflections of many comrades in the struggle for dalit empowerment who have also engaged with the group relations framework for their learning and to take the struggle forward. The ideas here are also a result of numerous conversations over many years. I would like to specially and gratefully acknowledge Paul Divakar, Wilson Bezwada, Anuradha K, Annie Namala, Vincent Manohar, PL Mimroth Ruth Manorama, Vimal Thorat, Fr Aloysius, SK Thorat, Jhansi Geddam, Leslie Martin, SDJM Prasad, Suresh Lelle, Sabrina Francis, Anand, Sudhakar, Thomas Pallithanam, TD John, MC Raj and Jyothi Raj. My colleagues and friends in group relations work Gouranga Chattopadhya, Zahid Gangjee, Rina Tagore, Dipankar Banerjee, Paul Divakar, Anuradha Prasad, Annie Namala, Ganesh Anantharaman, Bhanumathy Vasudevan, Shelley Ostroff, Erika Stern, Alastair Bain Joy Mercy, Yawar Baig and K T Suresh as well as the courage

and generosity of my husband Vish and daughter Tanuja and our families have contributed a lot to my thinking on this issue.

16. When the group of senior dalit leaders in Dappu read Jean Reed's (then Hutton) (The Grubb Institute) paper on "Working with the concept of organization-in-the-mind" one of them exclaimed and said—this was written for us!
17. Dare to think the Unthought Known Ed Ajeet Mathur Aivoairut Oy 2006.
18. GRC in India are mostly sponsored by the premier institutions such as the Institute of Management in Calcutta and corporate sponsorships and was seen as an elite or privileged learning space. One of the challenges continues to be to make this learning available within the reach of people from a wide range of sectors in terms of the fees and the language in which conferences are offered.

# SECTION IV

## POST CONFERENCE REFLECTIONS

This is a particularly unique section which reflects the heart of the Group Relations thinking, namely the capacity to learn through experience. Each of the four chapters in this section deals with the experience of the narrators during the conference events themselves, drawing new insights from these experiences.

The first in this section, by Zachary Gabriel Green and Nick Papadopoulos, reflects on an action they took during an intense moment in the exploratory event. The two writers offer a fascinating analysis of their 'walk out', creatively interweaving psychoanalytic, leadership and culture theories with a powerful introspection of their personal-yet-not-private action.

The second chapter, by Gerard van Reekum and Doris Gottlieb, also takes as the focus for their reflections the exploratory event, with a key question around understanding—or rather confusion—of its purpose and particularly the way it was managed. van Reekum and Gottlieb reflect on their experience of the unexpected design of this event and bring out interesting associations to it from existential and familial points of view.

The third reflective piece in this section is by Ellen L. Short and Jeanne M.S.T. Woon. These authors focus on their experience of crossing the multiple boundaries, both tangible, such as a geographical transition, and intangible, such as the meaning underlying the geographical transition (e.g., identity, citizenship and so on) into the Belgirate conference. Considering themselves as 'inexperienced', they discover as the conference unfolds that they are in-experience and that in that place everyone can learn, grow and teach others.

In the final chapter Gordon Strauss compares his experience of the first Belgirate conference to this second one. Being in Belgirate for the second time, Strauss notes feeling more authorized and purposeful, but although clear on what he wanted to get out of the conference he left realizing yet again that learning from and through experience is a never ending task.

CHAPTER ELEVEN

# A walk out before mourning dawn: Reflections on innovations and adaptations at the boundary

*Zachary Gabriel Green and Nick Papadopoulos*

> *All true things must change, and only that which changes remains true. Everything ages and needs transformation and renewal.*
>
> C.G. Jung

## *Into the abyss: A walk out in slow motion*

*Walk out—an act of civil disobedience aimed at challenging a given social order, a method of fighting the status quo*

*Walk-out—an unconscious form of acting out whereby groups or individuals take flight from situations or circumstances subjectively experienced as anxiety provoking*

*Walk-out—a calculated act of defiance by an individual or collective with the express objective of defying the moral authority of a powerful force often viewed as oppressive*

*Walk-out—a conscious path of liberation whereby parties seek to create and transform familiar forms of discourse through making permeable the boundaries of interaction*

One classic interpretation of people walking out of any kind of experience is that they are expressing a form of public protest. Through action rather than words, they make their presence known by becoming absent. We were not the first to walk out. We were not the second to walk out. With so few minutes remaining in the closing Exploratory Event plenary, in many ways it would have been easier simply to remain until the end of the session. Yet something began to rise in the Exploring Absence group. One of our number began to speak to members of our group while yet another of the ineffectual voices from another group tried in vain to capture the attention, farbeit the imagination, of the membership. Though challenged for this "norm" violating behavior, he continued to speak with growing intensity and volume, insisting that something needed to be done. Moments later one of our few female members spoke with passion and tears about the shadow side of group relations life; the threats, attack and violence that too often characterized our conferences and our work with each other. By this time the three of us were just standing there erect in the midst of it all, poised for some action but still immobile and impotent. In this moment we appeared to be a human shield for our female colleague, though she did not seem on any level to seek or require our protection. Then one of us said, "Let's go." First checking to see whether there were objections within our ranks or further numbers who sought to join in the defection, we once more turned to each other and began what seemed like a slow motion stroll across the length of the room. The movement began with no option of return.

Met with cries from our colleagues of, "At least say why you're going..." and "No matter what kind of conference, there is always the attack on management," we continued our silent quest for what would be revealed by our exit—and absence. We opened the door. We crossed the boundary. We walked out. We looked again to each other anew. What could be learned by what we had done?

Our first and prevailing paranoid fantasy came nearly as soon as the door closed behind us. *Clearly we acted out and were now to be outcasts for the remainder of the Belgirate II event. Unwilling to express the unconscious processes coursing through us or incapable of managing the anxiety within us, our collective valence invited only one option—flight.* Initially comfortable with these facile and rudimentary interpretations, we remained content to allow it to rule the moment for the moment. Just as quickly, more began to dawn on us as we simply took the time to look at each other and what we might represent. Many things were obvious. We were all within the same half decade in age. We were black and white. We spanned four continents and five countries in residence. Our group relations experience ranged from marginal to central in our respective national contexts. We received projections and were in reality a spectrum of sexual orientation. Of all of these, the most noteworthy discovery was that we had each recently moved to a new country within months of the conference. In short, we were intimately familiar with the challenges, perils, and experience of crossing new boundaries to make our way in the world.

As the session ended and a select few ventured towards us to voice their queries, objections and curiosities about our departure, we offered our working hypothesis about the experience. *It seemed that the system had selected a set of recent emigres with a range of group relations experience to challenge the authority of the management and perhaps express some dissatisfaction about the absence of leadership demonstrated to support the learning and facilitate mutual exploration in the event.* This formulation seemed sufficiently robust for the duration of the conference but did not hold for us.

## A working hypothesis: More than an attack

After numerous iterations, our final hypothesis became a realization that *our walk out was primarily an attack on the person of the named director of the Leicester conference, Eliat Aram. On a manifest level as a young, Jewish, Israeli woman who was appointed, and perceived as anointed, to lead the conference, our trio stood as a counterpart of her representation. We were men of the middle generation, coming from all the places where she did not, who had been "skipped over" for a director who had not yet seen her 40th birthday. Despite proclamations to the contrary where the network had claimed authority for group relations work at Belgirate I, the behavior evidenced by the walk out continued to suggest that the authority for group relations work remained with the Tavistock Group Relations Program and, symbolically, in the person of the Leicester director. We were chosen to launch the attack, ironically because we were relatively safe repositories for the unconscious, unexpressed primitive rage at the appointment of this particular director—a young Jewish immigrant in Europe, an unwelcome and certainly illegitimate interloper into a privileged place others had worked for years to earn. As younger and more polymorphous men of this "skipped" middle age, more likely to be allies with the new director, our attack would not be seen to be as brutal as that of older men who had already earlier questioned whether women could indeed be conference directors. We also served as a convenient mask for the fury of the women directors, with whom our group allied in the Exploratory Event. Surely any one of them would have been a more suitable choice than the Chosen One. When their most senior woman walked out, it was not seen as an attack, but a personal choice by a seasoned director. Similarly when she was proceeded by the previous director of the Leicester conference on account of illness, only concern for his well-being could be observed and expressed, not the symbolic meaning of his abandonment of his chosen successor.*

We were the fellow émigrés, willing foils to hold projections that could not and were not made available at any time in any public forum at Belgirate II. The collective mourning was for the lost opportunity that now could not be realized. Death had come so soon and without notice while so many believed themselves to be alive. The last gasp came as an attack before dawn. It failed to stop the new day.

## A conference dream: Sacrifice at dawn

Our confirmation about this hypothesis came in the form a "conference dream" that came shortly after Belgirate. It helped illuminate and clarify our thinking:

*I had not remembered any of my dreams during the conference .... This one felt vivid [and] a little frightening... I was part of an isolated group of people wandering. It felt like we were walking through the desert (already a Jewish theme—though I am not Jewish there was some confusion during the conference as to my religion). In the dream we as a people had transgressed some unwritten law or code that called for a human sacrifice to have this sin forgiven. After much wrangling among the group, a young woman was chosen who had known more than one culture. With this choice the group it seemed felt a tremendous sense of relief, though I remember feeling dismayed that we had to in fact have a sacrifice. The sacrifice was going to take place at sunset, which was fast approaching. I remember pleading, "This is too soon! Isn't there something else we can do instead?" I was getting drowned out despite all my efforts, but I also felt a sense of relief that it wasn't me that was going to be sacrificed.*

Our associations to this dream are linked to our hypothesis and one meaning that can be attached to the session from which we walked out. The young woman being sacrificed was Eliat Aram, the then future director of the next Leicester conference. When Mannie Sher and Rose Miller, the elders, walked out it symbolically left the "middle generations" to wrangle among themselves while preserving the place of other seniors who were not truly parties to this succession drama in the "desert." Eliat represented the by-passing of this middle generation. The transgression was in how leadership in the group relations world got passed on from the elders to the grandchildren, creating a murderous rage among those passed over. The oppressive aridity of how the collective group functioned in the closing plenary of the Exploratory Event was an effort to act at "sunset" before there was any chance of "dawn." In other words, if Eliat's leadership could be effectively killed off at Belgirate, if she could be made a sacrifice at this sunset for so many of the middle generation, then there would be no need to face the envy in the emergence of her ascension into a symbolic and real seat of leadership in the group relations world.

In this respect, our walk out represented both the middle generation who "should" have assumed leadership and the "younger" "envious" ones who were overlooked. We offered ourselves and were used to represent alternative leaders from the two generations, enacting and carrying the envy, jealousy, rage, and rivalry that were disowned. Perhaps most curious and paradoxical of all, the walk out served as an alternative form of sacrifice. With our exit as willing scapegoats, the action for which the dream screamed came to be. The unconscious need to sacrifice the anointed one at this sunset was not revealed. Dawn was free to rise … .

## *Stumbling anew: Creative destruction and destructive creation*

In no way do these associations suggest that the action to walk out was any less an "attack." Yet it does make more evident that the one we sought to protect may not have been the young woman in our group as much as it was the one who the group relations world secretly sought to sacrifice without conscious examination of its own wish to do so. Indeed the subtlety of the attack was rather profound. Given the walk out at three points in this one plenary, a trinity of sorts became revealed. This particularly Christian imagery in the face of a Jewish leader is quite complex. At one level it can be seen as yet another denigration of the successor at Leicester. More precisely, it can be seen as the classic messianic wish that comes through a pairing dynamic. The departure of the pair of elders made evident the need of the Belgirate membership to find its Messiah. The walk out of the Trinity of men (though two have names associated with the birth or life of the Messiah) can likely be viewed as marking and obscuring the annunciation.

This trinity of departures also represented three generations of Group Relations—the elder, middle and new. In this trinity was also likely a tension between broadly three approaches to group relations work: one that embraced and cherished the framework in its traditional form, another that valued this more traditional way of work and sought ways to move deeper within this known frame, and perhaps a third way that sharply challenged the more traditional ways and engaged in active forms of breaking the frame to make room for innovation and greater access of the thinking by new populations. At Belgirate II, none of these ways prevailed, yet the unspoken anxiety may have been that with the presence of the new leadership of Leicester the third way now revealed itself and had, indeed, already arrived.

## *Theory into action*

In the context of an experience that had "innovation" as an explicit theme and focus, our actions both conformed with and challenged prevailing theory. In particular, it is commonplace in organizational development literature that a distinction is made between transformational and transactional change. Transactional change refers to change happening within an existing paradigm or framework whereas transformational change involves changes to the existing paradigm, often with another emerging paradigm supplanting and eventually replacing one that had previously prevailed (Porras & Silvers 1991; Burke & Litwin, 1992; Weick & Quinn, 1999). Similarly, innovation and adaptation are viewed as distinct constructs. Innovation treats the existing paradigm as part of the "problem" while adaptation involves working within the confines or boundary of the known paradigm. It also highlights the importance of "destructive creation" and "creative destruction," not as a duality but as different points in a process in the tension between innovative and transformational potential (Kirton, 1992; Hung, 2004). In this respect, authentic innovation involves assaults on the boundary of what is known and familiar. As such a walkout operates at the edge of two seeming contradictions: the transformational potential of destruction/creation *and* an iconoclasm within the boundedness and boundaries of institutional support. The action marks the space and highlights the tension that requires resolution.

From a systems psychodynamic perspective, development and change essentially occur at the boundaries. It is the location where the issues arise and the solutions are sought. These boundaries include task, role and authority boundaries as well as time, territory and external boundaries (Miller, 1990; Green & Molenkamp, 2005). The tension within group relations consultation is when and how to interpret incidents or challenges to boundaries as "destructive" attacks and a form of acting-out while holding onto the possibility that the same behaviour could well represent some form of "creative" expression. In dealing with such a dilemma, a consultation needs to acknowledge that a paradox may be present (Smith and Berg, 1995). By focusing only the 'destructive' component and not the paradox, consultations may stifle the transformational potential of creative-destructive 'boundary' incidents and thereby innovation from potentially taking shape.

More to the point, innovation does not occur in a vacuum. It requires leadership and the harnessing of institutional support to challenge the prevailing culture and status quo.

Schein (2004) contends that culture and leadership are two sides of the same coin. His basic argument is that formal and informal leadership play a critical role in innovation.

As such cultures begin with leaders who impose their own values and assumptions on the group. If that group is successful and the assumptions come to be taken for granted, that culture defines for later generations what kind of leadership is acceptable. When the group runs into adaptive difficulties whereby its environment changes, assumptions are no longer valid, and innovation is required, leadership comes into play again. In this scenario, the role of leadership is marked by the ability to step outside a culture that was previously adaptive to begin a process of evolutionary change in order for the culture to survive. The challenge to the underlying assumptions and beliefs that guide the culture become the essence of leadership, which will be experienced as destructive to the way the culture has been known by its own members. The work of leadership also must evolve to understand and manage culture as it absorbs the changes that determine its transformational potential. The ultimate act of leadership is to destroy the culture when it is viewed as dysfunctional (Schein, 2004).

When applied to the group relations world, adaptation at the boundaries requires options beyond that of ultimately destroying the actual container. While Belgirate II was itself well subscribed with a staggering majority of the participants in the 50–70 year old range, much was made of the declining enrollments in conferences offered by nearly every organization represented. One interpretation is that reduction in conference memberships and the lack of younger people at Belgirate II suggests a crisis in the ability of the group relations world to adapt and remain relevant to a rapidly changing external environment. As such there is the risk of group relations work being conserved and preserved as a cherished oddity of an older generation, a kind of fundamentalist altar for its true believers rather than a relevant and powerful learning modality in the world.

As such the walk out became a form of "acting out" when a more traditional psychoanalytic interpretation is offered. The trio of departing men could be seen as representing the third way, breaking the frame to see what else may emerge. An alternative way of seeing the same action is that of "acting-in," borrowing a perspective from other contemporary psychological models. As "acting in" the trio could then be seen as taking on the projections of the group, semi-consciously, in service of learning and new insight. In this way of thinking the "attack" was on traditional approaches, insights, interpretations, and approaches within group relations that can be viewed as having their own orthodoxy—or perhaps fundamentalism. The challenge of Belgirate II in particular was the presence and tension of remaining within known, familiar frameworks and territories of group relations work while being invited to engage and present innovations that define and challenge existing boundaries.

## *The (un)ease of boundary adaptation*

While the interpretations offered about the walk out highlight the importance of understanding action in multiple ways, more can still be seen. Beyond "acting out," the declaration where many group relations consultations would essentially end, there is something about the action of crossing a boundary that creates and invites the beginning of new learning. When anything other than being held in a prescribed way occurs, there is a change in the boundary—a boundary adaptation. In this respect, the walk out represents a boundary adaptation that reveals unexpressed and unconscious elements of a current moment that can be understood in multiple ways. These boundary adaptations are described here as *extrusion, expansion, and expression.*

### Extrusion

There is initial relief in the system at the elimination of those elements represented by what is extruded. Such extrusion allows the system to work in new and different ways. Implicit in extrusion is the experience within the system, real, imagined, or projected, of there being toxicity that can no longer be contained for the system to function. The toxicity is experienced as a form of anxiety that grows uncontrollably in texture, growing and spreading, not unlike a potential lethal malignancy. In an effort to preserve itself, the system seeks out the location(s) of the toxicity, unconsciously projecting into these places until "it" can be extruded. Not unlike in biological models of vulnerability to disease, those members of the system with the most resonant representative valence to carry the toxicity can be used to export it. Their extrusion allows the system the fantasy that it has preserved itself. More accurately the processes used to extrude paradoxically reveal the underlying, unmetabolized vulnerability within the whole system (May be akin to fight-flight).

*The walk out team as alternative "gay men" could also represent another minority group mobilized by the group to make an attack on the "elevated" youth—taking the heat away from the overlooked middle generation. The large group therefore locating its disowned feelings of envy into a minority group like the Jews.*

### Expansion

The purpose of the walkout can be seen as more than "breaking" the boundary, but also an adaptation where there is expansion of the boundary of possible work and action. In this thinking the boundary indeed includes both the open space beyond and the tension between the internal world that is being departed and the external world that is being approached. The boundary adaptation of expansion begins with an initial phase of exploration. As the central metaphor for this process, again those with a valence of going beyond the known are selected by the system to venture into the unknown. Though much of the anxiety of extrusion may also by present in this adaptation, as well as much of the experience of life-and-death peril, the difference is in the hope for the return. As such rapprochement is implied and desired by the system.

The "explorers" in the quest for expansion carry with them the hope that a boundary beyond the confines containing the current system can be discovered and inhabited by the larger system. With our return to the system in some form in other events, the system gains the benefit of what is learned through our exploration of absence.

In the Belgirate context, the boundary expansion adaptation was aided when earlier two noted elders walked out. Given that they were male and female, white and black, representing Britain and the United States, Tavistock and A.K. Rice Institute—their absence was accepted, if not encouraged. With them also went the "black and white" clarity of the boundary along recognizable and tolerable dualities. They marked the known boundary. Our walk out, opened by their departure, launched the exploration and the promise of expansion towards a boundary beyond the known and familiar (May be akin to pairing).

### *Expression*

We can also think of the walk out as a form of "acting in," representing through our action some alternative expression of unexpressed dynamics in the system. We were the action of those who could not fully voice their wish/desire to do something quite different with the direction of the work. Perhaps best understood as a blend of the extrusion and expansion boundary adaptations, expression is the holding of the tension of what is within and beyond the known boundary. Like leadership on behalf of a system, expression represents voices of the system, speaking for the voiceless in visible, demonstrable, and potentially disturbing ways to this same system. In the Belgirate context, the expression adaptation is needed to face the fundamental tension between the richness and limits of the group relations tradition and the liabilities and promises of innovating it.

The walk out team could be seen as having introjected and carried the projected anger of the women onto the men, holding and expressing on their behalf the outrage as being "less than" as directors. We may have also represented those other men, younger, gay, black, middle generation, living on the "edge of cultures"—not seen and "sacrificed" in place of the young, female Chosen One. More simply, could we have also been an expression of innovation, a counterpoint walking out in protest to the deep psychodynamically driven discourse that continued to dominate the public forums (May be akin to dependency).

The three who "walked" were all members of the Exploring Absence group, and the group they had the most connection with during the event were the women directors. The three all represented alternatives to traditional male role models (and perhaps also traditional male GR role models). Of the three one was gay (and black) and the other two could be seen as androgynous, with all three in some way representing alternative models or perceptions of maleness. To what extent were these three representing an alternative to the maleness offered by two of the keynote speakers who could be seen as representing both a provocative and charismatic way of "directing" or of "being present"—and therefore what is it that is "absent"?

## *Leadership: Exploring absence and boundary adaptation*

The type of leadership taken by the two collaborators also differed significantly in terms of boundary adaptation. The more experienced (and significantly much staffed) collaborator took up leadership as mainly a representative of his sub-group attempting to bridge and create relationships between the different sub-groups, often in the expansion form. In contrast the less experienced one (who could be seen as part of the younger generation) took up leadership within the sub-group, creating room for alternative expression to emerge and become explored as part of the group's work. Was he only allowed to take up leadership because he was both younger and inexperienced within such an experienced group of mainly men (adding weight to the unexplored envy and uneasy relations between the sexes and generations hypothesis in group relations)? Yet the Exploring Absence group experienced a walk out of its own. Interestingly when he (the less experienced collaborator) took up leadership, two younger and less experienced members (not unlike himself) left the group, perhaps representing a parallel process with the larger system on issues of age and succession. A further irony is that the third member of our walk out team, absent as an author of this paper, may continue to represent the extrusion adaptation and, thereby, perhaps what group relations remains unable to own and contain as its own.

In combination, the boundary adaptations represented by our walk out allowed the use of "absence," its exploration and its expulsion, to provide a paradoxical container for the unconsciously extruded, largely unexpressed and seemingly intractable rivalries within the group relations world. If understood, the irony is that the walk out may contain within the boundary adaptation the potential for new expansion in the boundary of group relations work.

### *Classic acting out*

It would be an error to suggest that the walk out in no way represented classic acting out. No doubt our action also represented the collective inability of our triad to contain within ourselves and within the boundary of the event some element of the anxiety of the situation. Rather than find the words (at the time) to express what we were experiencing, the key to taking up creative leadership and helping the group work through the issues, we took a more regressive stance, literally and metaphorically, and walked out. This sort of preverbal response could be seen as an attack on authority. In particular we made an attack on the leadership or rather the lack of leadership that was being taken up by the "management" group. In this respect the acting out was an attempt to "speak to" the dysfunction in a group in a way that could be seen if not "heard" per se. In this closing plenary of the Exploratory Event, we hold that those in designated roles needed to demonstrate effective leadership. Instead what management modelled was traditional writ narrow, restrictive and constraining role boundaries, absent adaptation or innovation. Whether they defined these roles for themselves or had these roles defined for them by the system, the event mandated some form of adaptation that went beyond the known and familiar parameters. In our language, a boundary expansion adaptation, in particular was needed, which may have also offered the possibility for different expression to emerge. As such the dynamic could be named and thereby and contained. We acted out. We walked out. Classic dependency revealed. Enough said.

## *Implications for innovation and transformation*

Our action, while easily understood and restrictively interpreted as "acting out" was likely much more. Ours was an attempt to make a potent statement in a microcosm of the rapidly changing group relations world. Perhaps it could have been made another way. Yet at Belgirate II, only one person was under 40—the future director of Leicester. A handful were in their 40's and the greater majority were in their 50's and 60's. There was a fundamental tension between those who wanted to go deeper with the existing "traditional" model to discover the new boundaries within the frame and those (perhaps represented by us) who acted to move outside the boundary and find those "innovative" elements that could possibly be integrated.

Our effort here has been to suggest that there are multiple, concurrent ways of interpreting a given action. What may have been revealed by the walkout is the potential for the expansion of boundary in group relations work beyond rigidly held tradition and "reckless" innovation. We would prefer to think the tension between envy and attraction, competition and collaboration, destruction and generativity, antipathy and desire, not so much as polarities but as points along a continuum of creativity, are now available for study more globally among us.

Despite the feeling at the time, the formulations about boundary adaptation outlined in this paper on extrusion, expansion and expression may be helpful in highlighting the overall strength of the meeting. It is our premise that an ongoing, fuller exploration of these themes may well illuminate how the boundary of group relations is being adapted and expanded for the next generation of our collective work. The fact that all of this could be held is a testimony to how all of us were seeking to discover a new way to be together and keep the work we cherish evolving into the future.

## *References*


Burke, W.W. & Litwin, G.H. (1992). A causal model of organizational performance and change. *Journal of Management, 18*(3): 523–545.

Green, Z. & Molenkamp, R. (2005). The BART System of Group and Organizational Analysis. Boundary, Authority, Role and Task. http://www.academy.umd.edu/tle/BART/

Hung, S-C. (2004). Explaining the process of innovation: The dynamic reconciliation of action and structure. *Human Relations, 57*(11).

Kirkton, M. (1992). Adaptors and innovators: Problem-solvers in organizations. In: Gryskiewcz, S. & Hills, D. (Eds.), *Readings in Innovation*, Greensborough, North Carolina: Centre for Creative Leadership, 45–66.

Miller, E.J. (1990). Experiential Learning in Groups I. In: Trist, E. and Murray, H. (1990). *The Social Engagement of Social Science* Vol. *1*. Free Association Books, London.

Miller, E.J. (1990b). *Experiential Learning in Groups II*. In: Trist, E. and Murray, H. op.cit.

Porras, J.I. & Silvers, R.C. (1991). Organization development and transformation. *Annual Review of Psychology, 42*: 51–78.

Schein, E. (2004). *Organizational Culture and Leadership (3rd ed)*. John Wiley, San Francisco.

Smith, K. & Berg, D. (1995). Paradox and groups. In: Gillette, J. & McCollom, M. (Eds.), *Groups in context: A New Perspective on Group Dynamics*. Lanham, MD: University Press of America.

Weick, K.E. & Quinn, R.E. (1999). Organisational change and development. *Annual Review of Psychology. 50*: 361–386.

CHAPTER TWELVE

# Is group relations a good regulator? *Ritualization as a basic assumption mentality*

*Gerard van Reekum and Doris Gottlieb*

> *"I am no lover of disorder and doubt as such. Rather do I fear to lose truth by this pretension to possess it already wholly."*
>
> (William James, 1902)

In this chapter we work towards a hypothesis about how Group Relations conferences may help or challenge people to relate to something that is really new. For this purpose we focus on one series of events in the Belgirate II conference, the Exploratory Event. We consider this event as a fractal of the conference, like an Institutional Event is to represent the dynamics in the whole of a Group Relations conference. Therefore, this chapter deals with key concepts in systems theory: isomorphism and the Good Regulator theorem.

> The idea of isomorphism is that whole systems consist of subsystems with similar or even identical characteristics and properties of shape, structure and/or form. One of the founders of systems theory, Ludwig von Bertalanffy, introduced isomorphism as a strategy to accelerate the advance of science (1951). He proposed that different fields could be brought together in a unified science based on isomorphism of laws in disparate

> disciplines. This approach of mediating similarities and differences was taken up in cybernetics to analyze and regulate complex systems. Conant & Ashby (1970) coined the Good Regulator theorem that states, "Every Good Regulator of a system must be a model of that system".

Correspondingly, the Institutional Event in a Group Relations conference is designed in such a way that all elements and aspects of the conference as a whole may become discernable within the event. In the same spirit, the Belgirate conferences can be thought of as events that are designed in order to allow all elements and aspects of the Group Relations community or field to become discernable. Within the Belgirate II conference, the Exploratory Event may offer the same functionality, and perhaps its concluding plenary is a concentration of all that.

### *Adaptation and innovation*

The task for the exploratory event was

> "to explore conscious and unconscious forces and meanings underlying this conference and its themes: adaptations, innovations, theory, design and role-taking. The event will begin in plenary and, after five sessions, will conclude in plenary. The event will be managed by the Management and Administrative Teams of the conference" (2006).

Exploring innovations and adaptations together creates an interesting duality.

- *Adaptation* implies a further incorporation into something that already exists. One adapts to his or her environment, or situation; the process is internal, the environment is a given. Adaptations can change one's relation to the environment but in essence the environment drives the process. Organisms that fail to adapt will either have to move to another environment or face extermination.
- *Innovation* on the other hand refers to an altogether different process. This can be seen in the words that describe and define it, such as revolution, upheaval, new measures, breakthrough.

> In addition it is often related to changes that come about as a result of one thinking about something (undated).

The fact that the designers offered an event that bears so much resemblance to and therefore invites such strong associations with the Institutional Event in a conventional Group Relations conference format, poses a real challenge to the participants to either go along with this familiar image or actively do away with it—especially in a conference that aspires to explore adaptation and innovation simultaneously.

> At the plenary beginning of the Exploratory Event, people began to name the themes they wanted to explore and then subsystems began to emerge. The theme we were drawn to, and contributed to formulating, related to exploring absences in the conference. A conscious reason why we felt related to this theme was the absence of Erika Stern, our colleague and mentor who had planned to be present but was unfortunately unable to travel.
>
> Upon arriving in what would become our workroom for the rest of the Event we found ourselves with various people to whom the theme appealed in one way or another. As it turned out, many of us were members of IFSI, which as an institution was absent from the conference out of protest; hence very much present through its absence.
>
> The theme was also explored in a linguistic sense. The conference was held in one language, English, which sometimes made it difficult to grasp and express the contexts of non-native English speakers. The more so since a considerable number of members in our subsystem were nationals of one country and residing in another, including several Americans living in The Netherlands, a Greek Australian returning to his country of origin, an Italian living in the United States, and an Italian resident of Italy who expressed feeling in the conference as if he were abroad. All these voices were indicating an absence from one's own land made even clearer due to their presence in another.

## *Absence and representation*

When we consider the Belgirate II conference as isomorph with the Group Relations field and community, then the theme of our subsystem becomes significant for adaptation and innovation in that world. Looking at 'absence' and 'representation' as extremes of a linear continuum, the absence of a person or institution is a simple loss. He or she is not there, that's it. In the Exploratory Event, however, it became clear that it is possible for some person or institution to be extremely present in or even through absence. For understanding the state of the system in the conference, exploring such 'absent presence' or 'present absence' is just another way of looking at 'representation'. Thus it bears to mention some of the meaningful absences.

First there was the absence of two people, Rosemary Viswanath and Erika Stern, who were announced as presenters of parallel sessions. The mention of their names in the brochure now indicated that a series of thoughts could only make themselves present in the absence of their thinkers. In other words: the absence of these presenters did not mean that their thinking was not represented in and through the minds of those who were there.

> Rosemary Viswanath's paper, "Identity, Leadership and Authority: Experiences in Application of Group Relations Concepts for Dalit Empowerment in India," was read by one of the members of the Management Team. As such, in a literal though symbolic sense, these thoughts were made known and engaged with. There were people at Belgirate who, through their contact and work with the author in other contexts, marked their presence. And quite a few of them were in our subsystem of the Exploratory Event.
>
> The title of Erika Stern's presentation "Inviting the Unexpected" reflected the negotiations that preceded her acceptance of the invitation. Due to unforeseen circumstances, the planned presentation never took place. Yet this theme and its intended presenter were very much present in our subsystem, as we assume they were elsewhere in the conference.
>
> It is interesting to note that both absent presenters were also the only people who in the brochure identified themselves explicitly as being related to IFSI.

So secondly, when we look at institutional representation, we must also be aware that part of what is at stake is the political interest of institutions that contain and delimit their own spiritual beliefs and emotional experiences. Every conference is necessarily a joint effort, an organized collaboration of people who are usually associated with more than one institution. These institutions are then represented through their involvement in the temporary institution of the conference. The aforementioned political interests are expressed through the behaviour of the people deployed, including the consequences of restraints that limit their freedom.

In a Group Relations conference, typically the Institutional Event provides the proper context for exploring such political interests in conjunction with emotional experiences and spiritual beliefs. So it wasn't surprising that in Belgirate these elements came to the centre of attention during the Exploratory Event. One example of at least the political and psychological dimensions is the tenacity with which the absence of IFSI from the Belgirate conferences became subjected to exploration.

> Part of the history is that there actually *was* an IFSI meeting where it was agreed to not participate in the Belgirate conference, and keep each other informed should one decide otherwise. The justification for this organized boycott was the sponsors' decision that an IFSI representative was only to address a subsection of the membership, not the whole conference.
>
> The subsequent absence of IFSI was persistently discussed in our subsystem of the Exploratory Event, to such an extent that finally a member expressed annoyance and tried to put an end to it, admitting, "I'm disappointed, but actually also glad they're not here."
>
> Yet the absence of IFSI was a mere fantasy. At least one of the members of the MATs was known to have affiliations with IFSI. Two presenters had identified themselves in the brochure as being related to IFSI, one even as a member of IFSI's governance structure. Furthermore, over time it became clear that a distinct majority of the conference participants with associations to IFSI (institutionally and through involvement in IFSI-sponsored conferences, also in staff roles) were actually *in* our subsystem of the Exploratory Event.

Finally, the Exploratory Event offered various physical enactments of absence and representation as well. The following vignette describes another example of that.

> During a session somewhere halfway through the event, a female member excused herself and left the room, silently indicating it would only be temporary. Yet she didn't return.
>
> A visitor from another subsystem made us realize that her purse was still occupying what had been her chair, when he asked whether that seat was taken. This particular chair was right next to one of the Israeli members of our subsystem. The purse's design—an elegant little backpack—added a threatening quality to what her absence might represent.
>
> This reminded us of a rumour that the owner of the purse might well be a 'party crasher', meaning she had not held any staff role in a Group Relations conference and therefore didn't meet this criterion for membership. When a while later the purse was delivered back to her with an explanation of the circumstances under which it was found, her response remained limited to a polite 'thank you'. This seemed to confirm the rumour and fuelled an exciting exploration.

This episode of the illegal immigrant and her dropping out of our subsystem might well have been an enactment of how the Group Relations community deals with those who don't belong to the in-group. Frankly, we were inclined to pass judgment on this member for not knowing the ropes—our ropes, so primarily from an adaptation point of view. Such a judgemental frame of mind prohibits any other thinking about our field than as a given and undisputed territory, independent from the successfulness of its members' claims. We tend to overlook how integration of immigrants, legal or not, might be indispensable for discovering new and as yet unfathomable ways of thinking. Without such alien import, how could we even begin to bring about the innovation that is needed to support survival of the system as a whole?

The previous vignette exemplifies how the concepts we use to think are also structured by the way our bodies function in the world (Lakoff & Johnson, 1999). The body is a bridge between behaviour and belief, and that bridge is a dual carriageway. With our bodies we perform social acts. We move them into and out of groups, we use them to greet, fight, work, court, and so on. All these social behaviours express certain beliefs; every social act contains some symbolism that refers to such beliefs. For example: applause can be a single person's simulation of a handshake, a ritual that symbolizes embrace. But this meaning gets easily lost, especially in social settings where specific social acts become 'normal' over time. The meaning of a particular behaviour can then go under the radar of conscious exploration and may become experienced as if it were meaningless or has become something else. Such ritualization complicates emotional experience and implies overcoding of actions and behaviours, i.e., discharging a surplus of meaning or values. This surplus then becomes an attractor that draws attention away from exploring other topics in the here & now (Bell, 1992). Ritualization allows us to stop thinking and to create an illusory sense of similarity in experience and perception, excused from reality testing or even interpretation. By providing a set of repeatable behaviours, it allows people to get lost in the minutiae of getting the ritual form or understanding 'right' instead of searching for a plurality of meaning. In that sense, ritualization functions as a defense against exploration of what is really new. For example, in the episode of the member who left our subsystem and didn't return to secure her personal belongings, we were quick to stifle our not-understanding under the blanket of familiar interpretations like terrorist attack, illegal immigrant, etc.

### *Exploration and ritualization*

During the Institutional Event in a Group Relations conference, engagement between groups or subsystems with each other and with the management is essential for exploring what David Armstrong coined "*in*-actment rather than just *en*-actment" (2000) in the mind, "a response to something elicited *by* the organizational field and not simply *on* it" (2005). To achieve this, specific forms of communication in the Institutional Event emerged over the course of the years and have become common practice, including certain procedural characteristics. During the Exploratory Event in Belgirate II, we found evidence that such practices harbour a risk to ritualize engagement and replace sincere exploration.

> A rather dramatic example of such ritualization of engagement was encountered when our subsystem dispatched 'envoys'. As usual, transgressing the boundaries around subsystems provoked a bit of turbulence here and there, yet in one case the turmoil was of a special nature. It happened when one of us went into the room where a subsystem resided that identified itself as the female directors. This subsystem had embraced a way of operating that prevented anyone from speaking to its members unless some obscure procedure was completed. For this purpose, we were 'welcomed' by an official who said she would only talk to us off-territory and could "but take a message" on behalf of her subsystem. Clearly, this way of working was an attempt to reduce engagement to a ritual, masked like the conventional monitoring of boundaries in the management room of an IE. Our envoy refused to go along with this overcoding of the situation, not saying he rejected the command to leave the room but simply continuing to transmit the information he had come to deliver. Within a few seconds, most of the female directors found themselves shouting at the top of their voices—seemingly to drown out our envoy's words, but a closer look at the yelling revealed they were actually trying to overrule each other's instructions. The considerable effort it took our envoy to stand his ground, still resounded in his voice when he eventually was listened to.

We think this vignette illustrates that there was confusion as to whether the Exploratory Event was an opportunity to explore the Belgirate II Conference or a demonstration of isomorphism with the Institutional Event in a regular Group Relations conference. Caused by the turmoil over our envoy's lack of compliance with the proposed ritual, the internal confusion of this subsystem became fully exposed. Hence, it showed that at least one effect (and perhaps function) of ritualization in this case was to keep the subsystem's internal differentiation covered up. Now we should take into account that this subsystem of female directors was one of the earliest to form at the beginning of the Exploratory Event, a success that perhaps reflected its consistency in theme and membership. On the other hand, not all females who had held directorial roles in Group Relations conferences were taking part in this subsystem. So perhaps another way of looking at this subsystem was to understand it as the organization of envy over the Tavistock Institute's recent decision to authorize a relative newcomer on its payroll to direct the next Leicester conference: a young female who was also present in Belgirate, in role as member of the Management Team. This could explain how and why the subsystem of female directors had installed a ritualized version of IE-like boundary management, as a way to fix management in the Belgirate II conference.

In reality the Management and Administrative Teams were carefully trying *not* to overcode and ritualize the situation. There were clear indications that the MATs aspired to create a unique event, not a surrogate Institutional Event, to open and offer new channels for exploration. This attempt placed us in the position of starting to clarify what may have become a ritualized way of communicating that exists within the Group Relations field and community. The next vignette about our experience of interacting with the MATs during the Exploratory Event shows that we too were operating with a ritualized version of an IE in the mind.

> At one point a member of our subsystem decided to go to the MATs and upon return spoke of how they were acting oddly. You could just walk into the room without indicating in what capacity you arrived, they were curious and asking questions and interacting differently than what the member had expected. Upon his return a great deal of time was spent discussing this. There were references to the acronym MATs as being like a doormat, something to wipe your feet on and then waltz right in. Besides, they didn't know how to properly manage their territory…
>
> People ranged from feeling worried that the system was not going to be contained by this inadequate management, to feelings of elation at something new being created.
>
> Members from the MATs also visited our room twice. During these visits they didn't launch hypotheses into the system about the state of the conference. What they did instead was bring in their ideas and questions. Moreover, they even continued to stay with us to discuss! This was again experienced at once as both exasperating and exhilarating with thoughts about how the management doesn't know what it's

doing intermingled with the sense that we were genuinely experiencing something new.

So quite some time was spent exploring our difficulty in knowing how to interact with what many in our subsystem considered a strange and—so it seemed from the undertone of our discussion—inadequate management. In our subsystem we discussed whether we would send *them* hypotheses. There was talk of an absent management, perhaps without noticing the presence of what indeed was there. The MATs provided those participating in the Exploratory Event with a great deal of material with which to question whether we were indeed in a different, new, perhaps innovative event. What they encouraged relentlessly was maintaining an exploratory stance with regard to their joint leadership, actively providing—through behaviour—a contrast with the traditional (perhaps ritualized) understanding of management as a correctional or even punitive formation in the system, based on the supposedly unambiguous authority in a 'monarchical' leadership model.

## *Concentration and eccentricity*

Taking the idea of isomorphism one step further, we may think of the concluding plenary as showing a concentrated enactment of the Exploratory Event as a whole (and therefore of the conference, of the field, and of human relations as such).

The first striking characteristic of the concluding plenary was its seating arrangement.

> Upon entering the plenary room, we were surprised to not find the usual stacks of chairs for us to decide where and how to seat ourselves and our subsystems. Instead we found the room prepared with a novel arrangement of chairs. The structure was such that for each subsystem in the Exploratory Event there was a section with the required number of chairs, in a circular arrangement, with the edges of each subsystem on an inner circle and the other chairs curved back to the outer limits. This created a shape that looked like the diagram below:
>
> The structure was slightly open near the door, where we could enter this circular shape. In front of every segment there were pieces of paper on the floor, each with the name of a subsystem.

The members of the MATs were seated together. When we entered, there were already many people inside, thus we hadn't witnessed the situation from when the room was opened, but we presumed the seating arrangement and the labels were prepared by the MATs and set up by members of these teams. Later comments attested to a similar belief being held by members of other subsystems and these were never denied or contradicted. Whoever did it certainly demonstrated that they had an accurate model of the system, at least in terms of numbers.

Within a few minutes various interpretations of this structure emerged. One mentioned a flower, the subsystems being petals. Another recognized love booths in a dancing hall. But after these rather benign associations there were also expressions of anger and contempt, directed towards the ones who had "sat us like this"—with the clear insinuation of being set up. And others, again referring to the conventional practice of an IE, expressed feeling at a loss, not being allowed to choose one's own seating and thus missing the opportunity to understand what system was being created or enacted at the moment.

Instead of taking this concluding plenary as an opportunity to continue the task of exploration, the exchanges moved into the direction of accusation and regret. And instead of testing

> the particular properties of this seating arrangement, people complained about sitting with their backs to other participants. Some stood up to speak from a more central position. All the time, the accusation was of someone—presumably the MATs—not knowing the rules, and it seemed the job of those seated in the room was to alternately correct them, blame them, or feel hurt that such a digression had taken place. The mood changed into that of a tribunal or a people's court, a self-correctional mechanism like in a sect.
>
> Along with these negative feelings and images, it dawned on us that there was also something very innovative in this arrangement that we should test in practice. As a result, some people in our subsystem broke with the plenary culture of one-person-speaking-at-a-time and engaged in a public continuation of exploring among ourselves. Of course then it became impossible for everyone to take in everything equally. This intervention created a sense of disorder and multiple layers of sound, if not of meaning. The seating structure was practically demanding subsystems to do just this. But it appeared that many participants of other subsystems and even some of our own were so tied up with plenary culture, that they couldn't understand or accept our innovation as anything other than a destructive aggression against those who were still hoping to capture the whole system's attention. Could this also be a re-enactment of the IFSI-drama, and was the purpose of this spatial design perhaps to create a parallel precaution against anyone wishing to address the whole conference?
>
> As frustration accumulated and the anger towards the MATs became increasingly explicit, the system split into pro- and contra-innovation factions. The image of adolescent paranoia versus parental impotence came to mind. With the time boundary nearing, several participants started to leave the room on their own authority—members of our subsystem among them.

Consciously or unconsciously, the design principle for the seating arrangement in this concluding plenary was an attempt to favour eccentricity over concentration. There was, in a way, a circle with one centre. At the same time, there were as many circles as subsystems, each with a centre of their own. If you cared to see it, you could think that these centres were still distributed on the perimeter of the one large circle that held the structure together. We were all, at the same time, in the one large in-group *and* in our own little out-groups–or perhaps the other way around. Hence, concentration was not necessarily driven out when eccentricity would be accepted.

The human capacity to reflect demonstrates a fundamental duality: we are in the centre of our own experiences, and at the same time we know about this centre as if we were looking at it from a distance. We do not only experience, we are also aware of our experiencing. We are not where we think, and we think not where we are (Plessner, 1928). Indeed the idea of multiple centres, multiple ways of thinking also about our work in the field of group relations with its plurality of perspectives and conceptual frames, could have been represented in this formation. Nevertheless, this accomplishment of the MATs could not be recognized and acknowledged, and probably out of fear for the unexpected effects of innovation the old familiar 'concentration' drove 'eccentricity' out of the room again.

## Reflection

> *"It is a pity to shut oneself indoors in the country."*
>
> (Marcel Proust, 1913)

So this is where we are, near the end of our exploration: concentration begets adaptation, eccentricity begets innovation. However, in situations that demand new ways of thinking and relating, things aren't as straightforward as this statement suggests. Whenever we think we know how we are supposed to work in a conference, we run the risk of merely putting members through an obedience training exercise, craftily advertised as open exploration. As soon as we stop thinking and re-thinking our concepts, ideas and relationships to methodology, we'll fall into the pit we diggeth. Whenever we hold on to concepts we 'know' just because they are familiar instead of testing them with the reality of the moment (which necessarily means we may need to reject them), we are blinding ourselves. And more importantly, we'll be indoctrinating others to a kind of thoughtlessness about experience that we strive to work against.

If we ourselves don't dare to move, how can we expect members to arrive anywhere else than where we are? In terms of isomorphism, we associate this with the dynamics of dysfunctional families that keep replicating their problematic behaviours onto the next generation. Therefore, in this final section of our chapter, we focus on a fallacy we feel sufficiently eccentric about.

### *Familiarism*

In our writing the theme of 'familiarity' came up quite a few times. We think this incidence of familiarity has much to do with the fact that Group Relations is said to be the beneficiary to two different inheritances: post-war social systems theory and psychoanalysis with its roots in nineteenth century philosophy of science. People are so eager to believe that Group Relations is an "amalgam of psychoanalysis and ..." (fill in the dots),[1] that we don't dare to even think of testing this statement's reality. As much as we confuse ourselves and others by slapdash references to various and varied theories and methodologies that employ terms like 'systems' and 'systemic',[2] so too are we sloppy in clarifying how exactly Group Relations is indebted to psychoanalysis. Regardless of the value of psychoanalytic theory for understanding organizational and social dynamics, if we are not precise we may adapt to all sorts of unconsciously imported ways of thinking that keep us arrested in obsolete rituals and undermine our capacity to innovate (i.e., adapt to the contexts of today and tomorrow).

One example of such an arrest is holding the conference in mind as a place for intra-psychic exploration and personal growth (lest we are misunderstood, we are not opposed to such exploration and growth in itself).

> In all the conferences where we've worked, staff have had to wrestle with this issue. The quality of work in progress was often described in terms of new insights gained by this or that member into his or her personality, rather than in accordance with the formulation of the conference aim or 'primary task'.
>
> Worries concerning individual members, expressed during staff meetings, are another example. How often have we seen that members who were supposedly near-psychotic or worse

> and whose 'case' hijacked uneven amounts of reporting time in a staff meeting, failed to live up to these expectations the next day? The repetitiveness of such incidents, concurring with non-therapy invocations in the brochure, makes us think this is a ritual.

Families are social systems, but not all social systems are isomorph with families. Still, many of us use family relations as a metaphor or even as *the* concept to understand conference dynamics. Even if we scholarly endorse Bion's taking sides with the sphinx, in conferences we lace our interpretations with Oedipal imagery. Yet such familiarism is called into question. For example: "... instead of participating in an undertaking that will bring about genuine liberation, psychoanalysis is taking part in the work of bourgeois repression at its most far-reaching level, that is to say, keeping European humanity harnessed to the yoke of daddy-mommy and making no effort to do away with this problem once and for all" (Deleuze & Guatarri, 1972).

So we doubt whether the concept of isomorphism supports using the family as a proper model for Group Relations. The issue is nothing less than in what sense a Group Relations conference is a good regulator for learning really new things about conscious and unconscious forces and meanings underlying social systems. We run the risk of propagating a basic assumption mentality of ritualization in and through our conferences, when we don't critique the practice of familiarizing associated with our psychoanalytic inheritance. If we are serious about clearing a space for understanding social systems in other ways than as a derivative from family dynamics, we should dare to speak so boldly as Proust's character Charlus to his author: "A lot we care about your grandmother, you little shit!"

## *Afterthought*

In retrospect we discovered how the theme of our subsystem in the Exploratory Event, absence, is intimately connected with familiarism. The connection is mortality. Most social systems, especially those in the work environment, have great difficulty accepting the reality that members are mortal. Implicitly, organizational structures and cultures take into account that people grow, mature, age, and sooner or later will terminate their membership. But the stark reality that our bodies are subject to decay and are ultimately disposable remains hidden behind ritual. One social system, the family, is used by all others as a dumpster to deal with death—and families in turn pass their dead bodies on to the undertakers, who then become untouchable. There is no reason to assume that the global Group Relations community is different in this respect; evidenced by the affiliation of the two absent presenters and their subjects—the Indian 'Dalit' caste being considered to fall outside the system of Cosmic Man (Franz, 1964)—we are tempted to think that at least one of the dumpsters in this case was IFSI.

The passing on of leading figures is a continuous reality that cannot be denied as such, yet the actual experiences associated with death are wished away into the families concerned. Obviously, we can and do hold on to such feelings as anger over being orphaned, bereavement and mourning over the loss of a dear one, and fear for one's own end. It is through these feelings that the self-image of our community is—at least partly—transformed into that of a family. In addition there are also the less openly addressed envious impulses, similar to sibling rivalry, sparked by new *opportunities* in a system that needs to rejuvenate if it is to survive. To critique such parallels is a prerequisite for exploring alternative images and creating practices that are less dependent on ritualized behaviours transferred from family life.

## Notes

1. Here is a selection of phrases we googled: "psychoanalysis, Marxism and sociology" (the Frankfurt School), "psychoanalysis, medicine and behavioral science" (the theory of affect), "psychoanalysis, cultural analysis and deconstructive literary sensibility" (ethnographic writing), "psychoanalysis, cybernetics and artificial intelligence" (in 'Freud's Megalomania: A Novel' by Israel Rosenfield) or "psychoanalysis, religion and bullshit" (in a piece by John Sladek on Scientology).
2. Usually "open systems theory" is mentioned, but we also encountered "system theory", "social systems theory", "socio-technical systems thinking", "systemic thinking", "systems therapy", or "systemic therapy"—all quite different and some even incompatible, for all we know.

## References

(2006). Belgirate II—Adaptation and Innovation: Theory, Design and Role-Taking in Group Relations conferences and Their Applications (conference brochure), AKRI, OFEK and Tavistock Institute.

(undated). Webster's online Dictionary edition: www.websters-online-dictionary.org.

Armstrong, D. (2000). *Emotions in organizations: disturbance or intelligence?* Emotions in Organizations: The Contribution of Psychoanalytic Approaches, London, International Society for the Psychoanalytic Study of Organisations.

Armstrong, D. (2005). Organization in the mind: an introduction. In Organization in the mind: Psychoanalysis, group relations and organizational consultancy. R. French, Ed. London, Karnac Books: pp. 1–9.

Bell, C. (1992). *Ritual Theory, Ritual Practice.* New York, Oxford University Press, USA.

Bertalanffy, L.V. (1951). "General system theory—A new approach tot unity of science." *Human Biology: The International Journal of Population Biology and Genetics* 23(December): pp. 303–61.

Conant, R.C. & Ashby W.R. (1970). "Every Good Regulator of a System Must be a Model of that System." *International Journal of System Science* 1(2): pp. 89–97.

Deleuze, G. & Guatarri F. (1972). *L'Anti-Oedipe* (translation: Anti-Oedipus; capitalism and schizophrenia, 1977, Viking Penguin). Paris, Les Editions de Minuit.

Franz, M.-L. von (1964). The Process of Individuation. In *Man and his symbols.* C. Jung, Ed. New York, Doubleday: pp. 200–4.

James, W. (1902). *The Varieties of Religious Experience.* London, New York, Longmans Green.

Lakoff, G. & Johnson M. (1999). *Philosophy in the Flesh: The Embodied Mind and Its Challenge to Western Thought.* New York City, Harper Collins Publishers.

Plessner, H. (1928). *Die Stufen des Organischen und der Mensch—Einleitung in die philosophische Anthropologie.* Berlin/Leipzig, de Gruyter.

Proust, M. (1913). *Du côté de chez Swann, Tome 1 of À la Recherche du temps perdu* (Swann's Way—Vol. 1 of Remembrance of Things Past/ Translated from the French by C.K. Scott Moncrieff—1934). New York, Random House.

## CHAPTER THIRTEEN

# Crossing multiple boundaries: Reflections on the Belgirate II experience

*Ellen L. Short and Jeanne M.S.T. Woon*

### *Introduction*

In reflecting on our experiences of the Belgirate II conference, we perceive there to have been multiple boundaries at Belgirate II: boundaries that are tangible, such as the process of entering into the geographic territory of another country, as well as intangible boundaries related to identity, citizenship, allegiance and loyalty on personal and professional levels. As two women (one African American, one Asian) travelling to Italy from the United States, we believe our pre-conference interactions impacted how we entered the conference and the roles we took up as participants. Our commonalities in identity (as women, as persons of colour, in age, and in country of residence, for example), and differences (such as in race and country of citizenship), seemed also relevant in how we experienced some of the conference events.

This chapter combines narratives of our reflections of Belgirate II.

## *Tangible and intangible boundaries: Our journeys to Belgirate II*

### *Ellen's journey*

I crossed the geographic boundary of my home in New York to travel to Italy with some excitement and anticipation. I was aware of the first Belgirate conference three years before, and although I had been interested and had wanted to attend, my personal and financial situations at the time as a doctoral candidate, did not permit me the privilege of attending. However, having graduated, and improved my circumstances, I was in a position to not only consider attending Belgirate II, but to actually do it. As an assistant professor, my department had also offered to reimburse a portion of my expenses, which, in addition to helping me financially, also helped me recognize that attending Belgirate II was an important part of my professional identity development. The year had also been an interesting one for me regarding international group relations work, because I had also attended the Transformaction 2006 conference as a member in Paris (Marne-la-Vallee), France. This conference had been a powerful and stimulating learning experience for me and made me look forward to joining with and learning more from my international and American colleagues at Belgirate II.

Jeanne and I, who were group relations colleagues and friends, had communicated about meeting, pre-Belgirate, in Milan, Italy. Since all of my forays into international group relations conferences thus far had been on my own, I was very pleased to know that Jeanne would be at Belgirate and looked forward to our meeting in Milan. After arriving and settling in our hotels, we met for a dinner during which we re-connected, discussed and explored our experiences as younger generation women of colour who do group relations work. Our discussion encompassed aspects of reaffirming our connectedness and supportiveness of each other's work as well as our feelings of competitiveness and ambition. In hindsight, we believe this interaction created an opening for us to cross the Belgirate II conference boundary and take up our roles.

I had also committed to joining three other colleagues in Stresa, Italy, so while Jeanne stayed in Milan and spent time with colleagues who were also travelling to the conference, I took the train to meet with my group. In Stresa, I joined a group of three women who were senior to me, chronologically, as well as in their experiences in group relations work. Each of these women had also directed group relations conferences. Pairing was a significant part of our gathering. We were paired in a variety of ways—in our relationship to each other (as colleagues and friends), in our choices to share hotel rooms (each pair shared a room), and in our race—two of us were African American women and two were White women. I enjoyed my time with these colleagues, and I learned from them, specifically, about their experiences as conference directors and as women committed to doing group relations work. I marvelled at their continued excitement about group relations work, I was impressed by their physical, emotional, spiritual and intellectual strength and energy, and their generosity in sharing their experiences with each other and with me. I was also aware of the existence of the competition, envy, and cultural differences and similarities among us. I believe that the interactions I had with these colleagues, specifically related to female relatedness, authority, power and leadership, also created an opening for me to cross the Belgirate II conference boundary.

### *Jeanne's journey*

Born and raised in Singapore, I first came to the United States as a foreign student, with only the intent of earning a college degree and returning home. Several years later, with graduate degrees and a professional position, I decided to remain in the U.S. Having all but one family member in Singapore (and a sister in Australia), I made a new home in the U.S. but kept my ties to the old. Without the option of dual citizenship, I chose to retain my Singapore citizenship while holding U.S. permanent residency. Being primarily of Chinese descent, I would be in the racial majority in Singapore but have the daily experience of being in the minority in the U.S. Depending on the situation and context, therefore, my racial/ethnic identity—felt and perceived—could be Singaporean, Southeast Asian, Chinese, Straits Chinese, Asian, Asian American, person of colour, or American. In society as well as group relations work, these identities and perceptions contributed to a variety of roles such as foreigner, intruder, token, threat, and spokesperson.

I had only vaguely heard about the first Belgirate conference at the time that it took place. In the year prior, however, I participated in an international group relations conference in Australia (Lorne) as a member. It was a broadening experience to attend such a conference outside of the U.S. It expanded my curiosity, for example, about how much of what happens in conferences reflects historical traditions of group relations and how much stems from the context of the country, culture, or sponsoring organization(s). When I heard about the upcoming second Belgirate conference, I was keen to attend. I wanted the opportunity to participate in the exchange of ideas and experiences with international colleagues.

Cost was an initial barrier, however. The conference was not closely related to my work as a psychologist in a university counselling centre where I provide clinical services to students. While my supervisor and colleagues were supportive of this interest outside of my primary profession, any pursuit furthering it was at my own expense. I applied to AKRI for a scholarship from the Gabelnick Global Community Connections Fund and was fortunate to be awarded funds that helped make the conference and trip a possibility. Attending the conference with the support of a scholarship contributed to a sense of humility as well as responsibility, regarding my participation.

I learned from Ellen that she would be attending Belgirate II as well, and we arranged to meet up in Milan before the conference. Ellen and I met through group relations work. We have known each other since we both were graduate students in New York, even though we worked with faculty at different institutions that were actively engaged in AKRI and group relations work. We kept in touch even after I moved to Missouri some years ago and saw our connection first as fellow students shift into that of colleagues, and then into friendship.

My experience of dinner in Milan with Ellen resonates with what she has already shared above. During our dinner we shared our experiences of group relations conferences. In particular, we discussed our experiences as racial minorities in the U.S. while being perceived and treated as Americans first outside of the U.S. In relating to the similarities in some of our experiences, the topic of competition naturally arose, but in the process of owning it and sharing our feelings about it, a closer bond was formed. It also contributed to finding the space where we could be supportive of each other.

Like Ellen, I met up with other AKRI colleagues on another evening. What started out as a plan for two grew with others joining in and we ended up with a group of eight. The evening of dining and conversation was enjoyable and exciting in various ways. Although all were with AKRI, we came from different parts of the U.S. I did not see any of these people often even in the U.S., yet all were now dining together in another country. Nearly all were senior to me in group relations work and I felt both the honour of being included and the emergent responsibility of stepping in and stepping up. Both these pre-conference events contributed to a sense of being a part of an organization, on the verge of joining others in the larger international community of group relations at Belgirate II.

### *Belgirate II: Emerging themes*

#### *Jeanne*

One of the boundaries to be crossed prior to the conference was that of being accepted into the event. The application form included a category for 'Nationality', for which I stated 'Singaporean', while adding I resided in the U.S. It was noted that this data would be included in the list of participants, but it was not. Country of residence was tabulated in the demographics of the participants, but not nationality. I was disappointed because I had expected that at an international conference, the nationality of the participants would be relevant. I spoke to my experience at the Opening Plenary, that of having to choose from the multiple identities that I hold or, more to the point, of having one selected for me. Yet this experience was hardly mine alone, as I learned quickly from the participants, several of whom were also citizens of one country while resident in another. It seemed there was a complexity of identities and affiliations that could not be contained in the structure of the conference. It seemed, also, an example of the theme of allegiance and loyalty or rather, that of challenging one's allegiance and loyalty—"Where do you stand? With us or them? Pick one." This theme continued into the conference, for instance, with the discussion that emerged about the absence of participants from France.

The theme of generations and generativity was represented in the session where the keynote lecture, *Learning to Consult with Wonder: One Approach to Preparing Group Relations Consultants,* was presented. This was conveyed in the lecture itself, which described the process of development and the components of a formal program for certifying group relations consultants. It was also taken up in the discussion among the participants afterwards. At the tables there seemed to be much interest and also anxiety, as the topic of certification of consultants evoked questions about implicit values, traditions, and who would come after us in the work. As one who was to join the AKRI Training & Certification Committee shortly after, this was especially poignant.

During the exploratory events, without pre-planning, Ellen and I both spent several sessions in the 'Inexperience group'. Here, we explored our experiences of inexperience, which we related strongly to the experience of and openness to learning. The group was characterized by members taking up roles that balanced the individual and collective needs. There was a relatively clear but permeable boundary where members left and returned with information to share and where visitors were enfolded into the group, engaged with, and let go, but in a way that did not disrupt the core of our discussion. It seemed we could engage in conflict, explore and understand differences in experience, cultures, and organizations that emerged and that impacted or were impacted by our work in group relations, and that members used our individual, diverse experiences and competences to maintain the group. We noted that the group was not made up only of persons who were comparatively 'inexperienced', but there were those highly experienced and 'senior' (including women who have directed) and those more junior. Even when more senior members departed, the spirit of the group continued. It was dependent not on specific persons. As one member remarked toward the end of the exploratory events, the 'inexperience' group was hardly inexperienced—rather, we were '*in* experience'.

## *Ellen*

Upon my arrival at the conference, I was immediately aware of the excitement I felt within myself and from my colleagues about being together in what Jeanne previously referred to as "the larger international community of group relations." It was exciting to see people I knew and also those that I did not know but might meet and interact with.

One of the themes that immediately became apparent to me during the opening plenary was that of the boundaries between a conference that focuses on presentations to facilitate group learning and a group relations conference. The opening plenary felt much like the opening of a group relations conference and I felt a distinct blurring of the boundaries related to my role(s).

Another theme that quickly emerged was age. Jeanne and I both noticed some of the members' focus on age during the plenary, and expressions of regret that the membership did not contain a larger number of younger people (e.g., in their 20's 30's and 40's). This was interesting to us and reminded us of our own circumstances, as the "younger" members. For example, our awareness that we could not have afforded to attend an event like Belgirate only a few years earlier, and the inaccessibility (restrictive tangible and intangible boundaries) of group relations conferences for many individuals. The discussion about age in the opening plenary was also characterized by expressions of fear about the "death" of group relations work. This was also curious to us because we had initially experienced the excitement of journeying to Belgirate and arrival at the conference to be indicative of the durability and liveliness of group relations work.

The keynote lectures, although representative of important and insightful work and research in group relations, were, for both of us, with the exception of the final one entitled, *Learning to Consult with Wonder: One Approach to Preparing Group Relations Consultants*, challenging to hold onto. I recall being disappointed that only one of the presenters was female, and that she presented last. The theme of female authority and leadership, already very present, however, emerged more clearly in the first lecture, *"Doth my father yet live" Psychoanalysis and Group Relations Conferences: Revisited*, in which the presenters raised questions about the role of the female director, in relation to authority, leadership, and power. This was interesting to me because of the presence of many past female directors in the Belgirate II membership. I spoke with several women immediately after the lecture and during informal gatherings who expressed mixed feelings about this portion of the presentation. In spite of this,

I found it interesting that none of the women (including myself) openly commented and/or challenged the content of the lecture during the keynote session.

It was difficult for me to grasp where adaptation and innovation were being held in each of the keynote lectures. Thus, although my thinking was stimulated, and I appreciated the lectures, I looked forward to the parallel presentations and how they might further illuminate the conference's themes of adaptation and innovation. The parallel presentations did not disappoint; those that I attended (mostly focused on issues of identity and group relations) were quite interesting and innovative.

It was at the morning reflections and associations and exploratory events that the themes that Jeanne and I experienced as members began to more fully emerge. The themes were related to illness, aging, death, female authority and power, collusion of internalized oppressions, envy, and competition. It seemed to us that illness and the fear of death and dying was expressed repeatedly in the concern that the staff and membership expressed about the temporary deterioration of the health of one member in particular. Moreover, it seemed to us that the preoccupation with this member's health was, of course, related to more deeply held, unconscious processes of the conference. Belgirate II's blurred boundaries related to group relations conference work were also intricately connected to the themes of illness, aging, death and dying, regarding what seemed to be a group level fantasy of diminishing opportunities to consult and/or direct at conferences. However, there was also a covert focus on competition related to the very real diminished opportunity to be chosen for a specific role—that of director of the Tavistock Institute's Leicester conference.

It was also during the exploratory event that the emotions that had clearly been activated in the first keynote lecture about female authority, leadership, and power, came into play. In her description of this event, Jeanne elaborated on our group experiences as members of the "Inexperience" subgroup. We believe that the formation of both the "Inexperience" and "Female Directors" groups during this event were an unconscious group reaction and response to the keynote lectures, as well as unspoken conference dynamics related to female authority and power, and its relationship to aging, death, collusion of internalized oppressions, envy, and competition.

Some of the contemporary group relations literature concerning female authority, power, and leadership has focused on these themes, for example, the Group-As-Mother (G-A-M) and the members' fantasized relationship to the group as a maternal object (Rosenbaum, 2004). Other literature has focused on female authority as it relates to race, power and privilege, and the challenges inherent in taking up authority in the conference director role (McRae, 2004), and communicating and collaborating across racial-cultural boundaries at group relations conferences (Brazaitis, 2004; McRae, Kwong, & Short, 2007). Research on gender and authority in the experiential setting of group relations conferences and other systems for the last quarter of a century, has also been explored (Cytrynbaum & Belkin, 2004). It seems to us that what occurred at Belgirate II was an amalgam of the complexity of attempting to explore and manage all of these dynamics related to gender, authority, power, and leadership, in multiple contexts—historically, contemporarily, and in the unforeseeable future.

## *Conclusion*

The experiences that we had in Milan before Belgirate II turned out to be an important transitional space; having crossed the ocean and arrived in Italy, it was a time of preparing our minds, hearts, bodies, and spirits prior to the conference itself. The connection we had with each other supported our bringing voice to the conference, particularly to bringing in the gendered and racial/ethnic parts of ourselves. The interactions we both had with AKRI associates representing different 'generations' in the organization brought forth a sense of humility as well as responsibility in doing group relations work. It contributed to a still-growing sense of being in the 'middle' generation, with much to learn and work to take on.

Since Belgirate II, we have continued group relations work at conferences, in different roles, on staff as well as across the staff-member boundary. We believe that our experiences at Belgirate II have allowed us to continue to support and challenge each other, and to grow.

## *References*

Brazaitis, S.J. (2004). White women—protectors of the status quo; Positioned to disrupt it. In: Cytrynbaum, S. & Noumair, D.A. (Eds.), *Group dynamics, organizational irrationality, and social complexity: Group relations reader 3* (pp. 99–116). Jupiter, FL: A.K. Rice Institute for the Study of Social Systems.

Cytrynbaum, S. & Belkin, M. (2004). Gender and authority in group relations conferences: implications for theory and research. In: Cytrynbaum, S. & Noumair, D.A. (Eds.), *Group dynamics, organizational irrationality, and social complexity: Group relations reader 3* (pp. 443–455). Jupiter, FL: A.K. Rice Institute for the Study of Social Systems.

McRae, M.B. (2004). Class, race and gender: Person-in-role implications in taking up the directorship. In: Cytrynbaum, S. & Noumair, D.A. (Eds.), *Group dynamics, organizational irrationality, and social complexity: Group relations reader 3* (pp. 225–237). Jupiter, FL: A.K. Rice Institute for the Study of Social Systems.

McRae, M.B., Kwong, A. & Short, E.L. (2007). Racial dialogue among women: A group relations theory analysis. *Organisational and Social Dynamics, 7*(2), pp. 211–233).

Rosenbaum, S.C. (2004). Group-as-mother: A dark continent in group relations theory and practice. In: Cytrynbaum, S. & Noumair, D.A. (Eds.), *Group dynamics, organizational irrationality, and social complexity: Group relations reader 3* (pp. 57–79). Jupiter, FL: A.K. Rice Institute for the Study of Social Systems.

CHAPTER FOURTEEN

# Learning from experience: The two international group relations meetings in Belgirate

*Gordon Strauss*

Experiential learning is central to the group relations approach to education about the dynamics of groups and organizations. Most often this refers to "here and now" events at group relations conferences, but there is another aspect of experiential learning that has less to do with immediate experience in the here and now than with making use of previous experience. This type of "learning from experience" may explain, for example, why it is so common for a person attending their *second* group relations conference to report a quantum increase in their learning.

The reasons for this are not hard to identify: anxiety associated with novel learning environments is often high and no matter how well managed or contained, this anxiety exacts a toll. By analogy with riding a bicycle for the first time, the energy—physical and psychological—devoted to the most basic aspects of the task is enormous, but once one has the hang of it that state usually does not return.[1] While one may learn additional skills and improve those acquired the first time, this is usually accomplished without the initial anxiety.

Representatives of the international group relations community (i.e., those who direct, serve as consulting staff or administer group relations conferences) met in Belgirate, Italy, in the fall of 2003 for the first time and again in 2006 to discuss and explore the theory and practice of group relations (as a model or approach to learning). (Brunner, *et al*, 2006). The two meetings both included a mix of keynote plenary talks, smaller individual or panel presentations and events that had a distinctly "experiential" feel to them (though neither meeting was a group relations conference in the usual sense). In this chapter I will describe my experience attending both Belgirate meetings and reflect on how and why the second meeting was so different an experience. I hope to demonstrate how, in addition to the "learning from experience" that was connected with being there a second time, an analysis based on group relations principles (i.e., BART) can be used to understand the differences in experience.

The second Belgirate conference felt like a richer, more satisfying learning environment for me. Some of this was without question a function of having been to the first conference three years earlier. In 2003 I arrived in Italy on the morning the conference opened, saw no one I knew at the Milan airport and travelled to Belgirate by taxi, alone. In 2006 I arrived a day early and went to downtown Milan where I met up with a number of US group relations colleagues. Even though I met a host of new colleagues at both Belgirate meetings—including not a few from the US—the return of many of us from the first meeting made for multiple warm greetings during registration at the Villa Carlotta. By the time the conference opened, I was on familiar ground in more ways than one.

Belgirate I was a peculiar combination of modes: there were both group relations and non-group relations formats in what was most distinctly *not* a group relations conference. I know I was not alone in feeling frustrated at that attempt to adapt group relations elements in the service of something very different. It was easy to be critical of this attempt, as if we the participants were any less responsible for the outcome than those who had proposed the structure we used. Actually, six of the eight of us from the US did try to move beyond the given structure for the experiential part, but found that we could not engage others to join us.

During Belgirate II, not only was I less frustrated by a design that used some group relations elements, the management team also appeared to have made good use of the lessons from the previous meeting. Keynote talks were expanded from two to three and the Exploratory event was more free-form: instead of the pre-determined group themes used in 2003, this time we were given the opportunity to create groups with tasks of our own choosing. This was not only more like a typical institutional event or inter-group event opening, it gave the participants both the freedom and the responsibility to take this multi-session event where they wished.[2]

While the differences between the first and second Belgirate conference and my building on my first experience when I returned in 2006 were important factors in understanding why the second conference seemed so different, they are not sufficient. I believe crucial elements for me had to do with *task, role* and *authorization*.

In 2006, but not in 2003, the A.K. Rice Institute for the Study of Social Systems (AKRI) was a co-sponsor of the Belgirate conference. This appeared to have a dramatic effect on the proportion of conference members from the U.S., increasing from 15% (8 of 52) in 2003 to 30% (26 of 82) at Belgirate II. Members from AKRI were the largest contingent from any country or group relations organization. Because of both AKRI President Bob Baxter's role as one of the three who planned and managed Belgirate II (and AKRI Administrator Anne Marie Kirkpatrick's role and presence as the Belgirate II co-administrator) and AKRI's co-sponsoring the conference, participants from the U.S. had every reason to feel authorized institutionally.

For me this general institutional authorization went further. In the spring of 2005 I had been elected to a three-year term on the AKRI Board. As a Board member I was aware of and received regular updates about the processes leading up to Belgirate II. While my decision to return to Belgirate was individual—I received neither an official AKRI request to attend nor financial support from AKRI—I nevertheless was quite aware of being a representative of AKRI and its board.[3] Adding to my sense of institutional authorization was the fact that in the spring of 2006 I had been selected to direct the AKRI national group relations conference (so-called to distinguish it from group relations conferences sponsored by AKRI affiliate centers). Initially I was appointed to fill a one-year gap, but by the summer before Belgirate II I had sought and received a full three-year authorization.

So when Belgirate II got underway, I had what I experienced as a fuller sense of authorization. Some of this, as I have just explained, came from a combination of AKRI's role at Belgirate II and my role(s) in AKRI. However I came to the second Belgirate conference with a clearer sense of what I wanted to do this time; that is, I was clearer about my task(s). Some of these actually were not new, but were simply more fully conscious and more easily articulated. Meeting colleagues—both from the international group relations community and from the U.S.—and seeking learning about new ways to approach and do group relations work both had been goals in 2003 when I attended Belgirate I. My sense of pursuing these tasks more successfully the second time probably was a function of both the experience of Belgirate I (knowing what to expect as well as literally knowing many of the other participants returning undoubtedly allowed me to feel less shy and tentative and to feel greater self-authorization[4]) as well as of understanding more fully how these seemingly general tasks had specific value for me.

There was another aspect, however, to the impact of the roles and tasks I brought with me to Belgirate II. Because of my role as the next AKRI national conference director, I was very clear that more than anything what I wanted to do was to explore directing with other experienced conference directors. Being clear about this eliminated any indecision about which group to join during the Exploratory Event: especially since I didn't qualify for the group for women directors, the group focusing on directors and their dilemmas seemed tailored to my interests and needs. Indeed, I found it an excellent "fit". For example, Manny Sher, one of the members of this group, referred to a chapter he'd written about his first time directing the "Leicester" conference for the Tavistock some 6 ½ years earlier. (Sher, 2003) It turned out that I had brought a copy of the book containing his chapter and read it during the conference.

The sense of being at Belgirate II with this clear purpose carried over to discussions at meals and on many of the breaks. Inevitably there were conference members with director experience who were not in my Exploratory Event group. I also began to realize that some of the Belgirate members were expressing an interest in me at least in part because of my upcoming role as director of AKRI's conference. This was true not only for new U.S. acquaintances, but also for some of the Belgirate II members from other countries as well. The effect of all of this was to create a richer variety of roles and tasks for me. Put another way, I was more aware of subtle boundaries within and between the tasks I set for myself and the roles I took up within the conference.

Another example of how this affected my experience occurred in one of the parallel presentations. Two U.S. colleagues, Mary McRae and Zachary Green, described their work over eight years putting on conferences dealing with race and identity. Somehow I had never heard about what they had been doing with both the design and names of conference events. I came away from their presentation thinking, "Wow! I'd love to be part of what they are doing, but it sounds so different that I wouldn't feel I would want to work on the staff until I had been as a member."[5] What I also found fascinating was how their conference design innovations connected to solving problems that emerged as they grappled with the challenge of building on several years' experience with their conference themes. (This influenced my decision to stick with one broad theme—organizational transition—for all three of my AKRI conferences.)

Towards the end of the second Belgirate conference, during the Exploratory Event plenary, when all participants were gathered together in their respective groups to discuss the event and what had been learned, there were some comments that were striking to me, particularly in terms of "learning from experience." The gist of the comments was that it was surprising and perhaps disconcerting that a number of the participants had experienced and enacted dynamic processes like those seen in group relations conferences, as if this was something that Belgirate conference members with their years of group relations experience should somehow be beyond. The implication seemed to be that in this instance "learning from experience" meant that the learning would somehow inoculate or immunize the learners against being subject to the processes which we teach about in regular group relations conferences.

This was not the first time I had encountered this implicit belief in relation to what is learned from experience at our conferences. And it is not altogether incorrect: we *do* learn from our experience in ways that allow us not to repeat some things (this is probably the most common understanding of what it means to learn from experience in any context). But to believe, implicitly, that conference learning will keep us or any group from being subject to the forces that operate in groups, especially those processes outside conscious awareness, seems to me to be naïve. But more importantly, it reflects a misunderstanding of what group relations does offer by way of learning from experience (a "mislearning from experience").[6]

To think that the dynamics we teach about in group relations conferences somehow won't happen to experienced and senior group relations consultants and directors is folly as demonstrated by the "experiential" portions of both Belgirate meetings. This belief may be folly, but its origins aren't hard to understand. Who wouldn't like to believe that we can get beyond basic assumptions and the projecting of our group anxieties outward? However when this all-too-understandable wish is treated like an expectation, it can do real mischief. In group relations conferences this may show up as the sense that *this* is what separates members from staff rather than task and role—and experience.[7] However as the events at Belgirate II illustrate, learning from experience is a never-ending task.

## Notes

1. The exception to this generalization occurs when, again using the bicycle analogy, one must perform under changed or perilous circumstances such as riding in very narrow confines or on the shoulder of a road adjacent to fast-moving vehicle traffic.
2. The names of the resulting groups (Women Directors, Dilemmas Facing Directors, Chaos and Application, Absence, Cut Off and Inexperience) seem to me in retrospect to reflect both an attempt to engage the task creatively and an important tension in group relations between content and process.
3. I was not alone in this level of representation. Besides Bob Baxter and Anne Marie Kirkpatrick who *were* officially representing AKRI, President-elect Leigh Estabrook and fellow Board member Mary McRae also attended. Mary attended Belgirate I, but neither Bob, Anne Marie nor Leigh had.
4. This may be two ways of saying the same thing.
5. In fact I *did* go to their next conference as a member (for the first time in 29 years!). I had been thinking for some time that I should renew my member experience, and doing so before I directed my first AKRI national conference seemed especially apt.
6. Or, as an audience member suggested when a version of this chapter was presented at the AKRI Symposium in Chicago in May 2008, this may illustrate "the defensive use of experience."
7. This may occur despite considerable time and energy devoted by a conference staff to identifying parallel processes between member and staff groups.

# *INDEX*

For Product Safety Concerns and Information please contact our EU representative GPSR@taylorandfrancis.com Taylor & Francis Verlag GmbH, Kaufingerstraße 24, 80331 München, Germany